RHYTHM IN PSYCHOLOGICAL, LINGUISTIC AND MUSICAL PROCESSES

RHYTHM IN PSYCHOLOGICAL, LINGUISTIC AND MUSICAL PROCESSES

Edited by

JAMES R. EVANS, Ph.D.
Department of Psychology
University of South Carolina
Columbia, South Carolina

MANFRED CLYNES, D.Sc.
New South Wales State Conservatorium of Music
Sydney, Australia

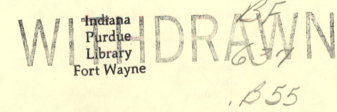

CHARLES C THOMAS • PUBLISHER
Springfield • Illinois • U.S.A.

Published and Distributed Throughout the World by

CHARLES C THOMAS • PUBLISHER
2600 South First Street, P.O. Box 4709
Springfield, Illinois 62717-4709

© *1986 by* CHARLES C THOMAS • PUBLISHER

ISBN 0-398-05235-2
Library of Congress Catalog Card Number: 86-1423

With THOMAS BOOKS *careful attention is given to all details of manufacturing and
design. It is the Publisher's desire to present books that are satisfactory as to their physical
qualities and artistic possibilities and appropriate for their particular use.* THOMAS
BOOKS *will be true to those laws of quality that assure a good name and good will.*

Printed in the United States of America
SC-R-3

Library of Congress Cataloging-in-Publication Data

Rhythm in psychological, linguistic, and musical processes.

   Bibliography: p.
   Includes index.
   1. Biological rhythms.   2. Psychology, Applied.
3. Language and languages—Rhythm.   4. Musical meter and rhythm.
I. Evans, James R.   II. Clynes, Manfred, 1925–
BF637.B55R45   1986   153   86-1423
ISBN-0-398-05235-2

CONTRIBUTORS

Manfred Clynes, D. Sc. Research Professor and Head, Music Research Center, N.S.W. State Conservatorium of Music, Sydney, Australia

William Condon, Ph.D. Department of Psychiatry, Boston University School of Medicine, Boston, MA

Charles T. Eagle, Jr., Ph.D. Professor and Head, Department of Music Therapy, Southern Methodist University, Dallas, TX

Charles A. Elliott, Ph.D. Associate Professor, Department of Music, University of South Carolina, Columbia, SC

James R. Evans, Ph.D. Associate Professor, Department of Psychology, University of South Carolina, Columbia, SC

Alf Gabrielsson, Psykologiska Institutionen, Uppsala, Universitet, Uppsala, Sweden

Madlyn L. Hanes, C.C.C., Ph.D. Associate Professor, College of Education, University of South Carolina, Columbia, SC

Thomas G. Holzman, Ph.D. Assistant Professor of Educational Foundations, Georgia State University, Atlanta, GA

Mari Riess Jones, Ph.D. Professor, Department of Psychology, Ohio State University, Columbus, OH

James G. Martin, Ph.D. Professor, Department of Psychology, University of Maryland, College Park, MD

M. Carr Payne, Jr., Ph.D. Professor, School of Psychology, Georgia Institute of Technology, Atlanta, GA

Mark S. Rider, RMT, MMT, Associate Professor, Department of Music, Eastern Montana College, Billings, MT

PREFACE

Interest in the concept of rhythm and closely related phenomena is as old as written history. It seems to be the common denominator in a wide range of topics, ranging from ancient scripture accounts of involvement of vibrations in the creation of life to present day scientific research in music and chronobiology. During the early part of this century much interest was shown in rhythm by pioneers in the field of experimental psychology. However, except for their research and that of a few music researchers, there was little scientific study of the concept until the 1960s and 70s when research on circadian (about 24 hour) and infradian (greater than 28 hour) rhythms became rather popular. In the meantime considerations of rhythm and related phenomena most often were limited to music theory and metaphysical speculation.

The last decade has seen a major increase in the scientific study of rhythm, and at least five major texts dealing directly with the topic have been published since 1981. With one exception, these concern primarily circadian and infradian rhythms. Faster (ultradian) periodicities have been relatively neglected even though there has been a substantial amount of research and speculation concerning them scattered throughout the literature of various fields.

The major purpose of this text is to bring together in one source some of the research and theoretical contributions of several pioneers in the study of ultradian rhythms and related phenomena. The chapters are organized into five general sections: (1) Chapter 1 provides a short introduction to the topic of rhythm, thus "setting the stage" for subsequent Chapters; (2) Chapters 2 through 4 deal primarily with rhythmic factors in psychological processes of attention, memory, perception and interpersonal communication; (3) Chapters 5 and 6 emphasize the roles rhythm plays in language—both oral and written; (4) Chapters 7 through 9 center around rhythm in music, and provide both theoretical and applied perspectives; Chapter 10 integrates information from other chapters into the notion of dysrhythmia as a basis of various human disabilities, and speculates on a wide range of phenomena to which rhythm may be closely related.

Circadian and infradian rhythms are neglected in this text. This is not due to failure of the editors to appreciate their importance. Those rhythms have been covered extensively in several other recent texts, and it was our intention here to concentrate upon the faster periodicities.

This text should be of interest to a wide range of professionals, including especially those from the fields of psychology, special education, language pathology and music theory. Throughout the book we have tried to minimize the use of technical terminology unique to any one discipline: The contents range from reports of well controlled research to theoretical speculation in a wide variety of areas. Thus readers should find it a rich source of research hypotheses and ideas to stimulate further "philosophizing" regarding the concept of rhythm.

JRE
MC

CONTENTS

RHYTHM IN PSYCHOLOGICAL, LINGUISTIC AND MUSICAL PROCESSES

Chapter 1.

RHYTHMIC PHENOMENA—
WHY THE FASCINATION?

CHARLES A. ELLIOTT

The study of rhythm has been a subject of fascination for both scholars and artists for centuries. Ancient Egyptian and Greek philosophers considered rhythm as a general concept that dominated aesthetics, psychology and metaphysics.

Why the fascination? It seems that humans are constantly engaged in trying to explain their surroundings. Indeed, an argument could be made that human-kind's principal on-going activity is that of attempting to explain the working of the universe, of seeking an understanding that will eventually bring order to the flux that seems, at times, to envelope us. This drive seems to be a basic and fundamental part of human nature.

Some scholars believe that an understanding of the very nature of the universe may eventually be possible and that clues to that understanding may lie in the study of rhythmic phenomena. Indeed, rhythmic phenomena appear to be all pervasive:

> Invisible rhythms underlie most of what we assume to be constant in ourselves and the world among us. Life is in continual flux, but the change is not chaotic. The rhythmic nature of earth life is, perhaps, its most usual yet overlooked property. Though we can neither see nor feel them, we are nevertheless surrounded by rhythms of gravity, electromagnetic fields, light waves, air pressure, and sound. Each day, as the earth turns on its axis, we experience the alternation of light and darkness. The moon's revolution, too, pulls our atmosphere into a cycle of change.(Luce, 1971, p. 1)

For the better part of this century the study of rhythm has been considered by many to lie in the domain of the arts—particularly music and dance. Outside of those disciplines, with the possible exception of some of the physical sciences, the study of rhythm and rhythmicity was often considered to be pseudo-science at best and at times outright quackery. However, despite the rejection by many in the scientific community, the thinking that rhythmicity was fundamental to an understanding of nature persisted, often at the intuitive level.

Perhaps biologists and physiologists were among the first in the human sciences to recognize the importance of rhythm. Cloudsley-Thompson (1961) writes that:

> The universe is not static: every component from an electron to a galaxy is continually moving and such movement cannot proceed forever in the same direction. Sooner or later it must complete a circle, or stop and return in the opposite direction. In either case, a continuously repeated rhythm, cycle or periodicity ensues, often resulting in a balance of centrifugal and centripetal forces. This applies equally to biological as to mechanical systems. Indeed, since the former are based essentially upon physicochemical processes, such as biochemical reaction systems or electrical nerve impulses, the situation could not be otherwise. (p. 1).

Actually, the phenomenon of biological rhythms had been observed at least since the time of Aristotle, when it was noted that " . . . certain plants (Legumes) stand with their leaves folded to the sides of their stems at night and raise them—as if in a pagan gesture—to the sun in the morning . . . " (Brown, Hastings, and Palmer, 1970, p. 3). However, "It was only about twenty-five years ago that a real interest in biological rhythms burgeoned . . . (Brown, Hastings, and Palmer, 1970, p. 3)." It is now believed that biological rhythms exist that are even independent of environmental rhythms and exist at all levels of the evolutionary series (Minors and Waterhouse, 1981, p. 1).

It is certain, however, that in the case of most living organisms rhythmic phenomena are linked to various types of environmental periodicity, the most notable, of course, being the alternations of day and night. "It is these daily rhythms that have become known as circadian, from the latin **circa** (about) and **dies** (a day) (Minors and Waterhouse, 1981, p. 2)." Today scholars in the life sciences generally agree that "perhaps the most ubiquitous feature of nature is that of rhythmicity (Minors and Waterhouse, 1981, p. 1)." The study of these biological rhythms has even resulted in the emergence of a science termed "Chronobiology."

While the various life sciences may have been among the first outside of the arts to recognize the importance of rhythm, a renewed interest in rhythm and rhythmicity is occurring in practically every discipline. This volume is a prime example of such a renewal of interest.

Though rhythm had been defined as a psychophysical phenomenon as far back as 1886 (Payne, this volume), recent research is showing that rhythmicity is likely basic to human perception and that an understanding of the nature of rhythm may be the key to an understanding of the human perceptual process. It is known that the rhythmic qualities of stimuli allow for those stimuli to be perceived not as individual items but as groups. Indeed, the tendency for humans to place stimuli into groups on a rhythmic basis is so fundamental that in a laboratory setting, subjects presented with a series of stimuli " . . . physically identical and uniformly spaced in time, . . . will perceive a series of groups with some member of each group being accented, provided the rate of presentation is not extremely slow or fast" (Payne, this volume). This tendency for humans to organize evenly spaced stimuli into groups has been termed **subjective rhythmization**. Apparently, the human mind assumes that a rhythmic principle operates in the whole of man's environment (Durr, Gerstenberg, and Harvey, 1980, p. 805).

This renewed interest in rhythmicity in the behavioral sciences seems to be opening a number of doors that have hitherto eluded researchers. Developmental psychologists are now telling us that as early as infancy humans have already assimilated many of the rhythms and cadences of speech. "These rhythms seem to be perceived during the first year of life and leave a mark even on the earliest, otherwise distorted, utterances (Gardner, 1973, pp. 137–138)." These findings contribute to the mounting evidence that language development and comprehension may have a rhythmic basis. Related research is showing that a possible connection may exist between certain speech impediments and various rhythmic dysfunctions and that a relationship may exist between reading comprehension and certain rhythmic abilities. Payne (this volume) cites a study by Zurif and Carson (1970) that " . . . compared normal readers and poor readers on the rhythm subtests of the Seashore Measures of Musical Talents (Seashore, Lewis and Saetveit, Series A, 1939 revision)."

> This subtest requires a subject to judge whether two rhythmic patterns tapped out in quick succession are the same or different. A similar visual task (direct translation of the Seashore subtest to vision proved to be too difficult for the subjects) was also employed. In the visual tasks there were three or four beats with short (1/2 second) or long (1 second) pauses between them. Both of these

tasks discriminated between normal and poor readers. Performance on the tasks was significantly correlated (Payne, this volume).

Payne concludes that " . . . rhythmic organization is an important factor
in acquiring an important human skill, reading (Payne, this volume)."

Another area of psychology in which the study of rhythm shows great
promise is that concerning the nature of memory. "It has been known
since the work of Muller and Schuman (1984) that metrical organization
makes it easier to remember verbal material (Berlyne, 1971, p. 239)."
Evidence now indicates that such rhythmic characteristics of stimuli as
accent, duration, and temporal spacing will effect both short and long
term memory.

Perhaps most excitingly, there are an increasing number of researchers
investigating the role of periodicity in neural activity in an attempt to
answer questions about the human brain that to this point have evaded
solution. Indeed, periodicity may play a key role in explaining the very
nature of the human brain and there is at least one theory of the brain
that has a temporal basis and that provides " . . . some basis for the
speculation that coherent temporal patterns in the average activity of
anatomically extensive neural ensembles may constitute the neurophysiological basis of subjective experience (John, 1972, p. 863)."

It is generally conceded, of course, that rhythm and rhythmicity
pervade much of the arts. "Poetry, music, dance, mime, and drama are
temporal arts and are therefore directly rhythmical (Durr, Gerstenberg,
and Harvey, 1980, p. 805)." With respect to music, Gaston (1968) writes:

> When the musics from all cultures of the world are considered, it
> is rhythm that stands out as most fundamental, **Rhythm is the
> organizer and the energizer.** Without rhythm, there would be no
> music whereas there is much music that has neither melody nor
> harmony (p. 17).

Rhythm, then, is likely the common bond that musics of all cultures
share, though it plays a more prominent role in some cultures and
musical styles than in others. For example, Davies (1972, p. 176) refers to
the rhythmic components of Western European Art Music as being
"tonalities' poor relation." Indeed, the rhythmic components of Western
European Art Music are considered to be primitive when compared to
the musics of many cultures, particularly those of Africa. As Radocy and
Boyle (1979) point out, however, this should not be construed to mean
that the study of rhythm has been totally ignored in our culture.

To the contrary, it has been studied both intensively and extensively from many perspectives. Winick's (1974) annotated bibliography of rhythm in music included nearly 500 sources. Innumerable definitions and explanations of rhythm and its various attributes have been offered (Radocy & Boyle, 1979, p. 67).

Despite this study, there is still little agreement among scholars as to the nature of rhythm and the role that it plays in music and in all of the arts. This lack of agreement is particularly glaring when compared to the study of the other components of the arts, as for example, the study of pitch and pitch relationships in music. It seems as if those theorists who elect to study rhythm in the arts invariably choose to study only one of its several aspects. Davies (1978), for example, argues that duration should be considered a characteristic of pitch and "... from a psychological point of view has nothing to do with rhythm (p. 177)." Fraisse (1982), however, in raising the question as to whether "... rhythm (is) the arrangement of durable elements, or ... the succession of more or less intense elements, the upbeat and the fall, ... (p. 151) answers by stating that both forms of rhythmic organization exist, often linked and interdependent.

The issue becomes even more muddled when one considers those art forms not directly temporal. For example, there are those who argue that rhythm does not refer entirely and exclusively to temporal aspects but it can possess certain "spatial" characteristics. Although one commonly thinks of rhythm in conjunction with such temporal art forms as poetry and music, it may be that there also are rhythmic features to visual art forms such as architecture, painting and sculpting. The latter involve spatial dimensions of symmetry and proportion which might be considered as features of rhythm in space— "visions of rhythm" so to speak. Credibility of the notion of symmetry and proportion as involving (or being) visual rhythms may be enhanced when considered in relationship to certain Pythagorean views concerning rhythm and number. According to such views rhythm and number essentially are synonymous, and the entire universe is arranged according to number, i.e., according to rhythm.

Definitions

The problem, then, seems to be one of precise definition, not only in those disciplines such as music where there is a considerable difference of opinion, but in all disciplines. Indeed, the operational definition seems to be rather common practice in much of the scholarly work done in the area of rhythm in practically all disciplines.

Is it possible, then, to arrive at a generally accepted definition of rhythm, one that will be all inclusive and will serve regardless of the discipline in question? At this point, apparently not, though there are some grounds for general agreement.

Etymologists tell us that the word rhythm is derived from the Greek words that mean "rhythm" and "to flow."

> **Rhythmos** appears as one of the key words in Ionian philosophy, generally meaning "form," but an improvised, momentary, and modifiable form. **Rhythmos** literally signifies a 'particular way of flowing." Plato essentially applied this term to bodily movements, which, like musical sounds, may be described in terms of number. He wrote in **The Banquet**, "The system is the result of rapidity and of slowness, at first opposed, then harmonized." In **The Laws** he arrived at the fundamental definition that rhythm is "the order in the movement." (Fraiss'e, p. 150.)

Fraisse, then, defines rhythm as "... the ordered characteristics of succession," and writes that rhythm exists "... when we can predict on the basis of what is perceived, or, in other words, when we can anticipate what will follow." (p. 150). He further cites, Martin (1972) who writes that "Inherent in the rhythmic concept is that the perception of early events in a sequence generates expectancies concerning later events in real time (p. 503)." Rhythm is occasionally used synonomously with "cycle." Ward, however, writes that:

> The word "cycle" comes from the Greek word for circle, and implies only that something is coming around again to its beginning. It does not have the additional implication that there is a regular period of time before it returns to the place where it started. When these time periods are reasonably uniform, the cycle is more accurately called a "rhythm" (Ward, 1977, p. 104).

Perhaps more specific definitions or descriptions will necessarily depend upon the context of the discipline in which those definitions are derived. The following list is summarized from Behrens (1984, pp. 35–36) and suggests some possibilities:

DEFINITIONS INVOLVING UNITS OF TIME

A periodic succession of events (Schwanda, 1969, p. 568).

... regular units of time or pulses (Spohn, 1977, p. 62).

... regular, equally spaced pulsations equivalent to the musician's term "tempo" or "meter" (Mikol, 1954, p. 240).

... the periodic succession or regular recurrence of events in time which constitute the organization of temporal relationships (Smoll, 1973, p. 232).

... a patterned cycle of events (Bond, 1959, p. 260).

... some sort of recurring and within limits, predictable event ... Rhythm in music is the pattern of organized sounds and silences (Radocy, 1980, p. 98).

... the organization of ... time relationships (Lundin, 1967, p. 111).

DEFINITIONS INVOLVING TIME AND SPACE

Motor rhythm. A periodic succession of events in time and space (Schwanda, 1969, p. 568).

Movement is a space-time organization of events (Smoll and Schultz, 1978, p. 838).

DEFINITIONS INVOLVING MOVEMENT IN TIME

Rhythm and motion may be analytically distinguished, the former meaning movement in time and the latter movement in space (pitch) (Apel, 1969, p. 729).

Rhythmic behaviors are those in which all or part of an animal's body moves in a cyclic repetitive way (Delcomyn, 1980, p. 492).

... movements of parts of the body or the whole body repeated in the same form at least three times at regular short intervals of about a second or less (Thelen, 1981, p. 238).

DEFINITIONS INVOLVING
THE ORGANIZATION OF MUSIC

... the organizational and dynamic force in music (Radocy and Boyle, 1979, p. 69).

... everything pertaining to what may be called the 'time' side of music (as distinct from the pitch side), i.e., it takes in beats, accents, measures or bars, groupings of notes into beats, groupings of beats into measures, groupings of measures into phrases, and so forth (Scholes, 1970, p. 872).

... an expressive pattern of accent, durations, and pause.... (but) not all rhythm is repetitive (Mursell, 1956, pp. 258–263).

... a generic term which includes a variety of concepts that bear directly or indirectly upon the organization of musical sounds in the dimension of time (Petzold, 1966, p. 184).

DEFINITIONS INVOLVING A SUBJECTIVE ORGANIZATION

... the subjective grouping of objectively separate events (Demany, McKenzie, and Vurpillot, 1977, p. 718).

The tendency to group stimuli by time or intensity, or both into pleasurable wholes (Schwanda, 1969, p. 568).

... the perception of a series of stimuli as a series of groups of stimuli (Smoll, 1973, p. 232).

... to relate ... respective durations in an order across time (Radocy, 1980, p. 98).

The ability to count, time discrimination, and loudness discrimination are all the three basic essentials (to rhythmic perception) (Thackray, 1969, p. 19).

... observation of rhythmic stimuli that may or may not involve overt behaviors (Radocy and Boyle, 1979, p. 79).

DEFINITIONS INVOLVING A MATCH OR A MOTOR RESPONSE TO AN EXTERNAL SOURCE

... to be at a specific point in space (spatial accuracy) at a specific point in time (temporal accuracy) (Smoll and Schultz, 1978, p. 838).

Rhythmic ability: The ability to maintain a steady tempo. Rhythmic accuracy: The ability to be in a specific point in space at a specific point in time. Rhythmic accuracy is contingent upon both spatial accuracy and temporal accuracy, each of which may be considered alone or with the other (Schwanda, 1969, p. 568).

DEFINITIONS INVOLVING A DETERMINATION OF DIFFERENCE

Differentiation between two or more rhythmic patterns as being either like or unlike in rhythmic organization (Schwanda, 1969, p. 568).

DEFINITIONS INVOLVING MOVEMENT QUALITY

... movement that is aesthetically pleasing to the observer as well as to the one being observed (Schwanda, 1969, p. 573).

This list of definitions should serve as an indication of the complexity and diversity inherent in any study of rhythm and rhythmic phenomena. As is usually the case, those who study rhythm frequently operate under certain assumptions, the most basic being that rhythmic phenomena do in fact exist in nature at all levels and that those phenomena can be observed. However, is it simply all an illusion? Is God really, "playing dice with the universe" as the Quantum theorists seem to be saying? Or, are we all unwitting participants in some great universal dance? Perhaps we will never know all of the answers. We must, however, continue the quest.

REFERENCES

Apel, W. *Harvard dictionary of music* (2nd ed.). Cambridge: The Belknap Press of Harvard University Press, 1969.

Bond, M. H. Rhythmic performance and gross motor performance. *Research Quarterly,* 1959, *30,* 259–265.

Behrens, G. A. In search of the long assumed relationship between rhythm and movement. *Contributions to Music Education,* 1984, *11,* 33–54.

Berlyne, D. E. *Aesthetics and psychobiology.* New York: Appleton-Century-Crofts, 1971.

Brown, F., Hastings, J., & Palmer, J. *The biological clock: Two views.* New York: Academic Press, 1970.

Cloudsley-Thompson, J. L. *Rhythmic activity in animal physiology and behavior.* New York: Academic Press, 1961.

Clynes, M. (Ed.). *Music, mind, and brain.* New York: Plenum Press, 1982.

Davies, J. B. *The psychology of music.* Palo Alto: Stanford University Press, 1978.

Delcoymyn, F. Neural basis of rhythmic behavior in animals. *Science,* 1980, **210,** 492–498.

Demany, L., McKenzie, B., & Vurpillot, E. Rhythm perception in early infancy. *Nature,* 1977, *226,* 718–719.

Durr, W., Gerstenberg, W., & Harvey, J. Rhythm. In S. Sadie (Ed.), *The new Grove dictionary of music and musicians* (*Vol. 15*). Washington, DC: MacMillan, 1980.

Fraisse, P. Rhythm and Tempo. In D. Deutch (Ed.), *The psychology of music.* New York: Academic Press, 1982.

Gardner, H. *The arts and human development.* New York: John Wiley and Sons, 1973.

Gaston, E. T. Man and music. In E. T. Gaston (Ed.), *Music in therapy.* New York: MacMillan, 1968.

John, E. R. Switchboard versus statistical theories of learning and memory. *Science,* 1972, *177,* pp. 850–864.

Luce, G. G. *Biological rhythms in human and animal physiology.* New York: Ronald Press, 1967.

Lundin, R. W. *An objective psychology of music* (2nd ed.). New York: Ronald Press, 1967.

Martin, J. G. Rhythmic (hierarchical) versus serial structure in speech and other behavior. *Psychological Review,* 1972, *79,* 487–509.

Merriam, A. P. *The anthropology of music.* Evanston, IL: Northwestern University Press, 1964.

Mikol, B. The effects of music and rhythm on the performance of a psychomotor task. In M. Bing (Ed.), *Music therapy 1953; Third book of proceedings of the National Association of Music Therapy* (Vol. 3). Lawrence, KS: National Association for Music Therapy, 1954.

Minors, D. S., & Waterhouse, J. M. *Circadian rhythms and the human.* Boston: Wright, PSG, 1981.

Mursell, J. L. Rhythm and musical growth. *Music education, principles and programs.* Morristown, NJ: Silver Burdett, 1956.

Petzold, R. G. Rhythm study. *Auditory perception of musical sounds by children in the first six grades.* Madison: University of Wisconsin, 1966.

Radocy, R. E., & Boyle, J. D. *Psychological foundations of musical behavior.* Springfield, IL: Charles C Thomas, 1979.

Radocy, R. E. The perception of melody, harmony, rhythm, and form. In D. A. Hodges (Ed.), *Handbook of music psychology.* Lawrence, KS: National Association for Music Therapy, Inc., 1980.

Scholes, P. A. Rhythm. In J. O. Ward (Ed.), *The Oxford companion to music.* London: Oxford University Press, 1970.

Schwanda, N. A. A study of rhythmic ability and movement performance. *Research Quarterly,* 1969, *40,* 567–574.

Smoll, F. L., & Schutz, R. W. Relationships among measures of preferred tempo and motor rhythm. *Perceptual and Motor Skills,* 1978, *46,* 883–894.

Smoll, F. L. A rhythmic ability analysis system. *Research Quarterly,* 1973, *44,* 232–236.

Spohn, C. L. Research in learning rhythms and the implication for music education. *Council for Research in Music Education,* 1977, *50,* 62–66.

Thackray, R. *An investigation into rhythmic abilities.* London: Novello and Company Limited, 1968.

Thelen, E. Rhythmical behavior in infancy: An ethological perspective. *Developmental Psychology,* 1981, *17,* 237–257.

Ward, R. R. If you look hard cycles are all over. *Smithsonian,* March, 1977, pp. 104–108.

Chapter 2.

ATTENTIONAL RHYTHMICITY IN HUMAN PERCEPTION

MARI RIESS JONES

Attending is a fundamental activity of living things. It is a selective activity that is exhibited by many different species and which allows the animal to pluck out and use one aspect of a complex and changing world structure while simultaneously ignoring others. One can attend primarily to one speaker while ignoring another, for example, (Cherry, 1953). Historically, these selective aspects of attending have played a major role in the development of psychological theories of attending (Broadbent, 1958; Eysenck, 1982; Treisman, 1964). Less attention has been devoted to other, perhaps concomitant, aspects of attending such as the energizing or arousal function of this activity, although Kahneman (1973) notably differs in proposing that both selectivity and arousal aspects of attending determine performance.

This chapter briefly and selectively reviews some current approaches to attending that direct basic research on this topic. Some of these approaches are shown to be relatively limited in scope and to ignore important features of dynamic attending. Theories that incorporate assumptions about time and rhythmicity both in the environment to which an individual attends and in the organism itself are shown to be more general.

I. Attending: Current Perspectives

This section considers three different categories of attentional models. The first category includes attentional resource theories which derive from the well-entrenched traditions of information processing. The second category includes schema theories which arise from a tradition established by Bartlett (1932). The third category includes more explicitly dynamic attentional theories in which rhythmicities play a primary role.

A. **Attentional resource models.** Information processing theories historically have placed great emphasis upon filter models to explain attentional selectivity. Thus, one attends selectively to a series of words or tones presented to one ear (i.e., information channel) by means of filters which are situated at some early stage of processing and which are tuned to a given physical channel. Filters could regulate (in an all-or-none fashion) the flow of information over the channel according to Broadbent's seminal proposal (1958). Originally simple filter theories out of this mold did not consider attentional selectivity as a time function—selectivity that might depend importantly on dynamic context (among other things). That is, the possibility that a person might adapt to a given rate or rhythm or that attending itself reflects a sensitivity to temporal relationships between presented items in a series was not considered. This is not to say that sampling-time and attentional switching rates were not important concepts in early filter models such as Broadbent's. They were. But the patterning of events in time and the possible temporal patterning of attending itself were not. Filters were not explicitly sensitive to, for example, the rhythm of a series of items.

Filter models of attention have been replaced by the now popular resource capacity models. This came about partly in response to data indicating that people actually "monitor" and respond to things presented on what filter-theory identified as an "unattended channel." People frequently will respond to their own name embedded in material presented to an unattended channel (ear); for example (Lewis, 1970; Moray, 1959). Although attempts to patch up Broadbent's model (e.g., Treisman, 1964) met with some success, ultimately accumulating data led to the abandonment of this line of theorizing. More detailed accounts of this decline are presented elsewhere (e.g., Eysenck, 1982; Massaro, 1975).

An influential treatise presented by Kahneman (1973) upon the function of effort and arousal in attentional theory also hastened the decline of filter theories. Kahneman introduced the concept of attentional energy as a resource, of limited capacity, that could be selectively marshalled to do "work" in various tasks. This amounted to incorporating not only a selective but also an intensive aspect to attention. Originally Kahneman advocated that attentional resources contributed to a central pool and thus tasks which require a division of attentional energy can interfere with one another because they both must draw from the same limited resource pool. Thus, if one must memorize digits while monitoring a speaker's utterances for a target phoneme, performance on the primary task may improve over time while performance on the secondary task declines due to limited capacity allocation and use.

More recently, theories which propose multiple, task-specific, resource pools have been developed (e.g., Navon & Gopher, 1979), largely in response to patterns of selective interference in divided attention tasks. For example, people required to form auditory images exhibited greater interference in an auditory signal detection task than people required to visually image (Segal & Fusella, 1970). Presumably, there are modality specific resource pools which explain such patterns of interference. Nevertheless, in all resource models, it is the limitation (general or specific) which tasks place on attentional resources that ultimately determines attentional selectivity.

A refinement on the resource model concept introduces attentional selectivity that does not arise directly from resource capacity limitations. Posner and Snyder (1975) proposed a distinction between automatic attending, which does not operate through capacity limitations, and controlled attending, which does. Automatic attending occurs in highly practiced tasks and without awareness whereas controlled attending involves conscious and deliberate focussing on relatively unfamiliar material (tasks). Automatic attention, for example, is revealed as the reply of "bird" to "robin." Conscious attending, however, would be reflected in a more thoughtful, time consuming, and original response such as "song." Recently, Shiffrin and Schneider (1977) and Schneider and Shiffrin (1977) developed this distinction in the context of a modified memory-search task of the Sternberg variety. They asked people to search visual displays of 1–4 items for a specified target (i.e., a letter). They argued that slow, controlled (conscious) attending happens whenever one must search an array item-by-item. However, if the target type can be identified categorically as "a digit" among a set of letters, for example, then attending will become extremely rapid and automated.

Resource capacity models are useful in raising the issue of attentional energy and in attempting to link this to attentional selectivity. In this, they offer greater explanatory flexibility than did the simple filter theory explanations of selectivity. Finally, however, none of these approaches directly addresses the nature of attentional energy. Nor do they attempt to specify determinants of energy capacity limitations in various tasks. That is, it is not clear from whence the resources, as attentional energy, come. Nor is it clear why and how these resources are actually task specific. This makes it difficult to predict in advance when a task will heavily tax particular resources.

This rather recently emphasized dichotomy between automatic and controlled attending oversimplifies the complex issue of skill acquisition and perceptual learning. Essentially the dichotomy suggests that people are either performing asymptotically in a highly skilled fashion, and hence using automatic attention, or they are akin to novices performing under high uncertainty and so with controlled attending. Thus, the distinction fails to even address how skilled attending develops with practice in complex tasks such as reading, writing, listening to music, etc. (Hirst, Spelke, Reaves, Caharack, & Neisser, 1980). Notably it could be argued that the failure to address the question of training-of-attending is related to the fact that much of the evidence used to support these models is based on tasks that lack a coherent structure to which people may gradually become attuned. For example, the tasks studied by Shiffrin and Schneider (1977) confront people with hundreds of arrays of randomly selected letters or digits.

Resource models of attention, like their filter-theory predecessors, fail to take account of the temporal context and its possible influence upon automatic and controlled attending (among other things). For example, resource models often conceive of time in terms of "processing time," namely the amount of time required to encode an isolated item. Thus, Massaro (1975), using one version of a resource model, suggests that a way in which resource limits can arise comes from constraints on available processing time. For example, he assumes that perception of an auditory sequence is time limited according to its rate. Longer time intervals between successive tones in a sequence will reduce limits on processing each tone, limits which arise from masking effects according to this model. Indeed, even in patterns where the time intervals between successive tonal onsets are varied in a patterned way within the sequence, Massaro (1975) and Massaro & Idson (1976) suggest that the amount of time allotted each tone determines attentional processing capacity. Possible effects of patterning in time (i.e., rhythm) are ignored here. The point is that absolute time, namely sequence rate, and not relative time, namely sequence rhythm, are assumed to determine attentional resources. Again the patterning in temporal context is ignored.

II. Schema Models of Attention

Schema theory, developed most elegantly earlier in this century by Sir Frederick Bartlett (1932), was not originally proposed as a theory of attention; it was a theory about remembering. Bartlett's hypothesis was not that people remember the general outline of an experienced episode, such as a story, and forget the details. Over time, even major structural parts of an episode get simplified and rearranged into a "good" form and this form is the scheme an individual uses to reconstruct the episode at a later time.

The idea that people may use simplified or distorted schemes to guide attention, and thereby influence perception, is a recent adaptation of Bartlett's ideas. Schema models of attention are less closely identified with a particular body of attentional phenomena than are filter or resource models. However, the most prominent contemporary proponent of this idea (Ulric Neisser, 1976), directly confronts the filter-theory account of attentional selectivity in the following way. "Organisms are active: they do some things and leave others undone. To pick one apple from a tree you need not filter out all the others; you just don't pick them." (p. 85, Neisser, 1976). The emphasis is upon selective anticipation. Neisser argues that certain acquired skills direct a person's attending and that attending is anticipatory in a way that prepares the individual to pick up new information. For Neisser, then attending is an activity engaged in by the organism that follows certain acquired patterns or schemes. It is inseparable from perception: "Attention is nothing but perception: we choose what we will see by anticipating the structured information it will provide." (p. 87, Neisser, 1976). Structured information may be complex and change over time. For example, the information afforded by visual movement patterns of players in a basketball game can be selectively tracked by viewers. This was shown in an experiment by Neisser and Brecklen (1975). Viewers watched a video of two different basketball games superimposed in full visual overlap. They were asked to attend to one of the games and ignore the other while they pressed a key to record each ball toss among participants in the attended game. The results indicated that viewers could perform such a task with high accuracy. According to Neisser, such selective viewing demonstrations illustrate that the "selection" in selective attending requires no special machinery (e.g., filters, resource pools, etc.) and that it is a process inseparable from everyday perceptual activities.

Attending and perceiving therefore follow acquired schemas. These schemas, in turn, selectively guide the future pickup of new and relevant information. In this way, Neisser accomodates perceptual learning. In contrast to resource models the schema approach views attending as a directed activity which prepares the individual in an anticipatory way and so enters into the refinement of skill. Accordingly, the model is more likely to be evaluated in environments where information is complexly structured and attention tasks are difficult. For example, Spelke, Hirst, and Neisser (1976) studied skill acquisition over a 17 week period in students required to concurrently read prose and take dictation. After six weeks, the two subjects became highly proficient in both tasks. Follow-up studies by Hirst et al. (1980) indicated that subjects were not automated in either task since they understood materials in both prose and dictation tasks. The authors argued that level of skill and not a fixed pool of resources determines performance even in controlled attending.

Schema models are useful in that they more directly call theoretical attention to the actual acquisition of complex skills than do many resource models. Paradoxically, however, the main explanatory construct, the schema, is often as vaguely specified as are resource pools. Indeed, a schema explanation of skill acquisition is unparsimoious if it adds nothing of predictive value to the banal observation that people improve with practice. For predictive value to obtain, there must be precise specification of both the nature of a schema and its environmental determinants, past and present. That is, what invariants in the environment, if any, "carry" a schema. Furthermore, how do they do this? Unquestionably temporal patterning in the environment should be among the determinants of schemas. Yet, there is a theoretical neglect of such determinants in general, and of time and rhythm in particular.

This neglect holds even in schema theories such as Neisser's which purport to be dynamic. It is especially ironic in the case of Neisser's model because schemas here are supposed to support responding that is **anticipatory** in time (i.e., dynamic). But without explicit incorporation of time into the schema itself, there is no theoretical basis for temporal anticipation. Because time is not explicitly incorporated as part of a schema or as part of its supporting environment the development of schema-based anticipations is not clear. The actual interplay of dynamic attending with a temporal context is not considered. Yet the temporal character of a schema relative to the surrounding environment is precisely what must determine a prepared attender and therefore an antici-patory responder!

III. A Rhythmic Model of Attending

A rhythmical approach to attending is one which assumes that people and other animals target attending over predetermined time intervals toward events in space and time in a rhythmical fashion. Attending is an energistic activity guided in part by explicitly dynamic schemes that are themselves set in motion or indeed synchronously driven by the ongo-ing temporal character of an environment (Jones, 1976; Martin, 1972). The main thesis of this approach is that attending reflects an **interplay** of a rhythmical organism with rhythmicities within the environment. Accord-ing to Jones (1976) the interplay depends upon excited rhythmicities, i.e., attentional rhythmicities, within the organism and their temporal relationship vis-a-vis temporal periodicities within the environment. That is, the interplay is manifested (usually in some overtly measureable way) by the way a person either anticipates (is early), misses (is late), or synchronizes attending with events that occur in the world. Essentially then the word "interplay" reflects the notion that a temporal relativity exists between time patterning of certain observable events in the world and the time patterning of attentional energy within an organism: attend-ing may either lag behind, be in phase, or run ahead of reference events in the world.

The approach differs from others in its emphasis upon the importance of temporal relationships that exist within an organism and in its envi-ronmental surrounds. It emphasizes the need to develop better ways to specify, manipulate, and assess the influence of temporal stimulation upon the behavior of a dynamic organism. The rhythmic approach to attending shares some features of resource and schema models, but it differs from each in important ways and these differences lead to new research issues. For example, while it incorporates the idea of intensive attentional energy, as do some resource models, a rhythmic model hypothe-sizes that this energy is patterned in ways that can (among other things) facilitate pickup of meanings through e.g. expressive intonation patterns. There is less emphasis upon capacity limits. Furthermore, while the rhythmic approach also incorporates the idea of dynamic schemes, here these are explicitly temporal so that the "selection" aspect of attentional selectivity is seen in terms of information pickup that is facilitated (or deterred) by **temporal predictability.**

Consider first some comparisons with resource models. Both resource models and the rhythmic attending approach engage the constructs of attentional energy and allocation of energy. But the interpretation and function of attentional energy differs in the two approaches. According to resource models, energy is an undefined construct that primarily limits work capacity in divided attention tasks. In contrast, in the rhythmical interpretation energy is explicitly tied to natural rhythmicities of living things. Energy is not metaphorical in this approach. It is potentially measureable in terms of heightened amplitudes (or increased recruitment) associated with excited brain rhythms of particular frequencies. Heightened attending thus is accompanied by heightened arousal which, if specific, is reflected by greater energy allocated to attentional rhythms that are sensitive to the spatio-temporal structure of the to-be-attended events. Attentional rhythms of variously graded frequencies determine the ability of an organism to lock-into environmental periodicties of various kinds. Heightened attention to one set of stimuli and not another reflects the differential assignment of energy to spatio-temporal patterning associated with the focussed stimulus set. Thus, by this account, attentional interference of two sets of stimuli or two tasks will depend upon a careful analysis of their structural relationships. A simple prediction is that tasks or materials which require two co-occurring serial responses (e.g., speaking and hand tapping) will be learned more quickly or performed with less interference if they possess harmonically related time structures, a prediction which is consistent with recent evidence (Kelso, Southard, & Goodman, 1979; Kelso, Tuller, & Harris, in press; Klapp, 1979, 1981). Harmonically related dual tasks should produce less temporally based interference.

According to the rhythmical approach then the energizing aspect of attending is linked to a structural analysis of the stimulation. This underscores the need to develop a formal language with which to analyze the dynamic structure of stimulation. But it also raises the related issue of structural ambiguity (Jones, 1981). A stimulus can be described in multiple ways. Which way is "correct"? Which structural analysis reflects the attended-to-aspects? In Gibson's terms an event affords many things. He argues that it is the **need** of the organism to perform a certain function which will determine an object's momentary perceived affordance (Gibson, 1979). Thus a given speech utterance will afford many different structural invariants that are respectively appropriate to different needs of a listener. One can attend to rhyming aspects within the unfolding speech sequence, or to the presence of certain phonemes, or to the meaning of the utterance depending upon the immediate requirements of a listener as Morris, Bransford, and Franks (1977) have shown. Nevertheless, the presence of structural ambiguity and of multiple, structurally-based, affordances presents a real practical problem to Gibson's theory of affordances as Cutting has suggested (1982). How does one determine, in advance, which structural affordance will predominate? More importantly, we need to explain precisely how one's need or goal selectively targets one affordance and not another.

With respect to the latter problem, I have suggested (Jones, 1976, 1981) that structural ambiguity is resolved, in part, by the way needs affect allocation of attentional energy to one or another spatio-temporal level. Often a temporal patterning or periodicity within the stimulus co-varies with its to-be-attended affordance. Temporal periodicities associated with speech phonemes, for example, differ from others associated with sentential meaning. Thus, if the need to monitor phonemes arises, e.g., for a person in speech therapy, this need will result in the individual learning (among other things) to heighten attentional energy to this (relatively small) time base. Alternatively, to catch the sarcasm of a speaker's utterance, which is associated with certain intonational inflections, attending is to longer and differently patterned time-based cadences in the speech stream. In this way, attentional selectivity is determined, in part, by temporal properties within the speech stream. This time-based selectivity suggests one way in which a need is translated into the selective targeting of one affordance and not another within a structurally ambiguous situation. Greater attentional energies specific to one need are allocated to the time patterning associated with that need. More generally this means that perceived needs may call forth within the organism particular "calibrated" shapes of energy over time and these attentional shapes selectively guide attending to "lock-into" matching affordances embedded within an ostensibly ambiguous stimulus pattern.

In other situations, the patterning of attentional energy is not called forth in advance by a need but is literally "shaped" directly over time by co-occurring spatio-temporal energy patterns within the environment. High energy environmental pattern can entrain matching attentional energy patterns within the organism, and thereby convey expressive meaning quite directly. This happens in communications between members of all species. Notably communications of courtship and territoriality among song birds certainly suggest the importance of primitive expressive energy patterns (e.g., Greenwalt, 1968). Similarly there are distinctive patterns of loudness over time revealed in human speech and music which convey, through intonation, intended (and sometimes unintended) meanings. Here meaning between speaker and listener is communicated at a tacit level through the attentional act of inner mimicry, a mimicry induced by entrainment of attentional energies of listener with intonations of the speaker. Through mimicry, emphathetic understanding is possible. In a sense, the listener partially "becomes" the speaker.

These views share more with those of Clynes (1978) than they do with current resource interpretations of attentional energy. Clynes has suggested that emotions are expressed through characteristic energy patterns which can be documented through studies of touch. In general, the rhythmical approach, through its emphasis upon dynamic energy patterns and their temporal interactions with environmental patterns, suggests a different kind of attentional energy with correspondingly different functions than is portrayed by resource models.

Consider next comparisons of the rhythmical attending approach with Neisser's schema theory. Again there are several commonalities. Dynamic attending is seen to prepare an organism for pickup of new information in both theories. And in both, people are assumed to acquire modes of attending over time that allow them to skillfully anticipate future events. For example, a skilled pianist acquires dynamic attending schemas that facilitate listening as well as piano playing. This means that in listening to a musical piece, the skilled listener will often be able to reasonably forecast certain upcoming notes and chords whereas the musically untrained person is less likely to do this. Among other things, this makes the skilled listener also better equiped to detect a musical change when it occurs. Both theoretical approaches essentially agree on these points.

The rhythmic approach differs from recent schema models, however, in its emphasis upon the importance of temporal invariants that control attending in skilled and unskilled individuals. It is more analytical about the relativistic interplay of a person's dynamic schema and co-occurring elements in the environment. One consequence of its greater commitment to temporal invariants is that the rhythmical attending theory predicts that synchronous attending is an important, and often overlooked, determinant of perceptual learning. Through synchronous attending the temporal aspects of a context, relative to the organism's attentional state, may silently pave the way for skill acquisition. Synchronicity, for example, ensures that one attends not only to the right place (or "thing"), but at the appropriate time. Attentional energy that is locked-into selected periods of an unfolding temporal context is more likely to be available at crucial times when new information, information useful for a desired goal, occurs. In short, the refinement of goal oriented attentional schemes that reflect different kinds of skilled behavior depends upon the relativistic temporal interplay of scheme and environment.

In summary, this section has presented a highly selective and explicitly comparative overview of three approaches to attending. The aim was to highlight similarities and differences between two of the more prominent approaches, namely resource and schema models, and the rhythmical interpretation of attending. In the following section, some preliminary evidence which derives from the rhythmical approach is outlined.

IV. Experimental Evidence for Rhythmic Attending

According to the rhythmic attending theory, people rely upon invariances abstracted from the temporal rhythmicities of a particular context to prepare attentionally for "when" forthcoming events will happen. Attentional energy is thus temporally targeted (Jones, 1976; Martin, 1972). Temporal preparation, in turn, paves the way for learning since a temporally prepared attender will have an advantage with novel or changed information. Learning, by definition, refers to one's changing ability to cope with new and unfamiliar material. According to the present hypothesis one copes better if new material happens at points in time where attentional energy is greater.

In much of our experience new material comes embedded within familiar material and both develop over relatively predictable time courses. But the temporal occurrence of new and significant information may often be signalled by the energy pattern of a surrounding context. Thus, a newscaster whose voice intonation falls to signal disclosure of the tragic demise of a prominent figure prepares the attender for this news. Among other things intonation is manipulated through accenting. And Bock and Mazzella (in press) have shown that intonation patterns in grammatical contexts effectively guide listeners to pick up the relevant new material which follows. Using sentences that induce accentuation on new information they found that these sentences were understood more quickly than sentences with a neutral intonation contour. In particular, in one study they found that faster comprehension times resulted when new information was accented and given (previously learned) information was not than when the reverse was true. Others have found that intonation patterns are picked up very early in language learning (MacWhinney & Bates, 1978). Related evidence (to be considered shortly) can be found in music recognition. Intuitively, this seems plausible for much of conventional musical listening involves relying upon relatively predictable temporal metrics to anticipate "when" forthcoming variations in harmonic and melodic patterns will occur.

In all these examples, an underlying component of a person's anticipations about forthcoming events involves the time dimension. People abstract certain temporal invariants from a particular context and use these time rules to synchronize or even anticipate not only "what" may happen but "when" it will transpire. Indeed, with sufficient uncertainty about "what" should occur, heightened attending during the expected time period is all the more crucial. And often an event does in fact violate specific expectations. For example, in attending to a speaker who says "I must run home to feed my . . . " a given listener may generate a specific expectation for the target word such as "dog," while the speaker may disconfirm this when she says "parakeet." Or in music one expects to hear a I chord but a III chord occurs. Such violations from expectation produce a contrast or novelty effect to the degree they differ from some anticipated outcome. But it is important to acknowledge that the novelty effect depends upon the individual's focussed attending at a given time. That is, the disparity between expected and observed is predicated on a temporal base. In this model, surprising things are only surprising within a temporal context. Furthermore, to the degree an unexpected event bears some lawful, albeit unusual non-temporal relationship to surrounding events this "surprise" becomes the basis for learning.

Relatively little research exists on the manipulation of temporal structure for the purpose of understanding the effects of timing and rhythm on people's attending to the environment. There is, to be sure, a long tradition of studies which manipulate musical rhythm or tempo in order to learn more about people's judgments of rhythm and tempo (Fraisse, 1978; Gabrielsson, 1973; Handel & Oshinsky, 1981; Povel, 1981). But less is known about effects of various rhythmic manipulations on people's ability to pick up different kinds of changes in their environment. Since this comes close to addressing the function of temporal context in perceptual learning I will review some of our own research which represents a modest initial attack on discovering the contributions of temporal determinants of attending in various tasks.

The research described here focuses primarily upon the issue of temporal preparation and its potential role in learning. To this end the contextual structure afforded by time patterns was carefully manipulated using both temporal and non-temporal rules. That is, the stimuli involved are structured patterns, not the arbitrary or random stimuli so often used in research on attention. In the present case, these patterns are often carefully simplified versions of more complex environmental arrays. Typically they are composed of discrete visual or auditory events that unfold in more or less predictable ways over time. With visual patterns, dynamic configurations of dots or lines are used. With auditory sequences, diatonic music-like patterns, involving carefully arranged melodic invariances, are used. In all cases, the influence of rhythmic patterning was also examined.

The question of interest was "Does temporal context affect a person's ability to pick up new or changed information in a pattern?" The manipulations of temporal context using a pattern recognition paradigm allowed us to answer this question. People who were exposed to a pair of patterns, had to judge whether or not the second pattern was different (i.e., contained a changed relationship) from the first pattern. Half the time it was different. A working assumption was the people attend dynamically to the second patterns largely using invariants abstracted from the structure of the first. We hypothesized that if these invariants are partly temporal in nature, then specific manipulations of timing should influence recognition of novel information regardless of whether that information itself is temporal or not. Thus, for example, if a listener is able to predict precisely "when" a V chord should occur within a melody, then he/she will be more accurate in assessing whether or not a I chord occurred at that point in time instead.

A. Temporal Context Effects on Time Judgments

Perhaps the most elementary issue concerns whether temporal manipulations have any effect on people's ability to judge timing itself. Clearly they should if the general hypothesis that temporal context facilitates the prediction of "when" things will occur is correct. Logically, one's ability to temporally anticipate successive events within a time pattern should affect one's skill at judging whether the time pattern has been changed or not. Furthermore, if temporal context as specified by particular time rules within a pattern is a determinant of anticipatory responding, then people should be more accurate in time judgments with contexts that involve highly regular temporal rules. For example, highly regular Isochronous rhythms will afford a more effective basis for temporal predictability than certain other rhythms which offer more complex temporal invariants. Thus Isochronous rhythmic contexts should more readily synchronize with internal attentional rhythmicities having stable beat periods.

Skelly, Hahn and Jones (Note 1) tested this idea. They varied (among other things) the temporal structure of unfolding circular arrays of eight radial lines in a time judgment task. Spatial configurations, such as in Figure 1, unfolded line-by-line over time according to one of two rhythmic patterns, Isochronous and Variable. The Isochronous rhythm involved a recurrent period of 200 msec between all successive line onsets. The Variable rhythm incorporated metrically lengthened durations of alternate lines (i.e., durations of lines 2, 4, 6, and 8 were greater than 200 msec). In both rhythmic contexts, however, the fifth line in the series normally (i.e., when not changed) lasted 200 msec. In the pattern comparison task used, viewers saw pairs of patterns that were identical in every respect except that half the time the timing of the fifth event in the second pattern was changed from its normal, 200 msec, value (by ± 50, ± 100, or ± 150 msec). And on each of a series of such trials, viewers tried to detect whether the two patterns differed in timing. They responded "Different" or "Same."

It was predicted that the context set up by the Isochronous rhythm should induce within the viewers a regular-internal attentional beat approximating the pattern's 200 msec onset-to-onset periodicity. The Variable rhythm, on the other hand, has greater structural ambiguity containing some event durations significantly longer than the Isochronous period. The Variable rhythm thus afforded a slower internal reference beat. A prediction is, therefore, that an Isochronous standard rhythm would tend to induce a highly regular 200 msec reference beat within viewers. If viewers used this beat to judge timing in the second (comparison) pattern, then their time discrimination performance would improve **symmetrically** for shortened and lengthened durations as these differed from the 200 msec value. On the other hand, if viewers judged new (i.e., changed timing) durations relative to a longer reference beat, then **asymmetries** in time discrimination accuracy should occur. In particular,

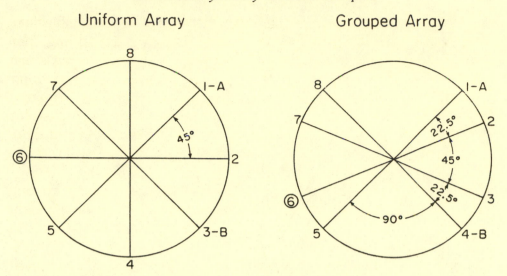

Figure 1. Two different spatial arrays of radial lines that were combined with different rhythms in the Skelly, Hahn, and Jones research (see text). The fifth line always gave the target duration (200 msec); the sixth line (circled) could, according to a masking account serve as a functional mask.

shortened comparison durations would seem more noticeable and lengthened ones less noticeable. Asymmetries in time judgments of the latter sort were expected more often in the Variable rhythm due to this contrast effect.

Figure 2 presents the results of Skelly et al. Proportion of correct judgments are plotted as a function of temporal deviation (from the 200 msec standard) and temporal context (Isochronous, Variable rhythm). The predicted temporal contrast effect was supported by a significant interaction of temporal context with temporal deviation. As shown in Figure 2, shortened events were more noticeable than lengthened ones in the Variable rhythm whereas this asymmetry was not apparent in the Isochronous rhythm. In the Isochronous rhythm people were likely to find a shortened event as noticeable as one lengthened by the same amount. So in a sense people were more "accurate" with Isochronous rhythm in that they were more faithful in their rendition of the standard duration. The nature of this temporal contrast effect suggests that with the Isochronous rhythms people use a reference beat which more closely approximates the duration of the fifth event, whereas in the Variable rhythm their internal standard for this event has shifted to a larger value. As a result, in this context, they "overestimate" the shortness of brief durations, and "underestimate" the length of longer targets.

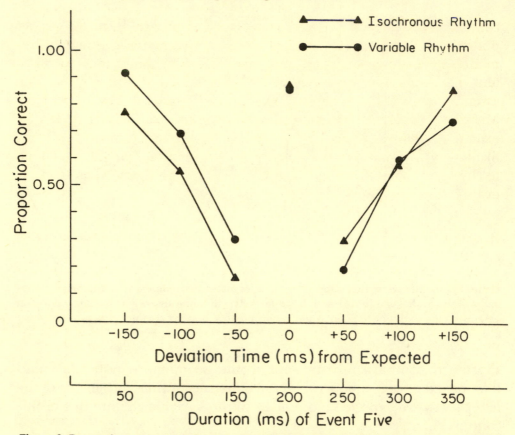

Figure 2. Proportion correct as a function of deviation from expected time (or duration) and rhythm (Isochronous, Variable) in the Skelly, Hahn, and Jones research (see text).

These and related studies with other rhythmic contexts suggested that Isochronous rhythms induce a stable and veridical "locking-into" the reference beat of the unfolding pattern whereas non-isochronous rhythms tend to induce reliance on a less stable and shifted reference beat. The resulting temporal contrast effects are interesting not only for what they tell us about the nature of rhythmically induced periodicities but also for what they show about viewer's use of "new" information. Novel events are evaluated with reference to an expected reference event which, in this case, was a beat period.

At a more general level, these studies were interpreted as support for the idea that people use context-sensitive dynamic schemes to generate expectancies. In this respect, the schemes are more explicitly temporal than Neisser has proposed. That is, the internal schemes are essentially temporal and reflect the relative time properties afforded by a particular context. This sort of dynamic expectancy approach also has greater potential for explaining the data then some versions of the resource models reviewed earlier. In several cases data were shown to be inconsistent with predictions generated by an information-processing model that assumed attentional resources are time-limited through backward masking. Masking models such as those proposed by Massaro and Idson (1976), for example, could not predict the observed temporal contrast found by Skelly et al. Thus, it is more parsimonious to assume that people attend to rhythmic (relative timing) invariants within a context and use these to evaluate new temporal information.

B. Temporal Effects Upon Perception of Non-Temporal Relationships

Time discrimination procedures involving rhythmic manipulations of dynamic visual patterns such as the one reviewed in the preceding section are useful for several reasons. In the first place, they indicate that temporal context does indeed affect a person's judgment about the "when" of future events. Secondly, in this particular illustration, they also happen to establish that rhythmicities are influential in visual as well as auditory patterns. Nevertheless, a time discrimination task does not establish that temporal context has any effect on one's performance in evaluating and using new information which is not temporal information. One could argue, for example, that rhythmic invariants will be more likely to affect judgments about timing than to affect judgments about non-temporal pattern features. According to the present perspective, however, timing is an indispensable (albeit silent) part of a person's interaction with all world events. So, it is theoretically interesting to discover if changes in timing that affect one's ability to anticipate "when" new non-temporal information will occur also affects one's perception of that information. Does rhythm influence one's chances of identifying a new relationship when it occurs?

Some recent research with simple musiclike auditory sequences speaks to this issue. In one of a series of studies, Gary Kidd, Marilyn Boltz and myself (1984) presented average listeners (i.e., people with no special musical background) with pairs of auditory patterns involving 10 (sine) tones each. The sequences were arrangements of notes from the C major scale where both members of a pattern pair were identical with respect to pitch intervals. The second pattern of the pair was always transposed one octave above the first to encourage attention to relationships between pitches. In the experiment of interest, listeners were to judge, over many trials, whether the second melody of a given pair reflected the same pattern of pitch relationships as the first melody. Half the time, one note (target note) was changed to an "out-of-key" note in the second (comparison) pattern (assuming the C major context), without changing the pattern's contour. Four different groups of listeners performed this task under four different rhythmic conditions (see Table 1). One group always received both melodies of pair in the same Isochronous rhythm (II); another received both in the same Variable rhythm (VV), a rhythm with time rules that rendered temporal predictability of the onset of the change note complex. Two other groups always received the two melodies in, respectively, different rhythms (IV and VI). In all cases, the durations and pitch values of the target notes were the same regardless of whether they occurred in the same or a changed rhythm. Furthermore, people in all groups were emphatically instructed to ignore rhythmic variations and to make their judgments strictly on the relative pitch patterns of the two melodies.

Table 1
Mean Proportion Correct Melody Recognition Judgments
in an Experiment by Kidd, Boltz, and Jones (Note 2)

Rhythmic Context	$\overline{PC}$	S^2
II	.71	.02
VV	.66	.02
IV	.59	.02
VI	.63	.03

It was anticipated that in spite of the instructions rhythmic properties might be hard to ignore. That is, this situation should be unlike that experienced by the viewers in the above-mentioned Neisser and Brecklen (1975) selective viewing study who could ignore one basketball team in favor of another. Here it was predicted that, because the rhythm of a melody is part of an integrated melodic-rhythmic object, listeners could not easily ignore the rhythm of the melody they must judge. This is because schemes assumed to guide melodic attending rely jointly upon melodic and temporal rules. Thus time is partly the basis upon which one can selectively ignore one pattern of (auditory or visual) motions in favor of another with a different time course. Within a given melodic pattern then rhythm becomes an integral part of the sequence, and separation of temporal invariants from pitch pattern invariants should be hard to accomplish. In the present experiment this was true. Often listeners judged patterns with the same rhythms, particularly in the VV group, to have the same melody. This reflected a simple rhythmic biasing effect. However, beyond these effects, there were also systematic effects upon melodic discrimination measures that indicated rhythmic influences on melody recognition. Table 1 shows proportion correct (PC) recognition judgments over the four groups. The II group performed best and the IV performed worst with the difference between these two groups statistically significant. These data indicate that shifts of the regular rhythmic base of a melody will disrupt attentional targeting and make it less likely that a changed melodic relationship will be detected.

Overall, this was a difficult task for these listeners for several reasons, including the fact that the melodies themselves were somewhat complex. Simpler melodies were used in another study conducted by Jones, Boltz and Kidd (1982). Again the purpose was to manipulate temporal context in a melody recognition task in order to discover if temporal predictability affected a listener's proficiency in identifying a melodic change. Here nine tone melodic patterns were created by following simple rules for arrangements of pitches into three groups of three tones each. The resulting patterns sounded relatively simple (although not especially interesting musically). One nice feature of these rule-generated melodies was that two kinds of pitch changes occurred within a sequence, one associated with lower-order rules (within group rules) and one associated with higher-order rules (between group rules). Figure 3a shows an example pattern composed of notes from the C major scale.

This study was primarily a melody recognition study in which listeners judged whether pairs of pitch patterns were identical or not. However, in this case, when the second member of a pair contained a change in pitch the change could either violate continuation of a lower-level rule (i.e., occur on the serial position of the sixth note, SP6) or it could violate a higher-order rule (i.e., occur on the serial position of the fourth note, SP4). In this regard, we posed the question "Could rhythmic contexts be devised that would direct attentional energy either toward or away from the temporal locations of these specific pitch-rule violations?"

Figure 3b shows the four different rhythmic contexts we devised. One was Isochronous, a second had certain events within the first and third melodic groups lengthened in order to induce accenting on the sixth serial position (UUA). A third, arranged times in the two surrounding

3a)   Sample   melody

C D E G A B F E D

3b)   Time   contexts

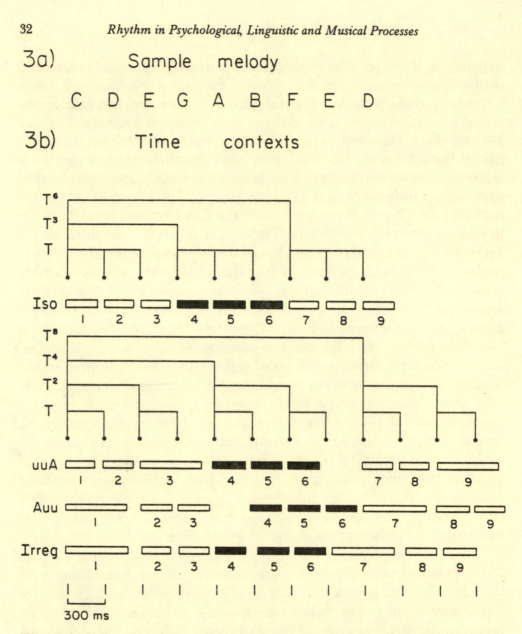

Figure 3. Melodies (example in panel 3a) presented in different rhythmic contexts were used to induce attentional targeting toward or away from tones embedded (darkened in 3b) within four different rhythmic contexts (Iso, UUA, AUU, Irreg).

melodic groups, to induce accentuation on the higher order rule transition at the fourth serial location (SP4). Finally, a control rhythm with an irregular time patterns was devised to shift attending away from the fourth serial location (Irreg). The important point to note here is that the central three tones remain identical in both melodic and temporal structure throughout the four rhythmic contexts. Only the surrounding temporal context was manipulated.

Table 2 presents the probability that listeners recognized unchanged melodic pairs (Same) and correctly detected in-key changes on SP4 and SP6 in these contexts. Simply put, rhythmic context significantly affects the likelihood that a listener will notice a change in a higher order pitch relationship. When the temporal context guides attending to the appropriate temporal location, as in Iso and AUU, the probability of correctly detecting a higher-order change is around .73; if attending is elsewhere in time, as in Irreg and UUA, then this probability drops to .59. Effects with lower order rule violations are smaller, primarily because overall performance is high at these points. Finally, however, the data clearly show that rhythms which help to target attentional energy to the higher-order rule transitions facilitated the detection of rule violations at these points.

Table 2
Mean Proportion Correct Different (SP4, SP6) and Same Judgments in Melody Recognition as a Function of Rhythmic Context (Jones, Boltz, and Kidd, 1982)

Rhythmic Context	n	$\overline{PC}$	S^2	SP4 $\overline{PC}$	S^2	SP6	Same $\overline{PC}$	S^2
Iso	12	.729	.04	.828	.05		.891	.02
UUA	12	.583	.07	.880	.04		.859	.02
AUU	12	.740	.06	.807	.07		.844	.03
Irreg.	12	.599	.05	.823	.05		.870	.02

To summarize, these and related studies indicate that temporal context is important in dynamically orienting a person's attention to things occurring at particular times. Temporal predictability is presumably offered by salient background beats (e.g., accents), by tempo of an unfolding patterns and by the durational figures or rhythms built upon a metric scheme. That is, rhythmic figures recur and so themselves lend predictability.

These studies have not addressed some of the larger issues that are suggested by the rhythmical attending approach. For example, they do not consider the degree to which certain melodic-rhythmic combinations convey, through their relational features, expressive emotions. Recent research along these lines (e.g., Clynes and Nettheim, 1982; Levi, 1982) suggests that there exist some characteristic dynamic shapes of auditory energy that enable certain musical patterns to reliably express emotions such as agitation, calmness, joy, etc. The focus of the present studies, however, has been upon the function that a dynamic pattern has in temporally preparing the listener. It is possible that the degree to which one responds to a given "level" of temporal structure, when present, is modulated by the emotion evoked by the piece. A joyous melody, for example, may be far more effective at engaging (entraining) attending. These questions, of course, are answerable only with future research. For the present, the importance of the silent component of attending, namely the time dimension, in perceptual learning is simply suggested and this opens up many avenues for exploration.

C. Synchronous Attending as Part of Perceptual Learning

Perceptual learning refers to the process of refining one's ability to distinguish among elements and relationships within complex patterns on the basis simply of repeated perceptual encounters with these patterns (e.g., E. J. Gibson). This section considers briefly whether timing and the mastery of temporal anticipation may play a role in perceptual learning.

We have seen that temporal context affects both the veridicality of time estimates and the accuracy of melodic recognition. These data have been interpreted to mean that the context in which people operate induces certain expectations about "when" and "what" events will happen next. These expectations, because they are partially based upon abstracted temporal invariants are dynamic schemes that assist in our exploration of the environment. New and unexpected things are uncovered when attending is oriented via contextually induced schemes. At the same time context can affect the very nature of one's evaluation of a new event. A brief interval which occurs in a "slow" context, for example, seems even briefer. Presumably this is because a context not only prepares one to attend at a given place and time but it also determines a **framework from which new information is judged.**

How does all of this relate to perceptual learning? Learning involves the acquisition of new information, information that will enable the individual to better prepare for events the "next time around." Consider the recognition study involving melodic rule violation discussed in the preceding section. This task only required detection of a change, if present. More skill would be required if the listener had to, say, reproduce, in musical notation, the whole presented pattern (e.g., Jones, Maser, & Kidd, 1978). Nevertheless, in both cases, part of learning to perform correctly involves recognition of familiar musical intervals and abstracting their regularity within a melodic configuration during listening. To the degree a melody follows simple rules it will conform to already acquired musical expectations of a skilled listener. It is the violation of these regularities which creates the setting for perceptual learning. How does one cope with surprise and the unexpected? If the listener must actually reproduce a melody that contains a deviant or unexpected relationship, then he/she must be able to relate that surprising occurrence to surrounding elements of the dynamic context. She must integrate the novel relation into the melodic line. One way this integration is facilitated is through temporal preparation: a listener who expects one note **at a particular time** but another occurs can evaluate this surprising event better because expected and unexpected co-occur in time. The co-occurring pitch difference between expected and observed is abstracted, leading to integration of the surprising event into the listener's attentional scheme. This is one way in which timing can influence perceptual learning.

Thus, temporal preparation may be an essential part of perceptual learning especially with dynamic patterns. One must attend at the proper time to pick up new information. Attending too early or too late won't do. Attending must be synchronously timed. And as the previous section indicated, synchronicity reflects the interplay between an organism and its environmental context. In a real sense, our environment contributes to the control of attentional energies. Fortunately, we have evolved multiple ways to achieve synchronicity with our environment; this inherent flexibility in attending undoubtedly contributes to our facility to learn, to adapt, and to change.

A significant part of this environment, in fact, is made up of other organisms. Adult members of our own species, children, pets, and even the wildlife around us afford many rhythmic patterns with characteristic natural time patternings, patterns to which we become adapted through experience. In a real sense we control and are controlled by this living rhythmical environment around us. Some of the more interesting evidence along these lines comes from work on interactional synchrony in which overtly synchronous behaviors are shown to obtain between interacting people. Condon and Sanders (1974), for example, found that even in newborn infants a delicate temporal interplay exists between overt motor gestures of the infants and speech and motor gestures of the nearby mother. The interplay reflects a precisely timed interactional synchrony relating the two individuals in a reciprocal dance of gestures. Other research on interactional synchrony suggests that the phenomenon may itself be taken as some reflection of the degree of tacit attentional control exerted by the dynamic patterns of one human over another (e.g., Condon & Ogsten, 1971; Kendon, 1977, 1983).

Connections between research on interactional synchrony and research reviewed here based upon laboratory work with "inanimate" auditory and visual patterns are provocative. But there is much that separates the two realms of findings. Kendon (1983) has suggested that dynamic visual patterns offered by humans are composed of various gesture categories, categories that are simply not realized by visual stimuli used here. Furthermore, even the leap from musical pattern perception to speech perception is tenuous. For example, isochrony may be a more straightforward matter in musiclike auditory sequences than it is in speechlike patterns. Recent work on the perception of isochrony with verbal materials (e.g., Marcus, 1981; Fowler, 1979; Tuller & Fowler, 1980) suggests that people introduce systematic biases into their judgments about speech isochrony. It turns out that patterns judged to be isochronous, aren't really. Yet there is an intriguing aspect to this research. Listeners reliably agree upon those patterns which "sound" isochronous and the resulting deviations appear to be systematic. Thus, there is nevertheless a common and controlling set of invariants to which people respond and which also afford a basis for very accurate predictions about "when" various speech elements in an utterance should occur (Shields, McHugh, & Martin, 1974).

Given that the gap between these various research areas may be narrowed in the future, general parallels and provocation possibilities remain. It seems not unreasonable, for example, to assume that a child in interacting with a parent or a person interacting with a friend is synchronously attending to the other individual on a variety of tacit temporal levels. This energistic interplay essentially paves the way for skill acquisition. Consider the possibility, for example, that a child learns to speak, to understand speech, song and dance, and to perform a variety of tasks by first attending to and, indeed, with people who are performing these tasks. Through synchronous orientation to these people, a learner's attentional rhythms adapt to the particular rhythmic gestures and patterns of gestures, both auditory and visual, that are afforded by the performer. Both child and adult may learn to selectively direct attending over those temporal periodicities afforded by another's gestures and thereby to prepare attentionally for the pickup of some aspect of the skilled performance of another. This attentional synchronicity, and the preceptual learning which accompanies it, reflect an unspoken internalizing of the behavior of others. This internalization begins with the abstraction of certain rhythmic invariants in the behavior patterns of others and the use of these to predict future timings. Finally, this internalization of another's gestures results in inner mimicry. It is a mimicry made possible by the entrainment of one person's attentional energies by another. This inner modeling is essentially temporal and it happens with the acceptance of the dynamic gestures afforded by others. It reflects an activity which allows one person to learn from another in ways that neither are aware of.

In conclusion, many contemporary theories of attending fail to include the time dimension either in their descriptions of to-be-attended material or in their assumptions about the attending organism. The viewpoint considered here differs in its explicit commitment to incorporating temporal variables into a theory of attending. Patterning of energy over time and space within the environment is the stimulus to which people and other organisms respond. The idea is that these patterns offer both means of guiding attending over time to prepare a learner to pick up new information "when" it occurs and they offer expressive frames with which a person communicates and comprehends.

NOTES

1. Skelly, J., Hahn, J., & Jones, M. R. Effects of spatio-temporal context on judged durations. Manuscript under review, 1983.
2. Kidd, G., Boltz, M., & Jones, M. R. Some effects of rhythmic context on melody recognition. *American Journal of Psychology*, 1984.

REFERENCES

Bartlett, F. C. *Remembering: A study in experimental and social psychology.* London: Cambridge University Press, 1932.

Bock, J. K., & Mazzella, J. R. Intonational marking of given and new information. *Memory & Cognition*, in press.

Broadbent, D. E. *Perception and communication.* New York: Pergamon Press, 1958.

Cherry, E. C. Some experiments on the recognition of speech, with one and with two ears. *Journal of the Acoustical Society of America,* 1953, *25,* 975–979.

Clynes, M. *Sentics: The touch of the emotions.* Garden City, NY: Anchor Press, 1978.

Clynes, M. & Nettheim, N. The living quality of music: neurobiologic patterns of communicating feeling. In M. Clynes (Ed.), *Music, mind and brain: The neuropsychology of music.* New York: Plenum Press, 1982.

Condon, W. S., & Ogsten, W. D. Speech and body motion synchrony of the speaker-hearer. In P. Kjeldergaard, D. Horton, and J. Jenkins (Eds.), *Perception of language.* Columbus, OH: Merrill Publishing, 1971.

Condon, W. S., & Sander, L. W. Synchrony demonstrated between movements of the neonate and adult speech. *Child Development,* 1974, *45,* 456–462.

Cutting, J. E. Two ecological perspectives: Gibson vs. Shaw and Turvey. *American Journal of Psychology,* 1982, *95,* 199–222.

Eysenck, M. W. *Attention and arousal.* New York: Springer-Verlag, 1982.

Fowler, C. A. "Perceptual centers" in speech production and perception. *Perception & Psychophysics,* 1979, *25,* 375–388.

Fraisse, P. Time and rhythm perception. In E. C. Carterette and M. P. Friedman (Eds.), *Handbook of perception* (Vol. 8). New York: Academic Press, 1978.

Gabrielsson, A. Similarity ratings and dimension analyses of auditory rhythm patterns. II. *Scandinavian Journal of Psychology,* 1973, *14,* 161–176.

Gabrielsson, A. Music psychology—A theory of problems and current research activities. Paper presented at a symposium arranged by the Royal Swedish Academy of Music, Feb. 11–12, 1981, Stockholm. In *Basic Musical Function and Musical Ability,* The Royal Swedish·Academy of Music, No. 32, 1981.

Gibson, J. J. *The ecological approach to visual perception.* Boston: Houghton Mifflin, 1979.

Greenewalt, C. H. *Bird song: Acoustics and physiology.* City of Washington: Smithsonian Institution Press, 1968.

Handel, S., & Oshinsky, J. S. The meter of syncopated auditory polyrhythms. *Perception & Psychophysics,* 1981, *30,* 1–9.

Hirst, W., Spelke, E. S., Reaves, C. C., Caharack, G., & Neisser, U. Dividing attention without alternation or automaticity. *Journal of Experimental Psychology: General,* 1980, *109,* 98–117.

Jones, M. R. Time, our lost dimension: Toward a new theory of perception, attention, and memory. *Psychological Review,* 1976, *83,* 323–355.

Jones, M. R. A tutorial on some issues and methods in serial pattern research. *Perception & Psychophysics,* 1981, *30,* 492–504.

Jones, M. R., Boltz, M., & Kidd, G. Controlled attending as a function of melodic and temporal context. *Perception & Psychophysics,* 1982, *32,* 211–218.

Jones, M. R., Maser, D. J., & Kidd, G. R. Rate and structure in memory for auditory patterns. *Memory & Cognition,* 1978, *6,* 246–258.

Kahneman, D. *Attention and effort.* Englewood Cliffs, NJ: Prentice-Hall, 1973.

Kelso, J. A. S., Southard, D. L., & Goodman, D. On the nature of human interlimb coordination. *Science,* 1979, *203,* 1029–1031.

Kelso, J. A. S., Tuller, B., & Harris, K. S. A 'dynamic pattern' perspective on the control and coordination of movement. In P. MacNeilage (Ed.), *The production of speech*. New York: Springer-Verlag, in press.

Kendon, A. *Studies in the behavior of social interaction*. Bloomington, IN: Indiana University Press, 1977.

Kendon, A. Gesture and speech: How they interact. In J. M. Wiseman & R. P. Harrison (Eds.), *Nonverbal interaction*. Beverly Hills: Sage, 1983.

Klapp, S. T. Doing two things at once: The role of temporal compatibility. *Memory & Cognition*, 1979, *7*, 375–381.

Klapp, S. T. Temporal compatibility in dual motor tasks II: Simultaneous articulation and hand movements. *Memory & Cognition*, 1981, *9*, 398–401.

Levi, D. S. The structural determinants of melodic expressive properties. *Journal of Phenomenological Psychology*, 1982, *13*, 19–40.

Lewis, J. L. Semantic processing of unattended messages using dichotic listening. *Journal of Experimental Psychology*, 1970, *85*, 225–228.

MacWhinney, B., & Bates, E. Sentential devices for conveying givenness and newness: A cross-cultural developmental study. *Journal of Verbal Learning and Verbal Behavior*, 1978, *17*, 539–558.

Marcus, S. M. Acoustic determinants of perceptual center (P-center) location. *Perception & Psychophysics*, 1981, *30*, 247–256.

Martin, J. G. Rhythmic (hierarchical) versus serial structure in speech and other behavior. *Psychological Review*, 1972, *79*, 487–509.

Massaro, D. W. *Experimental psychology and information processing*. Chicago: Rand-MacNally, 1975.

Massaro, D. W., & Idson, W. L. Temporal course of perceived auditory duration. *Perception & Psychophysics*, 1976, *20*, 331–352.

Moray, N. Attention in dichotic listening: Affective cues and the influence of instructions. *Quarterly Journal of Experimental Psychology*, 1959, *11*, 56–60.

Morris, C. D., Bransford, J. D., & Franks, J. J. Levels of processing versus transfer appropriate processing. *Journal of Verbal Learning and Verbal Behavior*, 1977, *16*, 519–533.

Navon, D., & Gopher, D. On the economy of the human-processing system. *Psychological Review*, 1979, *56*, 214–255.

Neisser, U. *Cognition and reality*. San Francisco: Freeman, 1976.

Neisser, U., & Becklen, R. Selective looking: Attending to visually specified events. *Cognitive Psychology*, 1975, *7*, 480–494.

Posner, M. I., & Snyder, C. R. R. Attention and cognitive control. In R. L. Solso (Ed.), *Information processing and cognition: The Loyola Symposium*. Potomac, MD: Lawrence Erlbaum, 1974.

Povel, D.-J. Internal representation of simple temporal patterns. *Journal of Experimental Psychology: Human Perception and Performance*, 1981, *7*, 3–18.

Schneider, W., & Shiffrin, R. M. Controlled and automatic human information processing: I. Detection, search, and attention. *Psychological Review*, 1977, *84*, 1–54.

Segal, S. J., & Fusella, V. Influence of imaged pictures and sounds in detection of visual and auditory signals. *Journal of Experimental Psychology*, 1970, *83*, 458–474.

Shields, J. L., McHugh, A., & Martin, J. G. Reaction time to phoneme targets as a function of rhythmic cues in continuous speech. *Journal of Experimental Psychology*, 1974, *102*, 250–255.

Shiffrin, R. M., & Schneider, W. Controlled and automatic human information processing: II. Perceptual learning, automatic attending, and a general theory. *Psychological Review*, 1977, *84*, 128–190.

Spelke, E., Hirst, W., & Neisser, U. Skills of divided attention. *Cognition*, 1976, *4*, 215–230.

Treisman, A. M. Strategies and models of selective attention. *Psychological Review*, 1969, *76*, 282–299.

Tuller, B., & Fowler, C. A. Some articulatory correlates of perceptual isochrony. *Perception & Psychophysics*, 1980, *4*, 277–283.

CHAPTER 3

RHYTHM AS A FACTOR IN MEMORY

M. Carr Payne, Jr. and Thomas G. Holzman

It is common knowledge that rhyme may be used as an aid to memory. For example, a common device for providing ready made organization for information to be remembered, a so-called mnemonic device, is to imagine items on a list to be learned along with items in some rhyme (Hunter, 1964; Wingfield & Byrnes, 1981, p. 79). People report that it is easier to remember a list once they have learned how to use the mnemonic than it was without such a device.

While such devices have been shown to be useful, they do not delineate the role of rhythm in memory. In the first place, the term rhythm may represent any of several characteristic organizations of stimulus materials. In the second, memory as a concept traditionally may be viewed from any of several viewpoints.

A popular current viewpoint, the Atkinson-Shiffrin model (1968), is to distinguish memory processes from memory structures. Memory performance is considered to result from those activities by which we put information into memory and those that later make use of that information. Acquisition, retention, and retrieval of information are considered as logically distinct processes in the act of remembering. Memory structures are concerned with the nature of memory storage itself as a product of the memory process. The model proposes that information initially is stored in a sensory memory (or memories) where it persists for a brief time after the physical stimulus has been terminated. The sensory memory (sometimes called sensory register or sensory store) is distinguished from other memory structures by its unprocessed sensory content, its brief duration (less than a few seconds), and the large amount of information it can temporarily hold. Information from a sensory memory can be encoded in some way into a short-term memory. Unless rehearsal occurs, however, the amount of information that can be held is limited. Finally, in long-term memory, events are coded in the context of other related events or concepts. This form of memory storage is presumed to be of the longest duration. Retrieval of information from long-term memory is not automatic but is an active process.

In this chapter we will employ this model of memory to examine effects of various characteristics of rhythm. For this purpose, we first must examine how rhythm itself has been treated as a concept, both psychophysically and psychometrically.

Rhythm

Psychophysics

Rhythm was clearly identified as a psychophysical phenomenon in Mach's **The Analysis of Sensation** (1886). Mach considered that we have knowledge only of sensations. He included as sensations temporal patterns, such as melodies, which are independent as regards form of any other particular qualities in which they appear (Heidbreder, 1933, p. 336). These were referred to as sensations of "time-form." Von Ehrenfels (1890) elaborated this idea by stating that "time-forms" (as well as "space forms") represent new qualities. They were referred to as **Gestaltqualität**. Despite changes in the sum of component elements making up "time-forms" or "space forms" the **gestalt** remained the same. For this reason, "time-forms" and "space forms" are something other than mere combinations of other qualities. "A configuration (gestalt) possesses properties over and above its parts and not derivable from them; the configuration is transposable since it does not depend upon any given set of elements" (Helson, 1925, p. 350). These are the criteria of **Gestaltqualität**: "(1) the inability of comprising them out of elements, and (2) the ability of transposing them like melodies" (Sahakian, 1975, p. 192). Thus, rhythm in this view exists as a form independent of the absolute character of specific elements which compose the rhythm. Psychologically, rhythm represents perception of series of stimuli not as individual items but a group of stimuli (Woodrow, 1951).

Objective stimulus conditions of rhythm are (1) relative intensity of specific elements (accent), (2) absolute and relative durations of the elements, and (3) temporal spacing (Boring, 1942, p. 584; Woodrow, 1951, p. 1232). When stimuli in a series are physically identical and uniformly spaced in time, a subject ordinarily will perceive a series of groups with some member of each group being accented, provided the rate of presentation is not extremely slow or fast. In general, a regularly recurring, greater intensity exerts a "group-beginning effect." That is, the stimulus series is perceived as being composed of groups of elements, the first of which is accented by possessing greater intensity, with an interval between successive groups. On the other hand, a regularly recurring greater duration produces a "group-ending effect." For example, when one element of three equally-spaced elements has a longer duration than the other two the series is heard in groups of three members with the longer one ending the group (Woodrow, 1951). Clearly, humans tend to organize evenly spaced stimuli into groups.

In the strict sense spoken English is arhythmic. However, the subjective impression is that it tends to be spoken rhythmically with recurrent alternations of stronger and weaker elements (Vanderslice, 1978). This apparently is due chiefly to the rhythmic nature of accents on syllables. Accent primarily is manifested by a change of pitch, but it also generally augments the duration and intensity of the affected syllable. To synthesize natural-sounding speech, in addition to temporal spacing, the following durational factors are needed: 1) accent (e.g., accented syllables are longer); 2) inherent syllable duration; and 3) location in a group (e.g., terminal syllables are drawled). Recurring differences in any of these factors may be loosely described as rhythmic, producing a perception of rhythmically spoken English.

Psychometrics

For years, recognition of auditory rhythm has been included as one of the highly regarded components of musical abilities. For example, the Seashore Measures of Musical Talents (Seashore, Lewis, & Saevert, 1960) contain a rhythm sub-test in which a subject must judge whether the members of a pair of rhythmic patterns of varying lengths are the same or different. Stankov and Horn (1980) showed that maintaining and judging rhythm is one of the factors in terms of which elementary auditory abilities are organized. Stankov and Horn selected tests and constructed others which seemed to involve the same thinking processes as are commonly involved in visual tests, but are dependent on audition rather than vision. These tests were administered and 44 measures based on them were factor-analyzed. Six separate categories were obtained, one of which was Maintaining and Judging Rhythm. This factor was defined not only by the rhythm sub-test of the Seashore Measures of Musical Talents and two tests of tempo, but also by incomplete words. It had little in common with general intelligence as measured by the Otis Intelligence Test or with educational level. This study helps to confirm that ability to recognize rhythm is one of the distinct elementary auditory abilities.

Relationship Between Rhythm and Memory

Subjects have been found to impose a rhythmic organization on material they attempt to remember even when that material is unpatterned (Neisser, 1969). Perhaps this is because a rhythmic pattern is a single structural unit, and may be represented by simple unitary codes in the response system (Lashley, 1951). Neisser (1967) hypothesized that unpatterned rhythm is the simplest form of organization available to a subject as a basis for active verbal memory. To test this hypothesis, Neisser (1969) ran an experiment in which memory span for 10 digits was compared when the digits were grouped in a triadic pattern, 3-3-3-1, or a quartic pattern, 4-4-2. Random permutations of the 10 digits from 0 through 9 were prepared with the restriction that the nth digit of a string was never identical with the nth digit of the string before, and that there were no natural runs of more than two digits (e.g., 456). Digits were spoken at a rate of two per second. Subjects listened to each string of digits over earphones and repeated back each string as soon as it was over. Serial intrusion errors were compared. These occur when the nth digit of a response is the same as the nth digit of the preceding string. When successive strings had the same rhythm, significantly more intrusion errors occurred than when they had different rhythms. Intrusions apparently represented instances where the subject had already forgotten the correct digit and emitted the intruding digit rather than guessing at random. The rhythm pattern served as a cue to the order in which the preceding digits were presented. When successive strings of digits were presented in different rhythm patterns this cue did not suggest to the subject which digit had occurred to the extent that it did when the strings of digits were presented in the same rhythm pattern.

In research studies, rhythm may be treated as an aid to encoding information into memory [as in Neisser's (1969) study] or one can ask how rhythm itself is processed and remembered. Most such rhythm research utilizes audition, although rhythmic patterns can be presented visually or tactually as well. Components of rhythm—accent, duration, and temporal spacing—may be considered separately. In the following sections, research on rhythm and memory involving each of these components will be discussed.

Accent

The relationship between rhythm and memory is of interest not only for its own sake, but also because of the importance of rhythm in language. Young children rely on rhythmic cues to comprehend speech (Dann & Bray, 1982). Intelligibility is related to speech timing, at least when a listener does not know in advance what is being said (Huggins, 1978). Free recall of brief English phrases appears to be organized in terms of stress rhythm, i.e., accent, of syllables (Robinson, 1977). In perception of speech sound inputs are temporally patterned, i.e., rhythmical. What is implied is that the locus of each element of speech along the time dimension is determined relative to the locus of all other elements in the sequence, adjacent and nonadjacent (Martin, 1972). Temporal locus, hence duration, is related to every other locus in the pattern. A pattern is a holistic unit characterized in terms of relative accent level and relative timing. Martin (1972) proposes rules about accents: (a) accent level covaries with timing, and (b) main accents remain equidistant. He supported these rules by a study (Shields, McHugh, & Martin, 1974) in which reaction time to a target phoneme was faster to accented than to unaccented targets in a sentence context, but did not differ significantly in a nonsense syllable context. Accent increased the predictability of the accented target phonemes. These findings suggest that memory for rhythm **per se,** at least in regards to accent or stress, is a major factor in memory for speech.

Accent rules have an influence on immediate memory. Sturges and Martin (1974) repeated either 7-element or 8-element patterns once. Elements composing the patterns were either high (180Hz) or low (150 Hz) tones presented at the same duration with the same inter-element silent intervals. Seven-element patterns were constructed by deleting one item from serial position 6 or 7 of a matching 8-element pattern. Some patterns were rhythmic as defined by Martin's rules (Martin, 1972). By these rules, 7-element patterns cannot have a simple rhythm, i.e., accents cannot be equidistant, while 8-element patterns can. Subjects judged whether the two patterns of a pair were the same or different and then wrote the entire sequence, an immediate memory task. They were told that each pattern began with a high tone and ended with a low tone. In each of three experiments patterns in which the elements were arranged in accord with Martin's rules ("good patterns") were recalled better than those which were not ("poor patterns"). In short, rhythmic patterns were generally easier to recall than nonrhythmic patterns.

Utilizing data in which subjects recalled patterns that they had correctly identified as the same, the authors examined serial position effects. When positions 1 and 8 were disregarded, the curves for "good patterns" were relatively flat while those for "poor patterns" showed a dip in the middle, typical of serial position curves for many sequences of memory items. This may be due to a response bias toward "good patterns." On the other hand, this finding is in accord with the view that rhythmic patterns are "gestaltlike holistic entities" which are processed in memory as entities rather than as individual elements. Thus, a pattern according with rhythmic accent rules, a "good pattern," apparently is easier to recall in immediate memory than a "poor pattern."

Some researchers argue that, in speech, accent acts on syllables rather than on phonemes (Shaffer, 1982). However, accent also affects the timing of all the phonemes in a syllable. Since ability to assign the beat to a given syllable was shown to be positively correlated with the degree of stress, i.e., accent, on that syllable in a short sentence (Allen, 1972), the syllable is obviously one unit of accent. Regardless of whether or not the phoneme is found to be as fundamental a unit for accent as the syllable, it would follow from the above studies that accent is a major rhythmic cue for memory. This should be true even if stimulus material were something other than words or sentences (such as musical notes).

Duration

Relative duration of elements has traditionally been considered to be a stimulus condition for rhythm. However, in some settings authors question whether duration of elements should be considered as an aspect of rhythm. For example, Davies (1978, p. 177) considers duration to have nothing to do with rhythm in music. He states that the order perceived as rhythm by a person is imposed solely on the bases of relative intensities (which appear as accent) and relative times of onset (temporal spacing).

Dowling (1973) investigated effects of rhythmic grouping on memory for brief melodies. Rhythm was defined in terms of patterns of element durations within a melodic phrase. On each trial a subject heard a sequence of 20 tones grouped rhythmically into four phrases of five different tones each, the original sequence. Tones within phrase differed in duration, either short or long, as well as pitch. A two second pause followed the sequence of tones. After the pause the subject heard a five-tone sequence, the test sequence. The subject was to say whether the test sequence was contained in the immediately preceding original sequence. On some trials the test sequence used the same rhythmic grouping as a phrase of the 20-tone sequence. On other trials rhythmic grouping of the test sequence cut across phrase boundaries of the original sequence, corresponding to the last three notes of one phrase and the first two tones of the next. Recognition was better when the test sequence was the same in rhythmic grouping as phrases of the original sequence. Bower (1970), and Bower and Winzenz (1969) had shown that the rhythmic grouping of a verbal list determines the form of subjective organization of the list into chunks which in turn determine how list items are stored in memory. Dowling's work extends Bower's position by showing that it applies to memory for tonal sequences in much the same way as in memory for verbal materials.

Hamill (1976) presented pure tone sequences patterned by short and long pulses. Subjects either selected a matching phrase, clause, or sentence to each pattern or generated one. The result was that there was a tendency for content words to be assigned to long-tone positions in the sequences and function words to be assigned to short-tone positions. This study also supports the presence of a relationship between rhythm, as defined by relative duration of elements, and language.

Payne, Davenport, Domangue and Soroka (1980) employed a variation of the Birch and Belmont (1964) task to examine recognition of patterns cross-modally or intra-modally. With this task a subject was presented two patterns consisting of three to five elements each in a sequential order, and was asked to identify whether the patterns were the same or different. Patterns were composed of combinations of three types of elements: Short and long pulses (approximately 0.3 sec. and 0.9 sec., respectively, separated from each other by approximately 0.125 sec.) and pauses (of approximately 0.3 sec. duration). There were approximately three seconds between the first pattern and the beginning of the second. Patterns were presented visually (pulses of a rectangular white light), auditorily (pulses of a pure tone), or tactually (vibrations of a plastic disk 0.7 cm in diameter). When both patterns were presented in the same modality (intra-modally) recognition performance was better than when each pattern was presented in a separate modality (cross-modally). When both patterns were presented auditorially, performance was better than when they were both presented visually or tactually. When the first pattern was presented auditorially, performance was better than when it was presented tactually or visually. Any condition in which the first pattern was presented auditorially discriminated between a group of children (third- through sixth-grade) who were normal readers and a matched group who were poor readers. These groups were equivalent on a vocabulary test but differed on scores on the Reading Comprehension Test of the Iowa Test of Basic Skills (i.e., scores of the Poor Reader group were at least one year, two months below grade level, while scores of the Normal Reader group were at grade level). The task in this study was a memory task. A subject had to process and store elements of the first pattern and then compare the second pattern with the memory of the first. It is known that a stored representation of auditory stimuli does not fade as rapidly as that of visual stimuli. This would account for the finding of superior performance when the first pattern was auditory rather than when it was visual or tactual, as well as the finding that intra-modal auditory comparisons were more accurate than those of any other intra-modal or cross-modal condition tested.

Findings of the Payne, Davenport, Domangue, and Soroka (1980) study suggest that an auditory sequential memory deficit is a major factor in at least some retarded readers' performance. This accords with Jones (1974) who showed that retarded readers were unable to hold an auditory pattern, a rhythmic pattern, in memory. However, neither of these studies allows one to discriminate whether the memory deficit may be attributed to a failure in trace retention (i.e., failure to store a pattern itself) or to a failure in trace formation (i.e., failure to code elements into a pattern). Payne and Holzman (1983) examined this question by employing a variation of the task used by Payne et al. (1980). Subjects were presented with two auditory patterns composed of three to five temporally separated elements. Elements were either long pulses (.75 sec.), short pulses (.25 sec.), or pauses (.25 sec.). Subjects were to say whether the two patterns were the same or different. Intervals between the patterns were varied. If poor readers had difficulty encoding the patterns as compared to normal readers, then the groups' performance would be expected to differ regardless of the time interval between the pairs. On the other hand, if the difficulty derived from poor retention of a properly encoded stimulus pattern, differences between the groups should be more apparent at longer intervals. Results showed that significant differences between the groups occurred only at a 10 sec. inter-pattern interval, but not at shorter intervals of 1, 2, or 5 sec. It appears that with this rhythm task in which there is no objective accent, poor readers have a deficit in short-term memory storage as compared with normal readers. This supports the thesis that short-term memory for rhythm is an important factor in learning to read.

Temporal Spacing

In studies of temporal spacing, elements of equal duration and accent are presented with the time between elements varied. A subject must store a pattern composed of temporally spaced elements and compare a second pattern with it. Klapper and Birch (1971) showed that this ability developed from ages four through 11 in a sample of white, middle-class children, although a ceiling effect may account for their results for children older than nine years. At each age younger than nine years, performance was better if stimuli were presented auditorily than if they were presented visually.

Zurif and Carson (1970) compared normal readers and poor readers on the rhythm sub-tests of the Seashore Measures of Musical Talents (Seashore, Lewis, & Saetveit, Series A, 1939 revision). This sub-test requires a subject to judge whether two rhythmic patterns tapped out in quick succession are the same or different. A similar visual task (direct translation of the Seashore subtest to vision proved to be too difficult for the subjects) was also employed. In the visual task there were three or four beats with short (.5 sec.) or long (1 sec.) pauses between them. Both of these tasks discriminated between normal and poor readers. Performance on the two tasks was significantly correlated.

The studies of temporal spacing in conjunction with those of duration indicate that rhythmic organization is an important factor in acquiring the important human language skill of reading. Short-term memory for temporarily organized material appears to be crucial whether elements of the patterns in that material are variable length stimuli or variable length intervals between stimuli. The rhythmic structure of the pattern appears to be the important variable.

Long-Term Memory

The memory research discussed to this point has dealt primarily with short-term memory phenomena which entail retention for only a few seconds. Relatively little research has been conducted on rhythmic factors in long-term memory, which involves relatively permanent retention of the sort that is typically required in instructional situations. However, during the past decade there have been a few attempts to determine whether and under what conditions rhythm influences long-term memory.

Laughery and Spector (1972) presented subjects with 48 auditory sequences of nine consonants at either a constant rate or temporally organized into four groups of one to four items each. Immediately following each sequence, subjects attempted to write the consonants in the same order as they had heard them previously. On this short-term memory task the rhythmic sequences produced better recall than the constant-rate sequences.

Laughery and Spector (1972) also studied how rhythm might influence long-term memory by presenting repetitions of consonant sequences to subjects. Each repeated sequence was separated by two non-repeating, "noise" sequences and their respective recall trials. Because of the two noise sequences serving as distractors and because approximately one minute interval occurred between each repetition, recall improvements across repetitions would be classified as long-term memory phenomena. Some subjects heard all consonants in all sequences at a constant rate of presentation. Other subjects heard temporally grouped sequences with the repetitions sharing the same grouping pattern. Finally, some subjects heard temporally grouped sequences with repeated sequences differing from each other in the patterns of their temporal groupings. Laughery and Spector suggested that if rhythm provides a basic structure for storing items in long-term memory and serves as a cue for retrieval, then repetitions of a sequence should most facilitate recall when the repetitions share the same rhythmic pattern. The results of the experiment indicated that recall in fact did increase across repetitions, but the extent of the increase was not influenced significantly by the consistency of the grouping patterns of the sequences. Laughery and Spector concluded that rhythm does not directly influence long-term memory, although it may cue other processes, such as stimulus recoding and rehearsal, that could, in turn, influence long-term memory. The conclusions of Laughery and Spector must be qualified, however, by a consideration of the nature of the stimuli included in the groupings.

Glanzer (1976) studied rhythmic influences on the recall of words that were either unrelated or associated as coordinates (e.g., **doctor-lawyer**), or subordinates-superordinates (e.g., **anger-emotion**). Subjects listened to sequences of 24 words that were grouped into triplets or quadruplets on the basis of the pitch and stress imposed on the sequences. The related words were always separated by a single intervening word. The related-word pairs were sequenced so that some occurred within a single rhythmic group and some extended across groups. Glanzer found that recall of words from related pairs was significantly higher than recall of unrelated words. Furthermore, for the early and middle portions of the lists (the parts associated with long-term memory), recall of related words was significantly higher when they occurred in the same rhythmic group than when they extended across groups. At the ends of the lists (the part associated with short-term memory), recall of related words remained higher than that or unrelated words, but the extent of that superiority did not change according to the location of the related words within or across rhythmic groups.

In agreement with Laughery and Spector (1972), Glanzer (1976) concluded that groupings per se improve short-term memory. However, Glanzer further pointed out that when the grouping is consistent with semantic relations (which could not occur in Laughery & Spector's consonant sequences), rhythmic grouping can also improve long-term memory. The grouping essentially packages information for further processing. If a package contains elements that fit familiar relationships in long-term memory, those elements may more readily become registered in long-term memory. On the other hand, if the contents of a package do not fit known relationships, they may remain restricted to short-term memory.

Given the possibility of employing rhythm to promote long-term memory of meaningful information, rhythmic processing may have potential as an instructional technique. Milman (1979) studied this application for academically deficient elementary school children who had particular difficulty with mathematical concepts and computation. Results were reported for two children trained to memorize multiplication and division tables by reciting them to the beat of a metronome. Approximately 25 minutes of this kind of training was devoted to each table. Both children were administered the Metropolitan Achievement Test, Elementary Arithmetic, at the end of Grade 4 and a parallel form at the end of Grade 5 with the metronome training occurring in the interim. One child's score on the comutational section increased 3.2 grade levels, and the other's rose 2.2 grade levels. Although this study reported data based on only two subjects, it suggests that some types of rhythmic training have promise for improving academic performance.

Rhythm is a multifaceted variable. The literature has suggested that the precise way in which rhythm functions may depend on what features of rhythm (e.g., duration, accent, temporal spacing) are involved in the stimulus material and what kinds of elements are being rhythmically organized (e.g., tones, digits, letters, words). The nature of the interaction between learning tasks and these dimensions of rhythm has not been sufficiently identified. Investigation of this issue has implications not only for better understanding of the learning process but possibly for instructional processes as well.

REFERENCES

Alln, G. D. The location of rhythmic stress beats in English: An experimental study I. *Language Speech*, 1972, *15*, 72–100.

Atkinson, R. C., & Shiffrin, R. M. Human memory: A proposed system and its control processes. In K. W. Spence, and J. T. Spence (Eds.), *The psychology of learning and motivation*. Vol. 2). New York: Academic Press, 1968.

Birch, H. G., & Belmont, L. Auditory-visual integration in normal and retarded readers. *American Journal of Orthopsychiatry*, 1964, *34*, 852–861.

Boring, E. G. *Sensation and perception in the history of experimental psychology*. New York: Appleton-Century-Crofts, 1942.

Bower, G. Organizational factors in memory. *Cognitive Psychology*, 1970, *1*, 18–46.

Bower, G., & Winznz, D. Group structure, coding, and memory for digit series. *Journal of Experimental Psychology Monographs*, 1969, *80*, No. 2, Part 2, 1–17.

Dann, L., & Bray, N. W. Effects of rhythmic cues in speech on comprehension of seven- and ten-year old children. Paper delivered at the Southeastern Psychological Association, New Orleans, Louisiana, March 27, 1982.

Davies, J. B. Rhythm: Tonality's poor relation. In J. B. Davies (Ed.), *The psychology of music*. Stanford, CA: Stanford University Press, 1978.

Dowling, W. J. Rhythmic groups and subjective chunks in memory for melodies. *Perception and Psychophysics*, 1973, *4*, 37–40.

Ehrenfels, C. Uber Getaltqualitaten. *Vierteljahrsschrift fur wissenschaftliche Philosophie*, 1890, *14*, 249–292.

Glanzer, M. Intonation grouping and related words in free recall. *Journal of Verbal Learning and Verbal Behavior*, 1976, *15*, 85–92.

Hamill, B. W. A linguistic correlate of sentential rhythmic patterns. *Journal of*

Experimental Psychology: Human Perception and Performance, 1976, *2,* 71–79.

Heidbreder, E. *Seven psychologies.* New York: Appleton-Century, 1933.

Helson, H. The psychology of Gestalt. *American Journal of Psychology,* 1925, *36,* 342–370.

Huggins, A. W. F. Speech timing and intelligibility. In J. Requin (Ed.), *Attention and Performance VII.* Hillsdale, NJ: Lawrence Erlbaum, 1978.

Hunter, I. M. L. *Memory.* Baltimore: Penguin Books, 1964.

Jones, B. Cross-modal matching by retarded and normal readers. *Bulletin of the Psychonomic Society,* 1974, *3,* 163–165.

Klapper, Z. S., & Birch, H. G. Developmental course of temporal patterning in vision and audition. *Perceptual and Motor Skills,* 1971, *32,* 547–555.

Lashly, K. The problem of serial order in behavior. In L. Jeffress (Ed.), *Cerebral Mechanisms in Behavior.* New York: Wiley, 1951.

Laughery, K. R., & Spector, A. The roles of recoding and rhythm in memory organization. *Journal of Experimental Psychology,* 1972, *94,* 41–48.

Mach, E. *The analysis of sensations and the relation of the physical to the psychical.* New York: Dover, 1959. (reprint of 5th ed. 1905)

Martin, J. G. Rhythmic (hierarchical) versus serial structure in speech and other behavior. *Psychological Review,* 1972, *79,* 487–509.

Milman, C. The metronome and rote learning. *Academic Therapy,* 1979, *14*(*3*), 321–325.

Neisser, U. *Cognitive psychology* (pp. 232–235). New York: Appleton-Century-Crofts, 1967.

Neisser, U. The role of rhythm in active verbal memory: Serial intrusions. *American Journal of Psychology,* 1969, *82,* 40–546.

Payne, M. C., Davenport, R. K., Domangue, J. C., & Soroka, R. D. Reading comprehension and perception: Intra-modal and cross-modal comparisons. *Journal of Learning Disabilities,* 1980, *13,* 34–40.

Payne, Jr., M. C., & Holzman, T. G. Auditory short-term memory and digit span: Normal versus poor readers. *Journal of Educational Psychology,* 1983, *75,* 424–430.

Robinson, G. M. Rhythmic organization in speech processing. *Journal of Experimental Psychology,* 1977, *3,* 83–91.

Sahakian, W. S. *History and systems of psychology.* New York: Wiley, 1975.

Seashore, C. E., Lewis, D., & Saetveit. *Manual of instruction and interpretations for the Seashore Measures of Musical Talents* (2nd revision). New York: The Psychological Corporation, 1960.

Shaffer, L. H. Rhythm and timing in skill. *Psychological Review,* 1982, *89,* 109–123.

Shields, J. L., McHugh, A., & Martin, J. G. Reaction time to phoneme targets as a function of rhythmic cues in continuous speech. *Journal of Experimental Psychology,* 1974, *102,* 250–255.

Stankov, L., & Horn, J. L. Human abilities revealed through auditory tests. *Journal of Educational Psychology,* 1980, *72,* 21–44.

Sturges, P. T., & Martin, J. G. Rhythmic structure in auditory temporal pattern perception and immediate memory. *Journal of Experimental Psychology,* 1974, *102,* 377–383.

Vanderslice, R. A rhythmic model of English. *Journal of the Acoustical Society of America,* 1978, *63,* Sup. 1, S55(A).

Wingfield, A., & Byrnes, D. L. *The psychology of human memory.* New York: Academic Press, 1981.

Woodrow, H. Time perception. In S. Stevens (Ed.), *Handbook of experimental psychology.* New York: Wiley, 1951.

Zurif, E. B., & Carson, G. Dyslexia in relation to cerebral dominance and temporal analysis. *Neuropsychologia,* 1970, *8,* 351–361.

Chapter 4.

COMMUNICATION: RHYTHM AND STRUCTURE

WILLIAM S. CONDON

Human history demonstrates the fundamental role of reason in human existence and identity. The universe is ordered and the human mind can perceive and know aspects of that order. Nature's structure and power become available for human purposes. That we can know, use, and communicate to each other about the universe implies a fundamental participation in the order pervading that universe. Observations from the sound-film microanalysis of human communicational behavior, which will be the central topic of this chapter, may provide insight into some aspects of that participation.

Humans evolved in a universe which has optical and acoustic properties. In this process eyes and ears developed. Eyes and ears are one form of Nature's expression of her optical and acoustic structure. Ears and hearing would probably not exist in a universe lacking acoustic properties. The ears and the acoustic properties of nature are distinguishable but not separate aspects of a unitary system within which "hearing" activity occurs. There must always be continuous and stable natural structures constituting and supporting human behavior. Intensive sound-film microanalysis of human speaking and listening behavior has revealed a linkage or participation of the organization of human behavior with the structure of nature. While speech is emitted by another human being and, at the present time, can be built into machines, the point of actual contact is through sound waves impinging on the listener's ear. This linkage involves forms of rhythmic synchronization. The present chapter will seek to explore this with observation from the microanalysis of speaking and listening behavior. The following paragraph briefly summarizes the material to be presented in this chapter.

A speaker's body is observed to move in organizations of change which are precisely synchronized with the articulatory structure of his own speech across multiple levels. This is a unified, rhythmic, and hierarchic

55

organization of great precision which has been called self-synchrony. Further, and surprisingly, the body of a **listener** moves in organizations of change which are precisely synchronized with the articulatory structure of a speaker's speech, and often with inanimate sounds as well. This has been called interactional synchrony or entrainment. It appears to be a universal characteristic of normal listener behavior and has been observed in many different cultures. It is also a basic characteristic of infant behavior and has been observed as early as twenty minutes after birth. The same organizational processes which mediate self-synchrony may mediate interactional synchrony. The organization of movement of the listener's body thus is in precise rhythmic synchrony with the rhythmic pattern of the speech of the person he is listening to. This occurs very rapidly, i.e., within the first frame following sound onset, which is 42 milliseconds (msec). Similar synchronization with sound has been observed in Rhesus monkeys and may exist in most hearing creatures. The hearing creature reflects the structure of the acoustic universe in which it exists. Human behavior and communication are also rhythmically organized and this will be discussed. The parallelism between the acoustic order of nature and that same order revealed receptively in human behavior implies a linkage with nature which may be basic to perception and the acquisition of knowledge. This would also be fundamental for human communication. Sound-film microanalysis of various disorders such as autism, dyslexia, hyperactivity, Huntington's disease, Parkinson's disease, schizophrenia, and stuttering has revealed "jumps" and "jerks" in the body following sounds. This lead to the hypothesis of an abnormal **multiple entrainment** to sound. The normal entrainment appears to be out-of-phase in these disorders, resulting in one side of the body entraining in a delayed fashion relative to the other. There are usually four such abnormal entrainments within the first second following sound onsets, hence the term "multiple entrainment." The existence of abnormal entrainment indirectly supports the general hypothesis of entrainment.

Communication

There is a translation of the order of the universe around us into forms of mental order. This seems to be achieved by the passage of forms of order through different kinds of media yet preserving the form of the order. Through a complex and little understood process the order constituting the speaker's thoughts (which may be microneuroelectric patterns) is transformed into ordered muscular operations of breath, vocal cords, tongue, and mouth, resulting in ordered vibrations in the air. The vibrations may also come from a loud speaker or a recording. In 1930 investigators listened in a distant telephone receiver to the output from a cat's auditory nerve in response to words spoken to the cat's ear and could clearly understand the speech. The airwaves, in turn, transport that order to a listener where forms of re-transformation occur. The listener's eardrum vibrates in synchrony with the ordered pattern conducted through the air. This order is then mechanically conducted through the ossicles to the oval window and then into the fluid in the cochlea which moves the hair cells. The hair cells transform the order into electrical impulses which are transmitted to the brain to become thoughts of the listener. This all occurs very rapidly. There is no vacuum between the speaker and the listener or between man and his universe. There is a translation of order from one form into another.

Method

The investigator's method often contains implicit perspectives which may blind him to many forms of order. This interferes with the observation of new forms. He tends to perceive what his own perspectives constrain him to perceive, obscuring forms which his method does not provide for. The viewpoint shapes the categories by which the material is analyzed. Many investigators select their units prior to analysis and look for connections between these a priori units. The experimental paradigm is of this type. The variables are selected in advance and controlled so that inferences about the relationships can be made.

An "intensive analysis" approach, where the data are studied over and over in the search for natural order and units (as in the writer's laboratory), can lead to the observation of new patterns. It cannot replace the experimental paradigm, but it can be very valuable. The universe is just as ordered outside the laboratory as it is in the laboratory. For example, a few years ago little was known about the micro-organization of natural, everyday human speaker and listener behavior. The first task was to determine the units and levels of units in that process. The method used was that of viewing sound films of human interaction over and over, often at the frame-by-frame level, for literally thousands of hours until the nature of the units of behavior was discovered. In time it became clear that it was not the individual body parts per se which constituted the units of behavior but characteristic **forms of organization** which the body parts seemed constrained to follow when they moved. These forms of organization were the only systematic and continuously present features of behavior at the micro-level which seemed to constitute units. In time this led to the development of an organizational view of the structure of human communication where forms of organization **as** organization were studied rather than discrete, atomistic items. The behavior had to be studied intensively over and over for the forms of organization which it exhibited. The investigator could not know in advance what they might be or how they would be manifested.

Speaker and listener behaviors need to be preserved or stored so that these complex and rapid communicational events can be studied intensively. The basic method used in micro-behavioral analysis is the sound motion picture film with special analyzing equipment. The films are frame-numbered, thus providing a unique number for each frame. Since there are a given number of frames per second, usually 24, the film also serves as a clock to time the behavior stored on it. The units of speech are segmented in relation to frame numbers at the one frame level using an Audio-Visual Analyzer (AVA). This requires linguistic training. The body motion of the interactants can also be analyzed at the same one frame level with a Time-Motion Analyzer (TMA). This is a 16mm movie projector which can be operated manually to study body motion frame-by-frame. How the body parts change in relation to each other and to speech can be evaluated in relation to the frame numbers (Condon, 1970).

The Micro-Units of Human Behavior

Human speech and body motion are rapid, complicated, and essentially continuous processes. Sound-film microanalysis, which covers an approximate range from 1/96th of a second up to two-or three-seconds, provides a "microscope" to study the complicated organization of both normal and pathological behavior. When a normal person speaks there are often many parts of the body moving at the same time. The arms, hands, fingers, head, etc., may be moving together almost constantly in complex, changing patterns. While this is occurring, speech is emerging simultaneously. This ongoing complexity, where several body parts are moving together simultaneously while speech also is occurring, must be faced by any investigator seeking the micro-units of behavior. A unit of behavior has to be something in the **relationships** these changing aspects of behavior have with each other since they are occurring at the same time. The units of behavior are not an arm unit, which is added to a head unit, which is added to a leg unit, etc. The body parts are not the units of behavior. The organization of the **relationships** of change of the movements of the body parts (and speech) constitute the units of behavior. A unit of behavior is a form of organization, and has been called a "process unit" to emphasize this (Condon, 1963). This is a new hypothesis concerning the nature of units of human body motion at the micro-level. It may also apply to most animal behavior. In summary, behavior is **already** organized at the minimal level and is not composed of pieces which are put together to form organized behavior.

Figure 1 illustrates units of behavior as forms of organization. It shows the sound-film microanalysis of a segment of a speaker's speech and body motion from a film taken at approximately 96 f.p.s. (high speed). It indicates the surprising amount of behavioral change that can occur within one second. Process units (which seem like pulses) are characterized by a "sustaining of a relationship together" for a brief period of time by whatever body parts happen to be moving at that moment. Behavior is a serial flow of such pulse-like forms. Body motion is continuous yet there are "discrete-like" unit forms (process units) within the on-going process.

In Figure 1 a young woman, approximately 25-years-old, is seated talking to a young man of the same age. As part of her conversation she rapidly says, "an so I'd get put back in that way." The process unit at the micro-level has the following characteristics, using the movements co-occurring with the /s/ of "so" to illustrate: there is a synchronous change of the body parts together, i.e., where they change direction and/or velocity. Not all body parts need change, some may sustain a given direction for a longer interval, which is part of a longer form (a higher order process unit in a hierarchy of units). The changes which initiate the beginning of a process unit always differ from the changes which indicate the ending of that process unit, which is also the beginning point of a new process unit.

The sustaining of the same movement by each of the body parts moving during that brief interval (which is also the sustaining of a relationship between them) forms the "content" of the process unit. This "quantum pulse" or "bundle" nature of organization always seem to be there no matter what body parts happen to be moving so that forms of

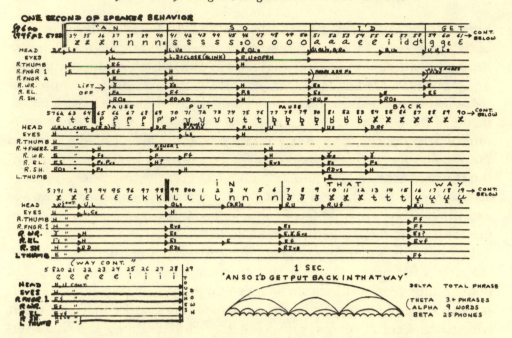

Figure 1. Sound-film microanalysis of the hierarchically synchronized speech and body motion of a woman saying, "an' so I'd get put back in that way." Film was taken at approximately 96 f.p.s. The notation is fairly simple. For example, E = extend, F = flex, U = up, D = down, AD = adduct, AB = abduct, S = Supinate, P = pronate, RO = rotate out, Q = incline of the head, etc. The lower case letters refer to speed: f = fast and s = slow.

organization are the most pervasive structural features of behavior. It seems obligatory that body motions follow these organizational forms. At the onset of the process unit co-occurring with /s/, for example, there is a change of direction in the head, eyes, fingers 1 and 2 of the right hand, and the right shoulder. There is a change in velocity of the right wrist and the right elbow. No change was detected in the extension of the right thumb which continued to extend. Again, that which forms the **content** of the process unit is the sustaining of the same relationship between the moving body parts. That these quanta or pulses of body motion also co-occur isomorphically with the units of speech provides additional support for their existence.

Across the emission of /s/ the head sustains a left and up slight movement, **while** the eyes move left, down, and the lids close beginning a slight blink, **while** the right thumb continues to extend, **while** fingers 1 and 2 of the right hand hold, **while** there is acceleration in the left wrist and elbow, **while** the right shoulder rotates out and adducts. One can sweep manually back and forth across these five frames with the analyzing projector and there is a smooth pulse or flow of motion where all the body parts are sustaining their relationship of movement together. No interstitial changes can be detected in any of the movements.

This "sustaining together" also illustrates another basic principle of the organization of normal behavior, i.e., interaction across multiple levels. The phones are emergently accompanied by a form of body motion (or process unit), the words are accompanied by other forms of body motion, and the phrases and sentences are accompanied by still other forms of body motion. It is this sustaining together of the units of speech/body motion across varying temporal durations which characterizes the hierarchic organization of speaker behavior. For example, fingers 1 and 2 of the right hand ceased moving at the end of the /n/ of "an," held their lack of movement exactly across the emission of the **total** word "so" and then began to flex at the beginning of "I'd." A model where discrete lower parts or pieces are put together to form larger parts which are in turn put together to form still larger parts is inadequate to deal with such organization. The process unit sustaining across /s/ differs from that sustaining across /o/. The /o/ process unit was not added to the /s/ process unit to create a larger /so/ body motion sustaining unit. There is no way the /o/ unit added to the /s/ unit could go back in time to create the hold of fingers 1 and 2 which sustained precisely across the entire word "so." This principle also applies to the larger forms of body motion which accompany speech across wider forms such as phrases. We seem to be dealing with a form of hierarchic organization where multiple levels are emerging together simultaneously. Behavioral organization is not "composed of" or "more than" these moving body parts and speech synchronized together, it is **in** all of them at all levels simultaneously. The investigator begins with organized behavior, the living, talking people in the film, and discovers their behavior to consist of many forms of organization integrated together. All normal behavior studied thus far is similar in organizational principle to that presented in Figure 1.

The precision with which the speaker's body accompanies his/her speech in a hierarchically organized fashion also can be seen in Figure 1. Most of the phone types have co-occurring process units. A speaker's speech at the minimal level appears to be formed of an on-going flow of unified speech and body motion process units. Both seem to be the product of a more basic neurological organization. The body motion process unit or pulse accompanying the /n/ of "an" has a sustained organizational integrity which is isomorphic with the articulation of /n/. This is different from a similarly sustained body motion organization accompanying /s/ and this, in turn, is different from that accompanying /o/, etc. The words also usually have different body motion forms accompanying them. Across "an" the head goes left, right finger 1 extends and the thumb extends. Across "so" fingers 1 and 2 hold, i.e., do not move. Across "I'd" the right elbow extends and fingers 2, 3, and 4 flex slightly, etc. There are three phrases that have co-occurring but different body motion forms. Her right arm which is resting in her lap sweeps up and right to shoulder height across the phrase, "an so I'd get." It sweeps left in front of her body during "put back" and then directly down to her lap across, "in that way," reaching her lap just as the utterance ends. The utterance, as a totality which lasts approximately one second, is accompanied by the right arm leaving and returning to the lap. As will be seen later, such one second movement forms also are characteristic of speaker behavior. Thus, normal behavior follows forms of structural organization. The study of pathological behavior also reveals forms of organization, but forms which differ from normal structural organization.

There is high reliability between independent judges in segmenting inanimate sound, speech, and body motion process units at the one frame level (Condon, 1981). For example, Plooij (in press) in speaking about self-synchrony says,

> "at certain moments (frames) in time several body segments such as the head, a hand, a finger or a foot change direction of movement. Condon calls these moments process-unit-boundaries. Personally I verified Condon's finding in newborn babies, although my study was not set up with this purpose in mind. Instead, I studied the development of preverbal communication in the human mother-infant interaction in a face-to-face situation. The main part of this study consisted of frame-by-frame analysis of filmed sessions. In doing so, one could not help noticing the self-synchrony. For instance, the eyes would blink and a foot would bend at the same time."

While more work needs to be done to demonstrate the ability of independent judges to reliably segment behavior at the micro-level, the work that has been done supports the ability to do so.

Behavior as Wave Phenomena

The hypothesis was presented that the normal speaker's speech and body motion are forms of organization which are precisely synchronized across multiple levels simultaneously. As a person talks he uses small sounds (the phone types) which are integrated together into words, the words into phrases, and phrases into sentences. The head, arms, fingers, legs, etc. move in complex patterns of sustaining and changing together which accompany these units of speech across multiple levels simultaneously. Speech and body motion also exhibit characteristic periodicities and can be interpreted as wave-like. Thus, the movements, gestures, and speech that one sees and hears when a person speaks can be interpreted as wave forms which are hierarchically organized. This also suggests that they may be produced by similarly synchronized brain processes.

In one analysis of phone types the mean length of 1055 consecutively analyzed phones was 1.61 film frames (or 15 per second using 24 f.p.s. film). Short, rapidly spoken words would also fit this periodicity at times, depending upon speed of articulation. In the word length analysis the polysyllabic words were divided into their component syllables. The mean length of 365 consecutive words (pauses omitted) from the same film was 4.5 frames (5.3 per second). Utterances are seen very clearly in body motion with a marked one second periodicity observed in one study. In that study 96 consecutive speech sequences from both speakers in an interaction were analyzed. The one second rhythm form was usually manifested by a head, or arm, or other body part sustaining a given direction across an utterance, or some aspect of the body moving from a given position then back to that position. Twelve of the 96 utterances were approximately ½ second in length and the others averaged 23.9 frames (24 frames equal one second). The range was from 19–29 frames (Condon & Ogston, 1967).

Another study was conducted to further explore the one second rhythm. One-hundred and eighty-eight (188) consecutive natural speech sequences from both speakers in another 24 f.p.s. filmed dyadic interaction were analyzed. Thirty of the 188 sequences consisted of one or two word replies to questions with "yes" or "no" or "um hum." These were excluded so that 158 sequences were examined. The major criteria for segmentation at this level were the sustained body motion forms, as described above, occurring during a spoken sequence. The mean frame duration of the 158 sequences was 24 with a range from 19–30 frames. Among the 158 sequences were 48 which occurred in relative isolation, i.e., the speech sequence was preceded and followed by silence. All of these fell within the 19–30 frame range, so that studying speech length alone (without the accompanying body motion forms) also showed a marked one second periodicity. The number of frames per word in the sequences examined ranged from 1–8 with a mean of 4.56 frames.

As noted earlier, it is as if there is an on-going, multi-level organizational rhythm hierarchy in terms of which behavior behaves. Both speech and body motion obey this hierarchic rhythm structure and are simultaneously synchronized across these multiple levels in their co-occurring. The on-going flowing and changing together of the body parts seems to reflect an underlying organizational structure. The characteristic form of order of the organizational flow of speaker behavior is thus quite clearly revealed to be that of an on-going process which is formed of several levels of waves emerging simultaneously. The behavior forming the longer wave begins at the same moment that the smaller wave forms begin. The smaller waves are integrated with the longer wave but are not added together to form it. Metaphorically, it is as if the organism were constantly generating an integrated, multi-level wave hierarchy which behavior necessarily followed. All behavior appears to be integrated together as a function of a basic, organized rhythm hierarchy, e.g., the speaker's eye blinks, which might seem to occur randomly, actually occur synchronously with the rest of the behavior and tend to occur at articulatory change points, primarily at phone boundaries. (This was seen in relation to the word "so" in Figure 1.)

Behavior appears phenomenologically to be both discrete-like **and** continuous simultaneously, without contradiction, providing an organizational form where the discrete-like is fused into the continuous. The smaller wave forms get integrated into the larger wave form. Furthermore, the speech/body motion wave hierarchy of normal speaker self-synchrony appears to exhibit periodicities similar to the Delta, Theta, Alpha, and Beta (DTAB) waves of the brain revealed by electroencophalography (EEG). This may simply be coincidence, but the similarities are striking. The DTAB waves may occur together at the same time in the brain (Duffy, 1981). This is also true of the behavioral waves. The brain waves are sequentially continuous and so are the behavioral waves. The body motion organization accompanies the phone types, **while** it accompanies the words, **while** it accompanies the phrases and sentences. This simultaneous multi-level accompaniment was seen in Figure 1. The present hypothesis is that human speech/body motion behavior can be interpreted as behavioral waves having continuous, hierarchically integrated series of waves. The analyses of behavior from 1/96th of a second up to one or two seconds are revealing forms of order which appear to link brain and behavior. If the hierarchic organization of the behavioral waves is synchronous with, or a reflection of, the brain waves, sound-film microanalysis can contribute to the study of how behavior reflects brain wave processes. For example, it may suggest that the brain waves are operating together synchronously and hierarchically like the behavioral waves. It would also suggest that the brain wave organization of a listener may entrain with the structure of the incoming speech of a speaker. This will be seen below in the discussion of listener behavior. A view is emerging that multiple aspects of human behavior and communication may be organizationally linked together. Behavior and the brain processes which mediate it are not separate systems, but may constitute an organizational integrity in the individual and between individuals.

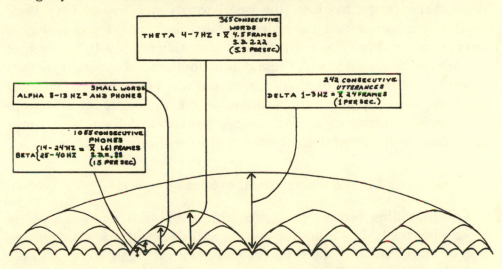

Figure 2. Illustrative schema of behavioral wave periodicities compared to brain wave periodicities.

Figure 2 presents a **speculative** schema of behavioral wave periodicities compared to brain wave periodicities based on phone, word, and sentence length analyses. The sentence length utterances tend to have a periodicity similar to the Delta waves. Words may have similar periodicity as Theta waves. Vowels, rapidly spoken short words, and syllables appear to be of Alpha frequency. Phone types seem to exhibit Beta periodicity. There is a great deal of flexibility, so that units of varying size can fit into the hierarchy.

Figure 1 illustrates the rhythmic pattern which is characteristic of speaker behavior. Rhythm is not a separate force added to this behavior from outside. It is a form of order or organization discovered in behavior and is an aspect of behavioral organization. Rhythm seems to provide predictable pulses or points which may facilitate synchronization of the sustainings and changes of the body parts which give rise to the process units. Speaker behavior is rhythmically organized and this appears to facilitate the emergence of hierarchically synchronized structure. In a sense rhythm adds power to behavior.

All aspects of behavior are integrated together and function together. Each serves as the context for the other during analysis. Rhythm, enabling behavioral changes to occur synchronously, may help link them in an organizational structure. Several levels of behavior seem to emerge simultaneously in terms of a rhythm hierarchy. The phone waves have their characteristic rhythms, the small words and vowels have their rhythm, the words have their rhythm, and the phrases and sentences have their rhythm. The body motion also exhibits levels of rhythms which are synchronized with these speech rhythms. The significant fact, however, is that these levels of waves are also **hierarchically integrated** together. This hierarchic integration, where the different levels are synchronized, provides a continuous organizational form which may contribute to the integration of smaller units within larger units.

Listener Entrainment to Speaker Speech

The preceding section concerned the sound-film microanalysis of speaker behavior. The following section will deal with the synchronization or entrainment of the listener's body motion organization with the articulatory pattern of the speaker's speech. The listener's body moves almost as synchronously with the speaker's speech as the speaker's body does. Entrainment of the listener's body motion with the speaker's speech occurs within a 42 msec latency, like a car following a continuously rapidly curving road. This suggests that there may be a basic short-latency, auditory-motor (striatal) linkage in the brain stem where the motor processes reflect the structure of the incoming auditory signals, especially speech. Figure 3 below illustrates the precision which is characteristic of entrainment. Two adult males who never met before are seated and talking. The sound film was made at 24 f.p.s. The speaker says, "Put the pressure on people on the job market." The word "pressure," which will be used to illustrate entrainment, exhibits a contrasting sequence of voiced and unvoiced segments. An oscilloscopic display of the speech is presented to show that the sound pattern can be displayed visually. The voiced / ð / sound terminating the word "the" is followed by the /p/ of "pressure" which is unvoiced and lasts two frames. This is then followed by the voiced /rɛ/ also lasting two frames. The /r/ flows smoothly into the /ɛ/, forming a unitary articulatory gesture. The unvoiced /š/ occurs next and lasts three frames. Finally, the terminal, voiced /r/ occurs, lasting four frames. The total word covers 11 frames or just slightly under ½ second. The body motion of the listener exhibits micro-movement organizations (process units) which occur isomorphically with the lengths of the units of the speaker's speech. This is seen particularly well in the listener's process unit that occurs with the three frames of /ššš/ in "pressure." Fingers 1 and 2 of the right hand had been flexing. They change direction and extend slightly across the three frame duration of /ššš/ and then flex again at the end of the segment. The head also moves down slightly in contrast to a preceeding upward movement and a following left movement.

The behavior of the listener in Figure 3 is not like that of a robot. His process units seen at normal projection speed transform smoothly into each other and cannot be seen by the naked eye. They are part of the flow of on-going behavior, but they are precisely synchronized with the articulatory structure of the speaker's speech. Such precise synchrony occurred constantly throughout this 12 minute sound-film. It has been observed in all normal interactants studied thus far, including films of many different cultures. The form of organization of the listener's process units seems to be modulated by the structure of the speaker's speech. Whatever body parts the listener happens to be moving at that moment will be organized and will follow the organization of the speaker's speech. Further, the listener's body often speeds up and slows down in relation to the softness or loudness of the speaker's speech. For example, there is accelerated listener movement with the voiced /rɛ/ and with the voiced terminal /r/ in contrast to the unvoiced /p/ and /š/. This is seen in the subscript f which means "fast." There is a precise isomorphism between the flow of the speaker's speech and the body motion of the listener. This occurs all the time and the illustration of it in Figure 3 is not an isolated instance.

The concept of **synchrony** is central to the hypotheses of self-synchrony

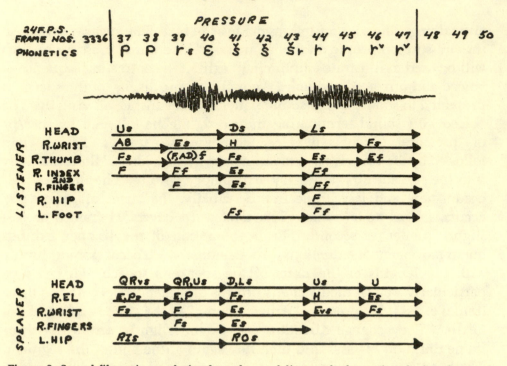

Figure 3. Sound-film microanalysis of speaker and listener body motion during the word "pressure" shows interactional synchrony or entrainment. The listener's process units entrain with the speaker's speech.

and entrainment. The units of speech and body motion are forms of organization or order. The patterns which form the process units of body motion during **speaking** behavior are forms of organization and are identified by their order and not directly by the specific body parts which happen to be expressing that order at a given moment. No matter what body parts may be moving during speaking they tend to occur with characteristic forms of order which are synchronous with the co-occurring flow of speech. This is also true of **listening** behavior, but the phone types and word levels are primarily entrained with, while larger movements covering phrases are rarer.

A normal infant as young as twenty minutes following birth can entrain with adult speech almost as well as an adult. This suggests a biological preparedness for speech and human communication. (Entrainment may even occur in utero.) An example of the phenomenon of entrainment in a two-day old infant is shown in Figure 4 (based on a 30 fps, 16 mm sound film). The infant is awake and alert lying in a crib. The male physician is standing to the infant's left out of view and says, "Look over here . . . hum . . . not over there." The infant's organizations of movement during "not over there" were microanalyzed and are shown in Figure 4.

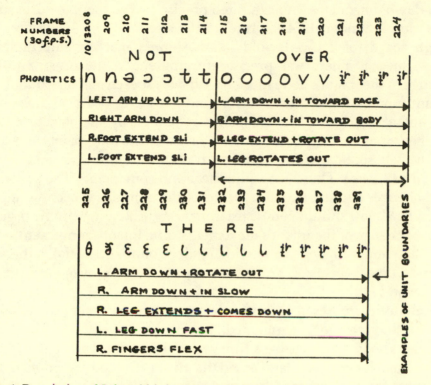

Figure 4. Description of 2-day-old infant's movements during "not over there" spoken to the infant by a male physician out of the infant's range of view.

The first word "not" lasts for seven frames or approximately ⅕ of a second. What can be seen most clearly is the left arm sweeping up and out through frames 013208–013214. The baby had been still and begins to entrain at the onset of the word "not." The second word "over" takes 10 frames, from 013215–013224. The left arm now moves back in toward the face and across it. The arms cross each other over the baby's face. As this is occurring the baby's left leg sweeps rapidly outward horizontally. Across the word "there" the left arm now moves back to the left. The word "there" occurs across frames 013225–013239. The left leg comes down rapidly toward the mattress and the fingers of the right hand flex.

The whole phrase lasts 32 frames or just slightly over one second and illustrates again how much movement can occur in such a brief period, even in a two-day-old infant. There are three clear process units which occur isomorphically with the three words uttered by the adult. This infant entrained in this same precise fashion across 89 consecutive words (in phrases) spoken by the physician. This infant was among 16 normal 2–4-day-old neonates who exhibited precise entrainment to adult speech (Condon & Sander, 1974). A recent intensive analysis of a 48 f.p.s. film (high speed) of a two-day-old infant showed marked entrainment to adult speech. There was precise entrainment of the organizations of change of the infant's body motion with both speech and tap sounds. The infant soon habituated to the tap sounds. It was as if the organization of the infant's body motion was being generated by the structure of the mother's speech. The infant exhibited micro-startle movements in response to the tap sounds within the first two frames following sound onset (within 42 msec). These were quite clear and convincing. The sustainings and changes of the articulatory units of the mother's speech were paralleled by almost simultaneous sustainings and changings in the organization of change of the infant's movements. The infant's movements would also accelerate in synchrony with louder sounds, especially the vowel sounds. (Speakers also characteristically accelerate movement with their own vowel sounds.)

Reliability studies have been conducted on entrainment. In an unpublished study, a judge segmented the speaker's speech blind from the listener's body motion using a film with only numbers and a sound track. The same judge then segmented the listener's body motion using a different frame-numbered film and without sound. This blind analysis resulted in an agreement of 97%. This procedure has obvious defects but is suggestive. In another more rigorous unpublished study 188 consecutive frames of two speakers' speech were segmented by one judge and the body motion of two listeners' behavior was segmented by another judge with an agreement of 87%. In a third study two independent judges analyzed the body motion of six normal children in response to 20 sounds for 10 frames following the onset of each sound. A significantly greater number of process unit boundaries occurred in relation to the frame following sound onset for both judges for all six subjects. In another study Condon and Ogston (1971) found that listener eyeblinks tended to occur at articulatory change points in the speaker's speech, thus further supporting interactional entrainment.

There have been a series of studies concerned with replicating interactional entrainment. McDowall (1978) conducted the first study on adult entrainment. His study had several defects. He used the wrong analyzing equipment, the wrong criteria for body motion change, and the wrong hypothesis. His study has been criticized by Gatewood and Rosenwein (1981) and Peery (1980). Austin and Peery (1983) conducted an intensive study of infant entrainment with adult speech, spending at least ½ hour on each of the 2400 frames of mother-infant interaction. They state, "This research corroborates the Condon studies which showed synchrony or entrainment between neonates and adults in interactional situations. It is possible that McDowell did not find such levels of synchrony because, as indicated before, his use of an electronically operated projector did not allow observations meticulous enough to detect the phenomena." Peery (1980) examined the facial approach and withdrawal between mother and infant. He states, "The most powerful relation is the simultaneous one. This simultaneity reflects the synchronous coordination of changes in direction of movement by the adult-infant dyad." He later says,

> "The same processes that produce interactional synchrony may be influencing the simultaneous regulation of the facial behavior we observed. In utero the fetus has considerable experience with adult (mother's) rhythms of movement and with the relation between adult speech and movement. This experience may provide the base for the high degree of movement coordination required in both interactional synchrony and the simultaneous changes in facial behavior reported here."

Kato et al. (1983) in Japan conducted an intensive replication study of infant entrainment to adult speech. His group studied 32 full term healthy infants. The mother, pediatrician, and a nurse were asked to talk to the infants using a carefully designed paradigm. The infants were videotaped and the results analyzed through linkage of the TV with a computer. The neonates were found to synchronize with adult speech but not with white noise, tapping sounds, and non-patterned sounds. They state, "Our work showed that the discrimination of voices was established within only the first week and that a neonate can correlate his movement with the voice not only from his mother but also from a doctor and nurse, who had been taking care of the neonates." And, further on they say, "Our results suggest not only that the organization of the neonate's motor behavior reacts to and is synchronized with the organized speech behavior of adults in his environment, but that the neonate's movements influence adult speech." Szajnberg and Hurt (in press) in a recent study of entrainment state, "These data suggest that infant's movements show both quantitative (total movements/second) and qualitative (growing and unipolar movements/second) changes in response to mother's speech." Kendon (1982) has studied human interaction intensively at the frame-by-frame level and states, "The phenomenon of synchrony has, in my view, been clearly demonstrated." Beebe et al. (1979) have found that mothers and infants can follow the movements of each other at a mean rate of four film frames (100 msec). In some instances this can occur as rapidly as one film frame. This seems to be visually mediated. Human infants also seem to be able to entrain to different languages. A two-day-old American infant was able to entrain to Chinese speech (Condon & Sander, 1974).

Entrainment seems to be an involuntary, **organized** motor reflex to sound stimuli, especially to speech in humans. It may exist in all hearing creatures. Entrainment may have species specific characteristics such that each species will entrain more readily to its own species vocal patterns. The listening organism clearly reflects the minute patterns of change in the incoming signal in its own patterns of movement. (There is some evidence that this may also be visually mediated and perhaps even mediated by several sensory processes.) This entrained and organized response on the part of the auditory-motor system may reflect the organization of the brain.

The highly speculative nature of the following comments on how interactional synchrony might be mediated between interactants must be emphasized. Since the speaker's behavior is rhythmic and the listener moves in synchrony with the speaker, the listener's behavior is also rhythmic. Human interaction thus appears to be fundamentally rhythmic in nature. Interactional synchrony has a dual nature with drive and rhythm aspects working together. The listening organism moves synchronously with the rapidly varying speech sounds of the speaker. It is difficult to imagine how the listening organism could predict these changes in advance, e.g., whether a phone type would last two or five frames or when a new sound might begin. This would seem to require a drive model. On the other hand, the rhythmic nature of the behavior, by providing expectable periodicities, could enhance the effectiveness of a drive model. Two organisms, having similar rhythm systems, might find it easier to entrain with an on-going drive process.

Different cultures exhibit different rhythm patterns. Over time the infant may take on the specific rhythm style of its culture. Subtle rhythm differences may cause difficulties when people from different cultures interact. In an unpublished study, eight people listening to a speaker were sound-filmed and found to move synchronously with the speaker's speech. This would suggest that audiences move in rhythm with the speaker. Each member of the audience would behave as an individual listener in relation to the speaker's speech. Since all were listening to the same speaker there would also be a group synchrony. Such group synchrony may create a new out-of-conscious-awareness phenomenon which is absent in dyadic interaction. If a listener could see many others in the audience they would all be moving, if they moved, in relation to the sound. This might create a richer participant effect. While it has not been studied, group synchrony may be occurring in situations such as the movies and watching television. Some speakers can arouse audiences more than others. Hitler, for example, was known for an ability to appeal to audiences. I once studied a close-up of a film of Hitler during a speech and at one point (and at the same moment) his right eye moved right and his left eye moved left.

Abnormal Entrainment to Sound

The existence of a basic auditory-motor reflex system which precisely, rapidly, and organizationally mirrors the pattern of both spoken and heard speech would suggest that this system might become disordered. This seems to be the case. An abnormal multiple entrainment to sound was postulated from an analysis of slight "jumps" and "jerks" observed in the bodies of dysfunctional children in relation to sound (Condon, 1974). In some cases of dyslexia, for example, the right side would entrain with sound within 42 msec as if normal, while the left side would entrain with the same sound after a delay which could range from 100 to 266 msec depending on the child. This multiple entraining gave the appearance of "jumps and jerk" in the body. The multiple entrainment pattern remained stable for a given child. A similar pattern was observed in autistic subjects, but the right side was delayed behind the left.

Continued intensive analysis revealed that multiple entrainment exhibited a characteristic pattern having four repeating entrainments within the first ⅔ of a second following sound onsets. Entrainment 1 occurs within the first frame following sound onset. Entrainment 2 ranges, as indicated, between 100 msec (3 film frames) and 266 msec (8 film frames) following sound onset. Entrainment 3 tends to occur at 333 msec (10 film frames) following sound onset. Entrainment 4 follows entrainment 2 by 333 msec (10 film frames). For example, one child might have a multiple entrainment of 1-4-10-14 frames and another a pattern of 1-6-10-16 frames. Speculatively, it appears as if there is a normal bilaterally synchronized 333 msec auditory input cycle from entrainment to orienting. The precision of the abnormal 333 msec pattern, where entrainment 4 follows entrainment 2 by 333 msec, suggests this. When a person is called by name his body begins to entrain to the sound within the first film frame following sound onset (33.33 msec using 30 fps film). Then, at approximately 10 film frames (333 msec using 30 f.p.s. film) from the time of onset of his name he will begin to turn toward the caller. In multiple entrainment it looks as if this input cycle is out of phase, with entrainments 1 and 2 being one 333 msec cycle and entrainments 2 and 4 being an out of phase 333 msec cycle. Several studies were conducted which strongly support the hypothesis of an abnormal multiple entrainment to sound (Condon, 1975; Condon, 1978). A similar pattern has also been observed in Huntington's disease, Parkinson's disease, cerebral palsy, schizophrenia, and stuttering. Multiple entrainment occurs in relation to most of the sounds occurring around such persons including their own voice.

Plooij (in press) studied an 11-year-old dyslexic child and his normal control in response to 58 random sounds using two TV cameras linked to a computer. At frame 1 following sound onset in both the dyslexic and the normal child there was a sharp increase or decrease of movement which supports the hypothesis of normal entrainment within 42 msec. The graphs of the dyslexic, however, were quite different from those of the normal control. The computer selected several peaks centering around frames 1, 4, 9–10, and 14–15 in the dyslexic child. Plooij states, "This is reminiscent of Condon's multiple entrainment." That a computer could pick-up an almost identical multiple entrainment pattern as that predicted is promising. The existence of multiple entrainment also provides strong indirect support for normal entrainment as a phenomenon.

Summary

An ability to participate within a shared order seems to be essential for interaction. In perceiving and knowing, the organism participates in the order of the universe in which it exists and replicates aspects of that order within itself. This involves a process of translation of that order through different media. "Sharings" of many kinds and at many levels

between interactants are primary factors in communicational maintenance and transformation. Sustaining movement together and sharing
posture are thought to reflect rapport in both humans and lower animals.
The courtship dances of the various animal species are examples. To
speak the same language means to share the same sounds and the same
grammar. A rapidly spoken foreign language is incomprehensible. Sharing or "sustaining forms of order together" is a fundamental principle of
the structure of the organization of behavior and interaction at the
micro-level.

In this chapter I have focused on the nature of the structure of
organization revealed by intensive microanalyses of behavior. Human
existence appears to involve a profound synchronization of the organism
with the universe in which it exists and with other human beings. A
speaker's body is precisely synchronized with his own speech across
multiple levels. And between human beings there is an exquisite, rhythmic synchronization. As indicated, the listener's body moves in rhythmic
organizations of change which precisely reflect the speaker's speech.
This is observable even in infants. Human communication is fundamentally synchronous and rhythmic. Synchrony and rhythm are primary
aspects of human individual and interactional behavior. They are not
separate forms added to the structure of behavior, but are forms of
organization discovered in behavior. They are elements in the structure
of behavior.

The temporal patterns (process units) of the organization of behavior
can be described. Synchronization is an essential aspect of the determination of the process units. These units also exhibit a characteristic
periodicity or rhythm. The boundaries of the higher level units (words,
phrases, sentences, and the body motion form accompanying them)
are precisely synchronized with the boundaries of the lower levels,
yet they are also rhythmic in nature. Synchronization tends to relate
to the determination of the unit boundaries and the sustaining of the
same relationship between the body parts (i.e., the content of the unit).
Rhythm relates to the length of time these relationships are sustained.
A boundary is the point at which a relational sustaining begins and
is not separate from it. Figure 1 illustrates this hierarchic organizational
process. What is revealed is a form of organization having multiple levels
of rhythms (where each level can vary slightly) which are, however,
synchronized together in a continuous, on-going fashion.

NOTE

This research was partially supported by BRSG Grant No. RR 05487.

REFERENCES

Austin, A.M. and Peery, J. C. Analysis of adult-neonate synchrony during speech and nonspeech. *Perceptual and Motors Skills,* 1983, *57,* 455–459.

Beebe, B., Stern, D., and Jaffe, J. The kinesic rhythm of mother-infant interactions. In Siegman, A. and Feldstein, S. (Eds.), *Of Speech and Time.* Hillsdale, N.J.: Erlbaum Associates, 1979.

Condon, W. S. Synchrony units and the communicational hierarchy. Paper presented at Western Psychiatric Institute and Clinic, Pittsburgh, Pa.: 1963.

Condon, W. S. Method of micro-analysis of sound films of behavior. *Behavioral Research Methods and Instruments,* 1970, *2,* 51–54.

Condon, W. S. Multiple response to sound in autistic-like children. Proceedings of the National Society for Autistic Children Conference, Washington, D.C.: June 1974.

Condon, W. S. Multiple response to sound in dysfunctional children. *Journal of Autism and Childhood Schizophrenia,* 1975, *5,* 37–56.

Condon, W. S. Asynchrony and communicational disorders. In Proceedings of Symposium on Research in Autism. Canada Society for Autistic Children. Vancouver: 1978.

Condon, W. S. Sound-film microanalysis: A means for correlating brain and behavior. Paper presented at Institute for Child Development Research Symposium. Philadelphia, Pa.: 1981.

Condon, W. S., and Ogston, W. D. A segmentation of behavior. *Journal of Psychiatric Research,* 1967, *5,* 221–235.

Condon, W. S., and Ogston, W. D. Speech and body motion synchrony of the speaker-hearer. In D. L. Horton, and J. J. Jenkins (Eds.), *Perception of Language.* Columbus, Ohio: Charles E. Merrill, 1971.

Condon, W. S. and Sander, L. W. Neonate movement is synchronized with adult speech: Interactional participation and language acquisition. *Science,* 1974, *183,* 99–101.

Duffy, F. Personal Communication, 1981.

Gatewood, J. and Rosenwein, R. Interactional synchrony: Genuine or spurious? A critique of recent research. *Journal of Nonverbal Behavior,* 1981, *6.*

Kato, T., Takahashi, E., Sawada, K., Kobayashi, N., Watanabe, T., & Ishii, T. A computer analysis of infant movements synchronized with adult speech. *Pediatric Research,* 1983, *17,* 625–628.

Kendon, A. Coordination of action and framing in face-to-face interaction. In M. Davis (Ed.) *Interaction rhythms.* New York: Human Sciences Press, 1982.

McDowell, J. Interactional synchrony: A reappraisal. *Journal of Personality and Social Psychology,* 1978, *36,* 963–975.

Peery, J. C. Neonate-adult head movement: No and yes revisited. *Developmental Psychology,* 1980, *16,* 245–250.

Plooij, F. The relationships between ethology and paedology. Amsterdam, Netherlands, In press.

Szajnberg, N. & Hurt, S. Infant cross modal movement response to maternal speech. (in press).

Chapter 5.

ASPECTS OF RHYTHMIC STRUCTURE IN SPEECH PERCEPTION

JAMES G. MARTIN

As scientists and scholars we recall those times early in our career when we were asked by our Aunt Olga or some other layperson to explain what it was that we "do." If we had an academic post there was no problem giving answers that would satisfy since everyone knew what teachers did. But the answer was harder if we wanted to give them some idea of what we were really doing most of the time, and why. My own solution was to refer to a scientific problem related to our own work, the perception of continuous speech, but which would be easier for a layperson to understand because of its enormous practical implications, namely the "voice-typewriter" problem. I explained that computers do so many incredible things, many of them much better than people do them, but that one thing a computer could **not** do was listen to a person talk and type out what was said. "And why not?" I would finish rhetorically, "That's the fascinating question!" Of course automatic speech recognition (ASR) is a fascinating problem. An illiterate child can listen to a sentence and repeat it back aloud, understood or not. A phonetician can transcribe a spoken utterance in an unknown language. Yet ASR fails when it is applied to normal continuous speech because it is not known how linguistic information is structured and distributed in the acoustic signal. We came to appreciate that problem in our own research.

Our earliest work with speech began with attempts to develop notions about a speaker-listener model by observing hesitation phenomena (e.g., Martin and Strange, 1968; 1971). In order to obtain the speech corpus necessary for this work, we recorded the responses of subjects as they described or otherwise talked about Thematic Apperception Test (TAT) cards which were shown to them. When we looked at the transcriptions we were producing in the course of our work we continued to be struck by the fact that the speech produced under these conditions was highly elliptical, grossly ungrammatical, or at least did not follow the received grammar of American English, yet upon listening it was very easy for us to understand what the speaker had in mind. Clearly the speaker was using syntactic and other knowledge in a "dialect" shared by us, however difficult this knowledge might be to describe linguistically. Eventually it seemed doubtful that the best approach was to continue to elaborate on models of what the speaker and listener were doing when so little was known about the acoustic signal that linked them. What appeared to be missing was any sort of detailed idea about the way linguistic information was distributed in the acoustic waveform. This was the problem that workers in ASR had faced and failed to solve. We should consider here briefly what the nature of the problem was and how it was approached.

In early work with ASR the goal was to take the continuous acoustic speech waveform as input and provide as output a reasonably accurate transcription of the speaker's intention. Such a transcription would consist of the string of symbols representing the phonetic segments (roughly, consonants and vowels), together with additional symbols representing the prosodic ("suprasegmental") aspects of the utterance, for instance, rhythm, tempo, changes in fundamental frequency, amplitude, duration, etc. Prosodic aspects are known to carry information about phrase boundaries, word stress, and other linguistic information not provided by the segments themselves. The task was seen as one of mapping between the linguistic and acoustic domains using the knowledge gained from decades of research with isolated syllables or words (e.g., Cooper, Delattre, Liberman, Borst and Gerstman, 1952: Liberman, Delattre, Cooper and Gerstman, 1954). Such research showed that each of the segments in a syllable or word could be recognized by combinations of acoustic cues, for instance, the silent interval preceding a noise burst when the lips were released to pronounce the stop consonant /p/. Similarly there were known acoustic correlates of the prosodic aspects of speech. Word stress, for example, was marked in the signal by greater amplitude, duration, etc. (e.g., Fry, 1968). Given this kind of knowledge gained from research with single syllables or words, and given the fact that initial attempts at computer recognition of isolated words was fairly successful it was thought that attempts to apply recognition routines to the continuous speech waveform should not be especially difficult. If continuous speech could be regarded merely as a longer string of segments when words were combined in a kind of building-block fashion, then the task for automatic recognition was primarily one of "segmenting" the acoustic signal into regions corresponding to the phonetic segments (hence the name) in a rough one-to-one acoustic-linguistic mapping. Prosodic aspects could be localized in the waveform in a similar fashion.

When the goal of phonetic transcription of continuous speech, as opposed to isolated syllables or words, proved to be elusive, the difficulties generally were laid to the fact that speech recognition by humans depends on knowledge of the language and of the world which is not shared by computers (Pierce, 1969). For instance, segments were often unclearly pronounced in normal continuous speech and hence were ambiguous from the point of view of speech analysis techniques. The human listener, however, could disambiguate such speech by her/his knowledge of syntactic, semantic and situational context. Work on models of continuous speech recognition by humans shifted attention away from the contribution of the acoustic stimulus to the contribution from the listener, that is, away from "bottom-up" approaches emphasizing acoustic decoding to "top-down" approaches emphasizing syntactic-semantic constraints. Work on automatic systems changed emphasis from recognition, which focussed on phonetic transcription to systems for "speech understanding" (see Klatt, 1977 for extensive review). This approach changed the nature of the automatic systems goal. First, heavy constraints were placed on the language input that the computer system was required to accept: The vocabulary of the language was limited to about a thousand words, the task domain was delimited, and an artificial syntax was used that was no more complex than that needed for the task. For instance, in one system where the task was document retrieval, an acceptable input sentence to the system was "How many articles are there in psychology?" Finally, accuracy of the system was based not on correct word recognition but on correctness of the response to the input. Under these very limiting conditions some understanding systems performed quite well but the original problem remained. It was not known how linguistic information was structured and distributed in the acoustic waveform of normal continuous speech.

As noted earlier, we saw this lack of knowledge about structure in the acoustic waveform as the initial obstacle in our work with spontaneous speech. However, we looked at the problem from the perspective of the psychology of perception rather than of linguistics or engineering, and hence we were doubtful about several assumptions behind the work with ASR. For one thing, while the difficulty with ASR might be that the speech signal was so phonetically impoverished that syntactic-semantic top-down processes were required to decode the signal, this interpretation was not necessary and in fact there was some reason to believe the opposite, that the signal was phonetically rich (e.g., Klatt, 1979). There was not much published evidence on the point, however, so to satisfy ourselves in an informal experiment we presented nonsense "sentences" spoken by a normal human talker over headphones to listeners and asked them to write them down. Examples of the sentences were:

(1) Guards play goods in the false room.
(2) A start from the screen for that brick hit forests.

Semantically-empty sentences like these are very hard to recall after a few seconds. However, in immediate recall the listeners scored over 90% of the content words correct (five per sequence). These results do not support the assumption that continuous speech is so phonetically impoverished that it can only be understood if it is semantically heavily constrained.

Far more important for continuous speech perception was the doubtful assumption of ASR that the relatively simple acoustic-linguistic mapping achieved with isolated syllables and words could be extended to the case of continuous speech. It did not seem likely that the segmental cues identified in isolated syllables or words would retain their same form in continuous speech context. Instead, they were in some sense more highly encoded; their invariants were of higher order and related by some system of transformations. Similarly the extension from isolated syllables and words to continuous speech was doubtful in the case of prosodic speech aspects also. In visual pattern perception it is commonplace that stimulus and percept are complexly related and that elements in context have different properties than in isolation. There was little reason to suppose auditory pattern perception would be different. We saw the continuous speech problem in that way—as one of auditory pattern perception, and more like recognizing faces than, say, reading—and we looked for a different way of characterizing the patterns of continuous speech. There were several hints that it might be fruitful to consider rhythmic patterns.

One of these hints was provided by linguistic theory in the form of the transformational stress cycle, an elegant device for assigning word and sentence stress solely on the basis of syntax of the sentence (Chomsky and Halle, 1968). For instance, the levels of stress in the following sentence are assigned by cyclical application of two phonological rules based on syntax:

(3) John's blackboard eraser was stolen.
      3   2   5   4   1

However, it seemed to us that the stress pattern of the sentence was a lot like the accent pattern in familiar musical cadences. We found that one could get the same result for sentence (3) by applying musical notation plus some assumptions about hierarchical structure implied by the notation and known tacitly by any musician. Moreover, the stress pattern could be applied on the basis of syllable durations or relative timing by means of a "rhythm rule" (Martin, 1970; 1972) and hence was independent of syntax.

Another hint from transformational grammar was provided by the center-embedded sentence used in psycholinguistic experiments (Fodor and Garrett, 1967) of which the following is an example:

(2) The window the ball the boy threw hit broke.

Possibly sentences like this are rarely spoken because they are syntactically difficult, but another reason might be that they are rhythmically awkward and hence harder to pronounce in a natural way. In this case the last four words provide four stressed syllables in a row, a rare sequence in natural speech.

These considerations and others led to the development of notions about rhythmic patterning in continuous speech and in behavior in general (Martin, 1972). The notion of rhythm has attractive implications for speech perception. Two of these have provided a guide for our research and may be characterized as follows.

The first concerns the stimulus. Speech, as a "natural" acoustic pattern produced by human movement, is seen as having internal wholistic organization; The sequential elements are organized in terms of relative timing and not concatenation. Hence there are constraints and temporal redundancy throughout the domain of the pattern. We thought it useful to regard the breath-group, a phrase-like unit, as the domain of the pattern; a notion that extends segmental concepts like coarticulation or context-conditioned variation to larger stretches of speech. Moreover, the segmental and prosodic aspects were integrally related, that is, the acoustic realization of the utterance is dependent on the identity and local context of segments as well as prosodic effects.

The second implication concerns perception. The perceiver expects as input an intact (as spoken) utterance and has an internal representation of the production constraints and temporal redundancy in the signal. Such constraints and temporal redundancy allow future pattern elements to be predictable in real time; early elements in a pattern generate moment-to-moment expectancies and hence an efficient perceptual device may be expected to have an anticipatory "feed-forward" component. Thus we thought of speech perception and production as dynamically related, with rhythmic action as the natural link between them. These notions focus emphasis on the wholistic pattern structure of the stimulus rather than on elements or parts, and accordingly they implicate a research methodology appropriate for wholistic pattern structure in work with continuous speech.

The remainder of this chapter describes some of the work that was done to give meaning to these notions. The next section describes experiments to determine the role of prosodic structure on the perception of speech, in particular, on the interaction or nonindependence of segmental-prosodic aspects. The second section following turns to segmental structure. In this case experimental work was done to determine the extent and structure of information, in particular, from anticipatory coarticulation, that specifies segments in continuous speech context.

Nonindependence of Segmental and Prosodic Aspects of Perception

Usually we characterize the input to speech production by a string of discrete and independent entities called segments. However, when a string of segments is encoded, the acoustic consequences are neither discrete nor independent. The acoustic realization of the string depends on the identity and local context of the segments themselves, and also on the effects of prosody. For instance, when speech tempo increases, segmental durations shorten and spectral cross-sections and rates of change vary also (Gay, 1978; Lindblom, 1963). Both tempo and segment identity are manifest in the acoustic realization of the segments. The talker cannot separate these factors during production; any given tempo difference modulates the segments to some degree, so that the resulting string carries information about both tempo and segment identity. Here we raise two questions, and describe an experiment that addresses each of them. First, are these two kinds of information separable during perception? Second, what is their domain?

The first question may be put in at least three different ways. (a) Is segmental information in local acoustics invariant across tempo changes? If so, then segmental and tempo perception should be separable or independent; all needed segmental information is extractable from the current time window independently of information extracted either earlier or later. Or (b), are tempo and segmental perception interdependent in the sense that segmental information is transformed under tempo change, and perception must take that transformation into account? Or (c), are tempo and segmental perception dependent only in the sense that they must be carried out simultaneously? Put yet another way, with respect to segmental and tempo perception we may ask: (a) Are they independent? (b) Are they dependent, with the dependency in the stimulus? (c) Are they dependent, with the dependency in the perceiver? On the grounds that segmental and prosodic information are inseparable in the stimulus, parsimony favors their inseparability in perception also, but experimental evidence was needed.

Our approach was to change or distort the tempo of a sentence within the sentence itself, then observe effects on perception elsewhere in the sentence. If the subject cannot ignore the changes in prosodic structure while listening for segmental targets there was a basis for concluding that segmental and prosodic perception are not independent. However, as will be seen, the experiment was done in such a way that we could pit our theory against other approaches, in particular, some current information-processing notions.

The 36 basic "sentences" in the experiment (Martin, 1979a) were six-syllable nonsense sequences of the form "DAS a LAS a GAS" or "a DAS a BAS a LAS." Either (a) one vowel in the sentence was lengthened or shortened by 50, 90 or 130 msec by computer-editing routines, or (b) the sentence was left intact (as spoken). The resulting perceptual impression from the time distortion was a change of tempo within the sentence. The time distortions occurred systematically across the sentence, in one of syllables one through five. Reaction time (RT) was recorded to assigned target segments /b,d,g/ in one of syllables one through six, and RT was compared to targets in tempo-change (time distortion) vs. intact sentences (these were acoustically identical except for the distortion). The listeners responded to over 2000 versions of the sentences.

Now consider the results we might expect from this experiment. When a vowel duration is distorted there at least are two effects. On of these is a change in the structure of the stimulus, with resulting change in **stimulus**

expectancy. The other is a change in what might be called warning or **processing time.**

Consider processing time first. When a vowel duration is distorted there is either greater or less processing time from sentence onset to target. Suppose that change in processing time is the only distortion effect. In that case we may predict slower RT following pre-target shortening, but faster RT following pre-target lengthening. Moreover, the effects on RT of **amount** of distortion, from + 130 msec through intact (nondistorted) to − 130 msec should show a linear increasing trend, as can be seen in Figure 1.

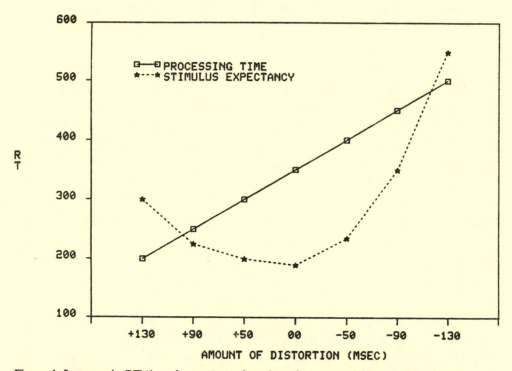

Figure 1. Increase in RT (interference) as a function of amount of distortion in pre-target syllable, predicted by the Processing Time and Stimulus Expectancy hypotheses. The units on the ordinate (RT) are arbitrary. As the text explains, the one function is linear, the other is quadratic (U-shaped).

The other effect of the distortion of the sentence is change in stimulus expectancy. That is, temporal redundancy in the stimulus permits (or drives) the listener to predict the future course of the waveform from correlated information in the part of the signal already heard. We assume that the expected input to perception is the intact (as spoken) sentence in both its prosodic and segmental aspects, and that any or all distortions degrade the stimulus to some extent at least. This view predicts slower target RT following **both** shortening and lengthening, on the grounds that relational aspects of the stimulus are distorted in both cases. On this hypothesis the effects on amount of distortion, from $+130$ msec through intact to -130 msec, should show a concave (U-shaped) quadratic trend. However, lengthening should disrupt RT less than shortening since for a given amount of change (e.g., 50 msec) added or subtracted, the **relative** change is less in the case of lengthening than in the case of shortening (i.e., $[X + d]/X < X/[X - d]$ where $X =$ sentence length and $d =$ amount of distortion). That is, the stimulus expectancy view predicts **some** linear trend also.

The combination of linear and quadratic trend therefore predicts, first, results like those shown in Figure 1. Second, stimulus expectancy effects (quadratic trend) should increase later in the sentence since expectancies become firmer with increasing prior context or redundancy gain. Third, linear trend should decrease later in the sentence since the need for warning time is greatest at sentence onset but diminishes later in the sentence. (Note here that processing-time and stimulus-expectancy hypotheses are not equally interesting; any theory predicts processing-time effects in an RT experiment. The hypotheses are distinguished here because they predict **opposed** effects across the time course of the sentence which can mask the separate contributions of each.)

The results of the experiment supported all three of these predictions from stimulus expectancy. The quadratic trend effects are crucial because they rule out effects solely from processing time. They also rule out effects from some sort of generalized distortion from intervention effects such as splicing, since that kind of effect would not predict a quadratic trend. These results support the stimulus-expectancy hypothesis for continuous speech perception; The expected input is the acoustically intact utterance in both its segmental and prosodic (here, rhythmic) aspects; there is little reason to believe that these aspects are perceived independently.

The next experiment (Martin, 1979b) considers the second question posed earlier. Given that the perceiver expects an acoustically intact utterance, what is its domain? On the present view, sequential or temporally-extended redundancy in the continuous speech waveform allows the listener to predict the future course of the waveform from correlated information in the part of the signal already heard. As more of the utterance is heard, there is increasing redundancy and therefore increasing ease in tracking the utterance.

This view implies continuity in perception when there is continuity in production but also that where there is discontinuity in articulatory flow there will be correspondingly a discontinuity in perception. One locus of relative discontinuity in production is a phrase boundary, which is often marked by lengthening of segments and other prosodic change. The present experiment shows that these discontinuities at the boundary in production are accompanied by a corresponding discontinuity in perception.

The experiment was similar to the one above. The sentences were nonsense strings consisting of six stressed syllables (e.g., "LAS a PAS a LAS, a GAS a LAS a BAS"). Each sentence was pronounced with a slight phrase-like boundary (indicated by the comma in the example) after the fifth syllable. The stressed syllables were either target carriers (PAS, BAS, KAS, GAS) or a dummy syllable (LAS). Hence there were six potential target positions, three in each phrase. Half the sentences contained targets in positions one, three and five; half contained targets in positions two, four or six. Each sentence contained three of the four targets; thus for a given target one-fourth of the sentences were foils. Figure 2 shows the results.

In general, target RT tends to decrease monotonically as a function of time into a sentence (Martin, 1979a; Shields, McHugh & Martin, 1974). Such a result is predicted by several hypotheses most of which, like processing time, are of little interest. Here, however, we see that the decrease in target RT as a function of time into the sentence was not monotonic. Instead, target RT decreased successively within the first phrase, but increased after the boundary before decreasing again in the second phrase. This "scallop" effect suggests a relative discontinuity across boundaries in **both** production and perception. Phrases are units in the sense that articulatory-acoustic sequential redundancy (correlation) is higher within than between phrases. In perception, such redundancy facilitates increased ease in tracking the successive syllables in the phrase until the boundary is reached.

These experimental results have implications for continuous speech perception theory. Evidence that the rhythmic and segmental aspects of continuous speech are not perceived independently suggests that a future model of speech perception by humans should incorporate at some early stage a rhythmic expectancy component. The expectancy component

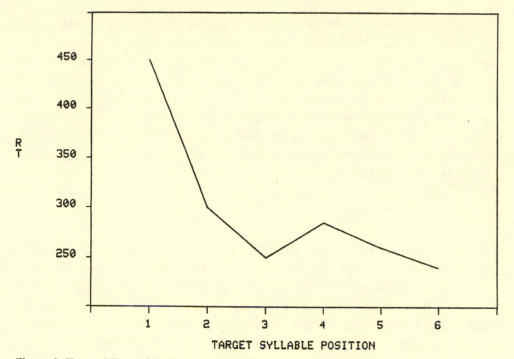

Figure 2. Target RT as a function of target syllable position. RT decreases with time into the sentence, then rises after the phrase boundary before decreasing again.

accepts as input an intact utterance, i.e., the output of a speaker's vocal tract. Starting from utterance onset, all extracted information is used to predict the outlines of the utterance as yet unheard, and expectancies extrapolated ahead within the constraints supplied by current information. Such a model can apply to human perception even if tempo and other prosodic changes leave segmental acoustics invariant. In this case the experimental results above reflect real-time constraints on simultaneous segmental and prosodic perception when it must be done by humans, i.e., the dependency in segmental-prosodic aspects of perception is in the perceiver, not the stimulus. If this interpretation is correct, then a future automatic speech recognition routine, if it is given an improved account of local acoustic variation, say, a good diphone dictionary (Klatt, 1977), and if it is not required to handle input with the same time constraints placed on the human perceptual process, will perform well even though tempo and other prosodic aspects of the signal are ignored.

On the other hand, it may be that much local acoustic variation is the result of higher-order phonetic segment encoding in continuous speech context. That is, as-yet-unexplained local variation is explainable by dependencies of higher order such as extended coarticulatory effects. If this interpretation is correct, there is a limit on what can be accomplished by analysis limited to local input. Improved machine recognition in that case will need to take into account segmental-prosodic interactions, higher-order dependencies and other wholistic aspects of the signal, just as humans apparently do. These unanswered questions provide the basis for the work in the next section where we turn to segmental aspects of continuous speech perception, in particular, to the perceptual effects of anticipatory coarticulation.

Nonindependence of Segmental-Phonetic Context in Perception

When a talker says "sloop," her/his lips are rounded or protruded as the first segment /s/ of the sequence is pronounced, or even sooner. However, when the word is "sleep," this does not occur. These examples illustrate differences in anticipatory coarticulation, that is, in the positioning and movements of the articulators to prepare for the pronunciation of segments later in a sequence. In the examples, lip protrusion occurs two segments or earlier before the "rounded" vowel /u/ of "sloop," but not before the "unrounded" vowel /i/ of "sleep." Articulatory studies of speech production have shown evidence for anticipatory lip protrusion across up to four segments (e.g., Kozhevnikov and Chistovich, 1965; Daniloff and Moll, 1968; Bengueral and Cowan, 1974; Bell-Berti and Harris, 1979). There is also evidence for anticipatory coarticulation preceding nasals. In this case the velum is lowered to open the nasal cavity several segments before the nasal segment is pronounced (e.g., Moll and Daniloff, 1971). Moreover, coarticulation has acoustic consequences that can be readily identified in the signal. In the classic acoustic study of vowel-consonant-vowel (VCV) utterances, Ohman (1966) showed, e.g., that formant transitions in the first vowel were conditioned not only by the identity of the consonant but also by the following vowel. That is, a given format in the first vowel rises to anticipate its target value in the second vowel if its value is high in that vowel, whereas it lowers to anticipate a low target value.

These studies and others (see, e.g., reviews by Kent and Minifie, 1977; MacNeilage and Ladefoged, 1976) show that the effects of coarticulation are not limited to immediately adjacent segments; the sequential constraints are often of a higher order. The articulation of each segment in a continuous utterance may be constrained by (or correlated with) the articulation of a number of upcoming and/or preceding segments. Similarly, the acoustic consequences of these articulations are constrained or correlated over time. Do these higher-order constraints in production and acoustic signal have a role in perception?

The perceptual significance of adjacent or first-order coarticulation effects has been established decades ago (e.g., Cooper et al, 1952; Liberman et al, 1954). However, attempts since then to show higher-order effects have generally reported negative results (e.g., Lehiste and Shockey, 1972). Such results led to the apparently widely-held belief that higher-order effects of coarticulation play no role in perception. Research on segmental perception focussed on local or first-order effects, and theoretical issues like categorical perception and feature detectors turned on questions of how information is extracted from the same local acoustics. The possibility of perceptual influences of higher-order coarticulatory effects was seldom mentioned. Indeed there was little need to consider them because the issues of interest could be and were usually examined using isolated syllables as the stimuli.

Recently attention has turned to models of perception in continuous speech context (Marslen-Wilson and Welsh, 1978). However, the majority of these models are concerned not with the acoustic signal but rather with top-down processing, that is, on how the listener's knowledge is brought to bear on decoding the acoustic signal. These models either ignore or take for granted the processing of the acoustic signal itself and therefore evade the fundamental problem of continuous speech perception (and automatic computer recognition as well), that the acoustic stimulus in continuous speech context may not be at all like the mere concatenation of isolated words, syllables or phonemes, but rather that every part of the continuous stimulus may be transformed by the context preceeding and following it. There is one model of continuous speech perception, an important exception by Klatt (1979) that explicitly deals with the acoustic signal of continuous speech. However, it does so by assuming that the acoustic differences between continuous speech and isolated syllables, etc., although real are not perceptually significant. According to this model, perception extracts the needed information to recognize "diphones" (roughly two half-segments) independently of the effects of earlier and later context, i.e., diphones are perceptually independent of context.

This theoretical orientation toward local acoustics in contemporary research stands in sharp contrast to the acoustic and articulatory studies cited above; theory has assumed that perception, unlike production, is sensitive only to first-order segmental constraints. However, this assumption seems unlikely both on theoretical and methodological grounds. From the standpoint of theory, simply put, the assumption suggests that the potential information for one segment is there, in other (nonadjacent) segments, yet this potential information is simply ignored by the perceptual mechanism. The methodological difficulty with this view springs from the fact that evidence against higher-order perceptual effects came from experiments which were unlikely to be sensitive enough to capture any subtle perceptual effects that might be present. For instance, in their influential experiment Lehiste and Shockey (1972) recorded VCV sequences like those used by Ohman (1966) and cut them in half within the (silent) closure interval preceding consonant release. Then they in effect discarded the second part and presented the first part to listeners. The listeners tried to identify the vowel in the discarded part but could not. While one possible conclusion from these results was that coarticulatory information in nonadjacent segments is ignored, another was that the method was simply too insensitive. For instance, it was quite possible that one segment (the first vowel) could contain enough information about another segment (the other vowel) to lower recognition threshold for the other segment, yet not contain enough to identify it absolutely. We thought the latter was the correct interpretation and therefore used a different methodological approach to find higher-order perceptual effects.

We have done a variety of experiments showing that there are perceptual effects from anticipatory coarticulation (Martin and Bunnell, 1981; 1982). The general approach and a summary of the results is as follows. The task for the listeners was target reaction time (RT) to the final vowel in a sentence. The stimuli were sentence pairs which ended in VCV and differed only in the final vowel. For example, one sentence pair was "I say poozee" and "I say poozah." A cross-spliced version of each sentence was created by exchanging all of the sentence prior to the final syllable /zi, za/ between the members of a pair. Crossed sentences were thus phonetically identical to their intact (as spoken) ecounterparts but differed from them acoustically in that any coarticulatory information prior to the crosspoint was now appropriate for (i.e., predicted) the other final vowel of the /i, a/ sentence pair. For instance, consider the first example sentence which ends with the final vowel /i/ but which has been crossed. It is preceded by the vowel /u/ as it does in its normal intact version but in this case any coarticulatory information within the vowel /u/ is now appropriate for the final vowel /a/. Hence the crossed sentence carries misleading information about the final (target) vowel, and therefore target RT should be slower in the crossed compared to the intact sentence.

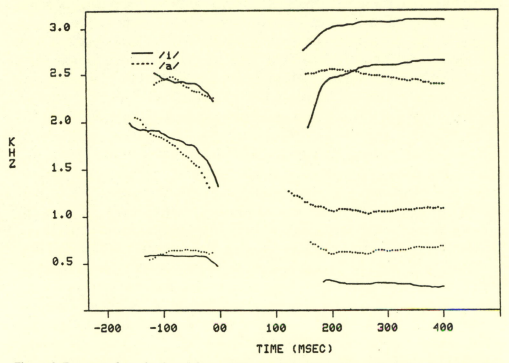

Figure 3. Formant plots of a /kaepi, kaepa/ ("*kaapee, kaapah*") sentence aligned at the crosspoint (zero on the time scale) and superimposed. The *solid* lines are (from bottom to top) the first, second and third formants of the intact /i/- sentence, respectively. The formants are discontinuous because silence precedes the /p/ consonant release. *Dotted* lines are the corresponding formants in the intact /a/- sentence. On the right side of the figure, note the very high second and third formants, and the low first formant, in the target vowel /i/.

Figure 3 shows the acoustic analysis of the VCV region of an /i,a/ sentence pair. The sentences are aligned at the crosspoint and superimposed. The solid lines are the first three formants in the /i/ sentence, the dotted lines the formants in the /a/ sentence. As can be seen, there is **anticipatory** formant movement in all three formants. The second and third formants are higher in /ae/ preceding /i/ than preceding /a/, and the first formant is lower. These differences arise as the tongue **during** pronunciation of the pretarget vowel /ae/ is being moved into position to pronounce /i/ later. Such movements do not interfere with pronunciation of the intervening stop. They do, however, change the exact **point** of closure, which of itself also has acoustic consequences. To the extent that such coarticulatory information is present in the sentences and is used in perception, RT should be slower to targets in crossed than in intact sentences. Furthermore, crossed sentences should attract more false alarms (responses to a **non**-target vowel) when they are foils (non-targets) since they contain information that predicts their assigned target vowel, yet they end with the (wrong) non-target vowel. In all experiments RT was obtained from listeners to the final target vowel and compared between intact and crossed versions. Measures of misses (negligible) and false alarms were also recorded. Acoustic analyses of all sentences were obtained so that differences in acoustic measures could be compared or correlated with perceptual differences.

The general pattern of results was similar in all experiments and shows that there were perceptual effects from anticipatory vowel-to-vowel coarticulation. Crossed sentences produced slower RT, whereas false alarm rates were higher to crossed sentences. Both of these results are predicted on the view that higher-order coarticulatory effects are perceptually significant. Acoustic analyses of the sentences also supported this view. Differences in degree of anticipatory coarticulation as measured by differences in formant frequencies in the first vowel correlated significantly with RT differences between the crossed vs intact versions. Finally, further experiments showed that it was possible to obtain **faster** rather than slower RT to crossed sentences if they contained anticipatory coarticulation effects predicting the target vowel. In these experiments we crossed sentence pairs in which both intact sentences ended on the **same** target vowel but in which one of them contained strong anticipatory coarticulation effects whereas the other did not. The results favoring crossed sentences (faster RT) in this case were further support for the general conclusion from all of these experiments that the acoustic effects of anticipatory coarticulation are used in perception.

Finally it is worth noting here that a potentially important alternative conclusion, namely, a sort of generalized perceptual disruption from sentence-splicing effects themselves, appears to be ruled out. Such an interpretation cannot explain the following facts: (a) Acoustic formant differences were correlated with amount of RT interference. (b) False alarms were more frequent to crossed than to intact foil sentences. The latter fact is particularily strong evidence in favor of anticipation from coarticulation effects and against the view that splicing effects alone produce slower RT. For one thing, the presence of anticipatory information for the "wrong" target vowel in crossed foil sentences appears to be

the only plausible explanation for that fact. Moreover, if splicing by
itself slowed down responding, there should have been fewer rather than
more false alarms to crossed sentences. Note that the well-known speed-
accuracy tradeoff, often a problem with RT, is used to advantage in the
present experimental paradigm. In the usual case, high false-alarm rates
reflect a low listener criterion and therefore cast suspicion on interpretations from fast RT. In the present paradigm, overall false-alarm rates
may vary with listener criteria, but listener criteria cannot account for
the distribution of false alarms, which is weighted toward crossed rather
than intact foils.

The results of these experiments have implications for current theories of segmental perception/recognition. As noted earlier, many current theories appeared to assume that the perception of segments in a
sequence, unlike the production of them, is sensitive only to local
coarticulatory constraints, and therefore that an adequate account can be
given by analysis limited to local acoustics spanning a half-syllable or
less (e.g., Klatt, 1979; Searle, Jacobson and Kimberly, 1980; Zwicker,
Terhardt and Paulus, 1979). Other theories ignore the role of coarticulation in favor of postulated invariant (context-independent) properties to
segment identity (e.g., Stevens and Blumstein, 1978). None of these
theories are well equipped to handle the perceptual effects of higher-
order coarticulatory constraints such as vowel-to-vowel coarticulation
found in our experiments. Moreover, such theories, most of which seek
support from experiments with isolated syllables or words, can be expected to encounter increasing difficulty as attempts are made to apply
them to the continuous speech signal. Segmental information which is
normally so salient in isolated syllables is obscured or attenuated in
continuous speech by the interaction of variations in stress level and
tempo as well as by the mutual, overlapping effects of phonetic context.
Therefore, if a given region of the continuous speech signal is isolated
from the rest of the signal for analysis, the information in that region
for identifying the segment normally associated with that region for
identifying the segment normally associated with that region is impoverished by comparison to the information in an isolated vowel containing that segment. Put another way, in a syllable spoken in isolation,
all its segmental information is contained in itself. If the syllable is
embedded in continuous context, some of the information about its
segments lies elsewhere; by itself the syllable (and its segmental
information) is impoverished. Moreover, it may contain information

about segments outside itself. Hence theories that ignore continuous context and focus on local intervals are in the position of attempting to extract phonetic segments from impoverished regions of the signal while discarding correlated data from other regions at the same time. This approach seems counterproductive, but it would seem forced on us if indeed listeners always perceived segments in this way. As the experiments above showed, however, there is little reason to believe this is the case.

A part of the motivation for studies of coarticulation has been the search for control principles in speech production (MacNeilage, 1980). For one thing, it had been hoped that the determination of the precise temporal reach of coarticulatory effects might reveal something of the relation between various linguistic entities (e.g., segments, features, syllables) and aspects of the speech production process. For instance, what are the "units" of production? Are they different at the various "levels" or "stages" of the process? And so on. However, the acoustic and articulatory evidence appears to indicate that the temporal scope of coarticulation is independent of the boundaries of such linguistically-defined units. Therefore there is little evidence that a sequence of feature arrays or segments in linguistic representation has physiological reality in the speech production process. Instead, the facts of coarticulation suggest that we view the production of phrase-like utterances, not as the sequencing of any sort of entity whether linguistic or not, but rather as the unfolding of a temporally-extended, integrated, hierarchically-organized, e.g., rhythmic act (e.g., Fowler, 1980; Fowler et al, 1980). When we turn from production to implications for perception it is clear that the consequences of temporally-extended coarticulation are not lost on the listener. Anticipatory mechanisms for production seem to be mirrored in perception by mechanisms which use information in the part of the signal already heard to continuously update the percept and in effect predict at least the outlines of the signal yet to come, including both segmental and prosodic aspects (Martin, 1972). Any theory that ignores these rhythmic mechanisms, or the information these mechanisms provide, must necessarily remain incomplete.

NOTE

1. The research in this paper was supported by NIH Grant NS 13645 and by the Computer Science Center, University of Maryland.

REFERENCES

Bell-Berti, F., & Harris, K. Anticipatory coarticulation: Some implications from a study of liprounding. *Journal of the Acoustical Society of America,* 1979, *65,* 1268–1270.

Bengueral, A. P., & Cowan, H. A. Coarticulation of upper lip protrusion in French. *Phonetica,* 1974, *30,* 41–55.

Chomsky, N., & Halle, M. *The sound pattern of English.* New York: Harper, 1968.

Cooper, F. S., Delattre, P., Liberman, A. M., Borst, J. M., & Gerstman, L. J. Some experiments on the perception of synthetic sounds. *Journal of the Acoustical Society of America,* 1952, *24,* 597–606.

Daniloff, R. G., & Moll, K. L. Coarticulation of liprounding. *Journal of Speech and Hearing Research,* 1968, *11,* 707–721.

Fodor, J. A., & Garrett, M. Some determinants of sentence complexity. *Perception and Psychophysics,* 1967, *2,* 289–296.

Fowler, C. A. Production and perception of coarticulation among stressed and unstressed vowels. *Journal of Speech and Hearing Research,* 1981, *46,* 127–139.

Fowler, C. A., Rubin, P., Remez, R. E., & Turvey, M. T. Implications for speech production of a general theory of action. In B. Butterworth (Ed.), *Language production.* New York: Academic Press, 1980.

Fry, D. Prosodic phenomena. In B. Malmberg (Ed.), *Manual of phonetics.* Amsterdam: North-Holland, 1968.

Gay, T. Effect of speaking rate on vowel formant movements. *Journal of the Acoustical Society of America,* 1978, *63,* 223–230.

Kent, R. D. Models of speech production. In N. J. Lass (Ed.), *Contemporary issues in experimental phonetics.* New York: Academic Press, 1976.

Kent, R. D., & Minifie, F. D. Coarticulation in recent speech production models. *Journal of Phonetics,* 1977, *5,* 115–133.

Klatt, D. H. Review of the ARPA speech understanding project. *Journal of the Acoustical Society of America,* 1977, *62,* 1345–1366.

Kozhevnikov, V. A., & Chistovich, L. A. *Speech: Articulation and perception* (JPRS No. 30543). Washington, DC: Joint Publications Research Service, 1965.

Lehiste, I., & Shockey, L. *On the perception of coarticulation effects in English CVC syllables.* Joint Publications Research Service, 1982, *15,* 500–506.

Liberman, A. M., Delattre, P. C., Cooper, F. S., & Gerstman, L. J. The role of consonant-vowel transitions in the stop and nasal consonants. *Psychological Monographs,* 1954, *68*(8, Whole No. 379).

Lindblom, B. E. F. Spectrographic study of vowel reduction. *Journal of the Acoustical Society of America,* 1963, *35,* 1773–1781.

MacNeilage, P. F., & Ladefoged, P. The production of speech and language. In E. C. Carterette & M. P. Friedman (Eds.), *Handbook of perception* (Volume 7). New York: Academic Press, 1976.

Marslen-Wilson, W. D., & Welsh, A. Processing interactions and lexical access during word recognition in continuous speech. *Cognitive Psychology,* 1978, *10,* 29–63.

Martin, J. G. Some acoustic and grammatical features of spontaneous speech. In

P. Kjeldergaard, J. J. Jenkins & D. L. Horton (Eds.), *Perception of language*. New York: Merrill, 1971.

Martin, J. G. Rhythm-induced judgements of word stress in sentences. *Journal of Verbal Learning and Verbal Behavior,* 1970, *9,* 627–633.

Martin, J. G. Rhythmic (hierarchical) versus serial structure in speech and other behavior. *Psychological Review,* 1972, *79,* 487–509.

Martin, J. G. Rhythmic and segmental perception are not independent. *Journal of the Acoustical Society of America,* 1979, *65,* 1287–1297.

Martin, J. G. Boundaries in the perception of continuous speech. In J. J. Wolfe & D. H. Klatt (Eds.), *Speech Communication Papers. Journal of the Acoustical Society of America,* 1979, 63, Supplement.

Martin, J. G., & Bunnell, H. T. Perception of anticipatory coarticulation effects. *Journal of the Acoustical Society of America,* 1981, *69,* 559–567.

Martin, J. G., & Bunnell, H. T. Perception of anticipatory coarticulation effects in vowel-stop consonant-vowel sequences. *Journal of Experimental Psychology: Human Perception and Performance,* 1982, *3,* 473–478.

Martin, J. G., & Strange, W. Determinants of hesitations in spontaneous speech. *Journal of Experimental Psychology,* 1968, *76,* 474–479.

Martin, J. G., & Strange, W. The perception of hesitation in spontaneous speech. *Perception and Psychophysics,* 1968, *3,* 427–438.

Meltzer, R. H., Martin, J. G., Mills, C. B., Imhoff, D., & Zohar, D. Reaction time to temporally-displaced phoneme targets in continuous speech. *Journal of Experimental Psychology: Human Perception and Performance,* 1976, *2,* 277–290.

Moll, K. H., & Daniloff, R.G. Investigation of the timing of velar movements during speech. *Journal of the Acoustical Society of America,* 1971, *50,* 678–684.

Ohman, S. E. G. Coarticulation in VCV utterances: Spectrographic measurements. *Journal of the Acoustical Society of America,* 1966, *39,* 151–168.

Pierce, J. R. Whither word recognition? *Journal of the Acoustical Society of America,* 1969, *46,* 1049–1051.

Searle, C. L., Jacobsen, J. Z., & Kimberley, B. P. Speech as patterns in the 3-space of time and frequency. In R. A. Cole (Ed.), *Perception and production of fluent speech.* Hillsdale, NJ: Erlbaum, 1980.

Shields, J. L., McHugh, A., & Martin, J. G. Reaction time to phoneme targets as a function of rhythmic cues in continuous speech. *Journal of Experimental Psychology,* 1974, *102,* 250–255.

Stevens, K. N., & Blumstein, S. E. Invariant cues for place of articulation in stop consonants. *Journal of the Acoustical Society of America,* 1978, *64,* 1358–1368.

Zwicker, E., Terhardt, E., & Paulus, E. Automatic speech recognition using psyco-acoustic models. *Journal of the Acoustical Society of America,* 1979, *65,* 487–498.

Chapter 6.

RHYTHM AS A FACTOR OF MEDIATED AND NONMEDIATED PROCESSING IN READING

MADLYN L. HANES

Direct discussion of rhythm as a factor in reading acquisition or as a function of acquired reading proficiency is made difficult by the lack of its specific consideration in existing accounts of how reading, (and particularly fluent reading) is acquired. Instead, in order to argue the role of rhythm in reading processes (the purpose of this chapter) we shall require the two-fold task of: 1) disclosing the correlates of rhythm that appear in explications of reading performance; 2) establishing linkages among these correlates to principles of rhythm. These principles are from theoretical accounts of speech and language learning and information processing and, to a lesser extent, from accounts of skilled motor performance. Such linkages permit a discussion of rhythm as a critical aspect of reading performance, including both mediated and nonmediated states of processing. As discussed throughout this chapter, mediation refers to strategic processing necessary when difficulty arises, e.g. unfamiliar words are encountered requiring decoding and/or semantic confusion is experienced requiring contextual approximation. Nonmediated reading, on the other hand, refers to fluent processing whereby comprehension is accumulating readily without the need to employ alternative "emergency" strategies. Mediated and nonmediated states of processing are interdependent and interchange periodically in skilled reading. However, the ability to mediate effectively and rapidly, to accommodate processing disruptions and to restore processing to a fluent, nonmediated state is a distinguishing characteristic of highly skilled reading performance.

The properties of rhythm as defined in language and speech behavior and in skilled motor performance (e.g. typing and piano playing) strike reasonable parallels in several accounts of acquired reading proficiency.

Of particular interest here are accounts of 1) psycholinguistic decoding (Goodman and Goodman, 1977; Smith 1977; 1982); 2) the onset of metacognitively-enlisted mediation/correction strategies (Flavell, 1979; Brown, 1980; Woods, 1980); and 3) automaticity of processing (LaBerge and Samuels, 1974). It is the intent of this chapter to examine rhythm as a constituent of each of these perspectives of reading. Rhythm may thus be seen as an important dynamic component of reading development, together with the emergence of proficient decoding, correction and mediation strategies and finally of nonmediated/automatic reading.

The test of a sound explication of normal acquisition is the extent to which it can dually serve to explain performance deficits or inadequacies. In reading development rhythm should facilitate the acquisition process through its healthy functioning, or be disruptive to proficient performance through disorder or inadequate development. With respect to the latter, clinical and applied research has documented the relationship of rhythm dysfunction and dysfunctions of language and reading performance (Mosse, 1982; Sparks, Helm and Albert, 1975; Sparks, 1976). Rhythminduced treatment is also well documented as having beneficial effects on reading and language processing (Heckelman, 1966; Martin and Meltzer, 1976; Samuels, 1979). A selection of such studies is presented later in the chapter. By far the most immediate challenge is to determine the role of rhythm in healthy reading performance. Aligning the various theoretical presentations of rhythm [borrowing largely from the works of Martin (1970, 1972) and Shaffer (1976, 1982)] with psycholinguistic, metacognitive and automatized accounts of reading is particularly challenging since these processes themselves have not as yet been brought into alignment. Enough compatability appears to exist among them however to encourage such an undertaking with some promise of success.

Prosody, Parsing And Fluency:
The Correlates Of Rhythm In Mediated And Nonmediated Reading

The principal linguistic correlate of rhythm is prosody. Prosody and its constituent features—stress, pitch and juncture—accompany running speech, generating an intonation contour which serves to bound speech production into meaningful units, i.e., phrasing (Restle, 1972). This in turn facilitates both the production and reception of language. The boundary effect created by the prosodic features yields another linguistic correlate of rhythm which is critical to language reception, including reading. This correlate, which is manifested in a syntactic-level skill, is the ability to parse sentences (written text) into meaningful units be it phrase, clause or sentence gestalts.

Evidence as to the unit of meaning most characteristic of effective and expeditious processing is as yet discrepantly reported, thus rendering the prime locus of processing uncertain (Rode, 1974–1975; Willows, 1974; Clay and Imlach, 1971; Vazquez, Glucksberg and Danks, 1978). Nevertheless, parsing enables the processing of information, probably within as large a unit as possible (Golinkoff, 1975–76), without losing meaning or taxing the short-term memory. In this way parsing facilitates efficient and ready processing. Moreover, when processing is difficult and mediation is necessary to sustain execution, parsing provides the loci for focused attention to begin the search (and re-search) for meaning at the unit level.

Fluency is a third correlate of rhythm. It appears to transcend measurement and definition as the single or combined effects of speed and accuracy (LaCoultre and Carroll, 1981; Martin and Meltzer, 1976). It may be understood as a natural correlate of rhythm in skilled motor performance, but may be even better understood within the context of comparing various models of mediated and nonmediated reading—one against the other. Automaticity, psycholinguistic and metacognitive models of reading all attempt to account for reading proficiency and its enabling characteristics or operations used by the reader to sustain comprehension. The models vary principally with respect to the performance demand on the reader and the state of processing each seeks to describe. Automaticity is the most demanding account of reading, requiring that the reader achieve comprehension rapidly and effortlessly. Reading with automaticity, in behavioral terms, means reading with fluency.

In essence, automaticity is a state of nonmediated processing, whereas psycholinguistics and metacognition are concerned with mediation. According to psycholinguistic explanation, uncertainty is reduced through linguistic expectation. The reader applies internalized language usage to written text to determine the linguistic constraints from which unfamiliar words and phrases can be approximated. Proficient decoding is attributed to the strength of syntactic and semantic skills (cueing). Reading from this perspective is a search-for-meaning process in large part dependent on syntactic knowledge including parsing and morphologic skill. In mediated processing, the reader calls to use this inherent linguistic competence to transcend less meaningful graphophonemic cues (Goodman and Goodman, 1977; Smith 1977, 1982).

Metacognition theory calls mediation the conscious selection and implementation of strategies to correct and search for lost or difficult-to-process meaning. Proficiency is attributed to the use of strategies deliberately enlisted to rapidly correct ineffective decoding. The correction process is activated by the reader's on-going ability to monitor the status of his/her processing (Flavell, 1979; Brown, 1980; Woods, 1980). Several rhythm-related strategies may be enlisted, for example speech recoding. Speech recoding, a type of inner speech, relies on prosody to echo parsed segments of the sentence when the limited capacity of short-term memory is taxed (Kleiman, 1975). Serving as a "place holder" speech recoding thus temporarily overcomes the constraints of the primary memory so that additional processing can continue through sentence completion and hence, across long-term memory. While its selection and use may be entirely conscious, the effects of the strategy on hierarchical processing most likely are not.

Certain parallels are noted between mediated reading, particularly psycholinguistic mediation and rhythmic structure as described in speech production and reception. Of particular interest are the properties of predictability and approximation attributed to rhythm in language functions. Nonmediated reading and rhythmic behavior associated with highly skilled motor performance share similar properties which are thought to bring about and sustain an automatic state of performance, i.e. fluency. Characteristic of automaticity is a heightened coordination and fluidity of movement yielding error- and struggle-free performance.

Relating Principles Of Rhythm To Reading

Two basic premises are involved in relating rhythm theory and reading theory. The first, a relatively conventional percept, is that language (production and reception of connected speech) provides the most ready avenue to link rhythm and reading. The relationship between rhythm and reading is derived from the study of the independent relationships between rhythm and language, and reading and language. This premise works well for the examination of rhythm in psycholinguistic aspects of reading. Rhythmic behavior and structure in accounts of connected speech as described by Martin (1970, 1972) and Shaffer (1976, 1982) bear close resemblance to the psycholinguist's description of the language process in proficient reading.

The second premise is perhaps more revolutionary in that it subscribes to an information processing model of rhythm which is hierarchical in structure rather than concatenated, with consequences for both motor and perceptual responses (Martin, 1972). Of particular interest is that rhythm appears to behave similarly in skilled nonlanguage (motor) performance as well as language performance. It is postulated here that the property of fluency in automatic reading is akin to the intrinsic sense of timing in fluid, nonlanguage motor functioning (which is rhythm).

Metacognitive strategies of reading are more difficult to relate to rhythm than are psycholinguistic and automaticity theories of reading. Exceptions are those correction strategies that use a morphosyntactic analysis and that have the effect of reconstructing and sustaining the accompanying prosodic contour. It may be fair, however, to postulate a localized and highly specific relationship between rhythm and metacognitive aspects of reading. The first premise will apply in identifying those strategies that employ linguistic correlates to rhythm, e.g., prosody, parsing. The second premise will help to propose how such strategies work to assist in the processing of information, in the detection and correction of errors, and in generalized processing dysfunctions. Such accounts should substantiate a relationship between rhythm and metacognitive reading behaviors.

Nature of Rhythmic Processing

Favoring a hierarchical organization of rhythmic behavior facilitates study of rhythmic activity in the processing of information. It also allows examination of the role rhythm plays in the preservation of processing under conditions of near "overload" or of dysfunction, and the contribution of rhythm to processing efficiency. Rhythm becomes vital in the processes that determine language and motor performance in both reception and production modes. The hierarchical view of rhythm presently may be the only viable basis for relating rhythmic and reading processes.

The notion of a hierarchical structure of rhythm is an extension from earlier concerns posed by Lashley (1951) about concatenated models of rhythmic activity. Martin (1970, 1972) continued the argument in support of a hierarchical rather than a serial account of rhythm and offers an ample description of rhythm from this perspective. Shaffer (1976, 1982) proposes similar attributes of rhythm, with an emphasis on an intrinsic timing capability in rhythmic movement. Fowler (1980) provides a strong defense of an intrinsic timing theory of coarticulation. This complements Shaffer's explanation of internal timekeeping applied to skilled motor performance, including speech production.

According to Martin (1970, 1972), hierarchical structure is applied to a wholistic unit of processing or "signal stretch," e.g., a string of syllables, meter of music or series of motor responses arranged to comply with certain temporal constraints. A more naturalistic examination of rhythm is likely to occur at the level of the wholistic unit, which, as he states, is analogous to "carving nature at the joints." Within the wholistic unit a pattern of relative timing between adjacent and nonadjacent elements is analyzed, anticipated and executed centrally. Martin postulates the use of accent and terminal rules which, applied in sequence, create the wholistic contour of accented and unaccented elements giving the impression of relative timing, a temporal pattern which is redundant and predictable.

Concatenated (as opposed to hierarchical) accounts of rhythmic activity presume that patterning unfolds in a successive or "left-to-right" series and limit its predictive power to adjacent elements. Control is peripheral as opposed to central. For Martin, the locus of relative timing is the accented element—the stressed vowel or syllable in speech. Information is carried (for the sake of perception) via the receiver's anticipation or prediction of the pattern of accented elements to the full stretch of the wholistic unit or "signal." Production in fluid motor performance is executed based on a priori analysis whereby the dominant temporal features are determined and targeted for time and movement. The intervening or less dominant elements are anticipated subsequently, completing the pattern. This translates into a schedule of motor commands that will govern the movement of the wholistic unit through completion. Production is aimed at achieving in real time a "reproduction" of the anticipated pattern in keeping with the constraints of the relative timing. Speech production, as will be discussed, is based on a priori decisions made first to determine accented syllables which have high-information yields. Production then becomes a series of motor commands governing the articulation program in which accented (stressed) syllables become the targets or time trajectories.

To anticipate the temporal pattern from such a brief encounter (scan) of the signal stretch requires that timing is calculated as a constituent of the temporal pattern, and is readily extracted. Additionally, the transition for analysis, expectation formulation and execution is no small task, given that efficient processing must accomplish rather fluid inter- **and** intra-wholistic unit transitions.

There appears to be an intrinsic sense of timing to the rhythmic activity which functions primarily for the purpose of keeping processing in transit. (Shaffer, 1976, 1982; Fowler, 1980). This attribute of rhythm allows the self-pacing necessary to adjust performance and perception "in-progress" so that fluid movement and on-going reception respectively are sustained. The intrinsic sense of timing acts as an official time keeper responsible in large part for moving processing forward. Moreover, it works in partnership with the relative timing of the rhythmic pattern in the following way. An a priori analysis (Martin, 1972) [what Shaffer refers to as intention (1976)] scans the wholistic unit to approximate the temporal pattern. The anticipatory power, which is consequently acquired, in effect increases the predictability of the temporal pattern for use in reception and in determining the schedule of motor commands for executing fluent movement of the wholistic unit. Shaffer refers to the latter as motor programming (1982).

Once anticipated, timing essentially becomes the goal or time trajectory of movement—perceived and produced (Shaffer, 1976, 1982). During processing the timekeeping capability enables continual adjustments in movement relative to the wholistic unit (or "signal stretch"). Adjustments in forward processing brought about by deliberate variations in speed (typically slow-downs to avoid potential bog-downs) are necessary to accommodate the relative timing of movement within the wholistic unit and across accented components in transit from one wholistic unit to the next. This flexibility and transitional coordination among time trajectories maintain the integrity of the relative timing of temporal patterns as they emerge and reflect the essence of rhythmic activity at its best.

Shaffer (1976) gives as examples of intrinsic timing the copy typist who appears to pace his or her output according to the "conditions of the stimulus" without notable pauses or sudden burst of movements, and the speaker whose intention is to exert emphasis for the sake of expression and does so by targeting (in real time) components of the prosodic contour that will accommodate the added emphasis, again without disruption to the flow i.e., relative timing of movement. Fowler (1980) provides for accounts of intrinsic timing of voluntary and involuntary movements accompanying coarticulation in speech. Lastly, Martin (1972) describes the listener's deliberate cycling of attention to those accented (stressed) syllables of speech which are thought to carry more substantive or "heavier" information than the unaccented elements of the pattern. The latter has been a repeated finding in studies of content vs. function words in information processing of sentences; the accented or stressed syllables of the temporal pattern naturally fall within the content words (i.e., time trajectories of the intended message) which are primary carriers of sentence meaning (Martin, 1972; Hammill, 1976). The predictability of the pattern coupled with the internal timekeeping capability eliminates the need for continuous attention. Instead, reception is forwarded and made easier by selected concentration in anticipation of the dominant time trajectories that will provide the most information with less expenditure of processing energy. These capabilities have great potential for aiding difficult language processing. Difficulty, once experienced, can evoke a heightened concentration (a gearing-up) in anticipation of forthcoming information signaled by the prosodic pattern. Attention also can be recycled to decode previous information during periods of low information.

Rhythm and Language

Rhythm has been said to be the natural link between production and reception of speech (Lashley, 1951; Martin, 1970, 1972; Shaffer, 1976, 1982). Martin's (1972) view of rhythm applied to speech supports

> ... the general notion that speaking and listening are dynamically coupled rhythmic activities, such that linguistic information is encoded rhythmically into the signal by the speaker and decoded out of it on that basis by the listener (p. 489).

From Martin's perspective, rhythm is based on a theory of motor functioning, suggesting that the articulation of accented syllables is the target of ballistic movements. Unaccented syllables are produced by "secondary articulatory gestures en route to the target syllables." The effects are relatively greater phonetic detail of the accented syllables, with reductions or deployments of the unaccented syllables. In running speech the apparent predictability of relative accents (which define the temporal pattern, i.e. prosodic contour) allows the listener to focus attention on those elements which ultimately will provide the most information, i.e. acoustic, syntactic and semantic, and to recycle attention as need be to approximate the reduced information within the wholistic unit and/or to decode previous information during periods of low information. The prosodic contour is extracted from the signal stretch separate from and prior to segmental detail. Upon its analysis, the linguistic constraints of the segmental information are thereby determined. Martin uses the following prosodic contour as an example:

> **John flew to WxYz,** in which W and Y are accented syllables, and x and z are unaccented syllables, rules out Boston and New York as possible destinations, as well as Minneapolis, assuming the latter is correctly pronounced, etc. (p. 500, 1972).

Assignment of accented syllables in Martin's hypothesis accordingly is based on the high-information yields and a priori decisions which are ascribed to syntactic and morphologic priorities, e.g., content versus function words, root versus affix. These priorities are determined by the relative "semantic weights" inherent in the linguistic structures and warrant top-level placement in the hierarchical tree.

> ... since the accented elements dominate the temporal organization of the utterance, they must in some sense by planned first. Intervening lower-level syllables then are planned subsequently in hierarchical fashion ... Planning here means at least selecting the time at which syllables will be actualized ... In this view one might think of accented syllables as the main targets in the organization of the articulatory program. The hypothesis then predicts that decisions concerning accented syllables will precede those concerning unaccented syllables, hence that decisions concerning "content" words will precede those for "function" words, and so forth (p. 499, 1972).

Studies examining slips of the tongue or transpositions of words within a given contour or hierarchical organization support the notion of top-down a priori decisions, since most frequent transpositions occur at equivalent levels of stress, typically between the dominant accented elements, e.g., content words transposed for other content words (Bomer and Laver, 1968; Fromkin, 1971).

Morpho-syntactic structures determine to a large extent the assignment of accented syllables (insofar as their semantic loads permit). Speaker control to exert intent and to provide localized emphasis also contributes (Martin, 1972; Shaffer, 1976, 1982; Bolinger, 1972). Martin and Shaffer do not delineate the relative strength of such contributions to the assignment of syllable stress per se. However, shifts in relative accents (creating in turn shifts in the temporal pattern) respond to shifts in the speaker's intent and to the use of linguistic variations such as regional dialect or "foreign accent," indicating that intent and linguistic variation can supercede stress assignments that otherwise would be projected for "normally" produced connected English speech.

With the assignment of accents made in advance such shifts in dominant accent are accommodated and the more crucial attribute of predictability is entirely preserved. The articulation program of motor commands is thereby set for production; and reception becomes a matter of forward listening in which "the listener, given initial cues, actively enters into the speaker's tempo" and adjusts "ongoing processing based on information about the future as opposed to present or past states of the signal" (Martin, 1972, p. 503). This perspective takes into account semantic influences and intentions of speech (Bolinger, 1972). For these reasons such hypotheses are insulated against criticisms leveled at stress rules that adhere only to syntactic constraints [the most noted example being that of Chomsky and Halle's Nuclear Stress Rule (1968)]; that is, rules generated without reference to a hierarchical or rhythmic model of stress assignment which insists on relative projections of accent adjusted in terms of arrival-time relationships within the linguistic string, e.g. wholistic unit of utterance—clause, phrase, sentence.

The rhythmic model applied to speech and language does not arise only from the work of psychologists concerned with the construct of rhythmic functioning in varied motor performance outlets such as skilled production of music, copy typing and physical execution of an athletic feat requiring coordinated movement. A rhythmic model of language has been substantially embraced by linguists as well and generative phonologists in particular (Lieberman, 1975; Lieberman and Prince, 1977; Selkirk, 1980). The work, primarily of Lieberman and Prince (1977) has revolutionized prosodic definition as separate and apart from phonologic segmentation, using arguments similar in concept to those that appear in the independent works of Martin and Shaffer reviewed here. The most noted is the concept of hierarchical versus concatenated allocation of syllable stress. Other similarities exist. The prosodic contour is viewed as the product of hierarchical organization of the phonology of connected speech. The principles of "relative prominence" and metrical alignment or "gridding" (Lieberman and Prince, 1977) satisfy functions similar to those served by the concepts of relative accent and wholistic unit, although the respective rules applied to assign syllables dominant stress and to align these and intervening elements into a metrical grid are significantly different from those of Martin or Shaffer. Lieberman and Prince propose that

> relative prominence is defined **between** phonological constituents, rather than **on** individual segments. Prominence so defined, is projected onto syllables by associating them with a 'metrical grid,' which can be thought of as a hierarchy of intersecting periodicities (rather than constituents), the structure of which is relative to phenomena of rhythm and timing (p. 333, 1977).

Lieberman and Prince attempt to preserve the stress-assignment rules of generative phonology, restricting their definition of the local properties of the hierarchical structure. In addition, assigning stress to structural constituents (as opposed to phonologic segments) allows relative prominence at a given level of the hierarchy to be preserved under embedding, "since relations defined on higher levels of structure do not affect lower-level configurations, all definitions being strictly local. Thus the relative prominence of **dew** in **dew-covered** is not altered in any way by the assignment of greater prominence to **lawn** in **dew-covered lawn**," (p. 256).

In contrast, Martin's use of a priori decisions in the planning of the relative accent assigned to the hierarchical structure (top-down planned first) accommodates seemingly varied principles, including the accent allocation of normally-spoken English stress patterns (morphosyntactic structures carrying heavier information loads receiving first-assigned accents accordingly) as well as intended shifts for the sake of emphasis.

Prosody, Parsing and Reading

Prosody is the most direct linguistic correlate of rhythm at work in running speech. It has capabilities of extraction and predictability in timing to enhance intelligibility via segmental analysis and approximation. Sentence parsing is a secondary linguistic correlate. Sentence parsing is more frequently associated with **reception** of language, or in the case of reading, the reception of text. In speech, parsing is the natural consequence of prosody and reflects the rhythmic patterns internal to the hierarchically-organized contour. In reading written text, where prosody is only minimally represented at a graphic level through punctuation, parsing is evident as a characteristic of fluent automatic reading and in use during mediation to accomplish the breaking down of the linguistic string into meaningful chunks. Parsing is regarded as a syntactic-level skill (Rode, 1974–1975; Kleiman, 1979; Restle, 1972), and may be the principal means through which the reader can reconstruct in mediation the prosodic contour (the flow of language inherent in the text) in hopes of entering or reentering a more automatic state of reading processing. It is through such studies that a relationship among reading, language and rhythm is suggested. Some actually suggest a relationship between prosodic features and the "organization of the response repertoire of the reader," e.g. hierarchical processing that is linguistically and temporally arranged has been said to be a more likely possibility for the better reader (Clay and Imlach, 1971; Vazquez, Glucksberg and Danks, 1978). It is somewhat less clear, however, the extent to which these investigations, particularly earlier ones, have **formally** acknowledged prosody as a linguistic correlate to rhythm.

Attention to prosody appears to systematically distinguish good and poor readers. The reader is thought to attend to prosody when the prosodic features are preserved in keeping with the "intent" of text meaning. With respect to the notion of the preservation of prosody in studies dealing with oral reading behavior, parsing (sometimes expressed as a measure of syntactically-appropriate juncture, i.e. pause durations, or phrasing) is often cited as concomitant behavior (Stice, 1978; Clay and Imlach, 1971; Kleiman, 1975, 1979; Golinkoff, 1975–1976). The distinction between good and poor readers suggests a significant role of prosody in the acquisition process. Furthermore, studies of prosodic behavior in older readers of college- and adult-age discriminate between comprehension performance as well. Of particular focus in these studies is the reader's use and recognition of contrastive stress in the oral and silent reading modes, respectively (Dearborn, Johnston and Carmichael, 1949; Stice, 1978).

Research also indicates that the ability to segment, i.e. parse linguistic material at syntactically appropriate boundaries, has beneficial effects on reading comprehension. Much of the related research in this area involves the examination of the eye-voice span (EVS) as a means of estimating the length and therefore the locus of the processing unit characteristic of good reading. EVS refers to the number of words or letter spaces which have been visually processed by the reader in advance of the voice, i.e. the site of oral reading delivery. It is as yet unclear whether a particular locus of processing exists that is predictive of greater efficiency. But better readers at virtually all development stages are those who can "respond" to the largest segment of information stretch possible within a given linguistic context without sacrificing accuracy or time in processing (Buswell, 1920; Clay and Imlach, 1971; Willows, 1974; Rode, 1974–1975; Golinkoff, 1976; Vazquez, Glucksberg and Danks, 1978). Prosody and parsing serve similar boundary-setting functions, but, with the absence of the acoustic properties of prosody in written text (and the virtual absence of graphic conventions to adequately represent the prosodic contour), parsing must figure predominantly. In speech, of course, prosody carries more information than parsing alone contributes to reading. This is true particularly with respect to the assistance rendered by the relative accent or contrastive stress features of the contour. The absence of prosody from written text has been regarded as the root of reading difficulty in cases where the reader is unable to compensate for the lack of prosodic information through parsing skill (Kleiman, 1979; Schreiber, 1980), rendering the task of reading in context unwieldy and unnecessarily cumbersome.

Parsing assigns the stretch or unit of processing, establishing syntactic constraints from which the able reader derives the semantic constraints and identifies (approximates) detail related to words and word-parts. Judging from fluent oral reading descriptions wherein contrastive stress and language-like phrasing are distinctively evident, it seems very likely that the reader recreates the prosodic contour with the application of parsing. Contrastive stress is discovered (or rediscovered), and with it the immediate detailing of accented syllables and subsequently of unaccented or intervening elements, i.e. words or word-parts (Dearborn, *et al.*, 1940; Clay and Imlach, 1971; Stice, 1978; Vazquez, *et al.*, 1978; Kleiman, 1979). In reading, as in speech, parsing and prosody appear to sustain an interdependent relationship, but with reverse dependencies.

The argument surrounding the locus of processing in language most often involves the clause versus the phrase unit (Rode, 1974–1975; Vazquez, *et al.*, 1978). However, evidence from a number of studies employing text "intrusions" positioned between line boundaries of otherwise intact text strongly suggests that the good reader's tendency to scan for meaning will often extend beyond single phrases as well as clause boundaries, accommodating substantially larger stretches of linguistic text, e.g. sentence gestalts and partials (Willows, 1974; Buswell, 1920; Kolers, 1971). Inasmuch as the inclusive limits of the scan (as evidenced by the length of the EVS and site of fixation) adhere to syntactic boundaries, parsing appears to facilitate the proficient reader through appropriate syntactic cueing. Good readers, in addition, appear to sustain selective control of parsing (Willows, 1974; Vazquez, *et al.*, 1978). Such attributes—syntactic cueing and selective use of parsing—are consistent with psycholinguistic and metacognitive strategies of mediation, respectively.

Psycholinguistic processing is dependent on the reader's attention to syntactic cues in the mediation of unknown words. In "miscue analyses" whereby word substitutions, i.e., word errors, are assessed for semantic and syntactic acceptability and graphic and phonic similarity to the target words, syntactic cueing is the most enduring of skill strategies (Goodman and Burke, 1972; Goodman and Goodman, 1977; Goodman, 1977). In psycholinguistic accounts of reading, otherwise proficient readers reading linguistic context that is beyond their cognitive and experiential reach still manage to read well-conjugated (and often prosodically appropriate) "nonsense" (Goodman, 1977). Rode (1974–1975) reported that good readers have a strong tendency to complete a "more comprehensive unit" despite instances where miscues become increasingly prevalent in the course of completing the unit. Such findings suggest that parsing, as earlier discussed, is an enabling skill to semantic approximation; at the very least it is a reliable processing skill which scans the stretch of linguistic material and locates the limits and thereby the site of processing activity.

In metacognitive processing the reader is deliberate in enlisting strategies to assist mediation. Selective control of parsing is consistent with clinical observations of readers who "intentionally" manipulate text organization to aid in difficult processing, e.g., within-line and between-line regressions (returns) to parsed units for repeated trials at processing, rearrangements or adjustments of parsed boundaries as needed to reduce processing difficulties (Hanes, 1984; Anastasiow, Levine-Hanes and Hanes, 1982; Buswell, 1920; Willows, 1974; Vazquez *et al.*, 1978).

Studies using EVS methodology involve eye movement photography to measure fixations and regressions. In addition to yielding a good deal of information about good and poor reading behavior these studies provide specific insights into the role of parsing as it operates in mediated and nonmediated states of reading performance. Drawing largely from Buswell's (1920) definitive work related to EVS and Golinkoff's (1975–1976) review of EVS studies, certain basic assumptions about parsing and unit of processing are concluded and shown to have been upheld in more recent studies:

1. The lengthier EVS's correspond to greater proficiency and efficiency in reading performance. Indicated here is that relatively more fluent reading entails fewer fixations and shorter fixation junctures. In other words, the units of processing tend to be larger in proficiency and characteristically more fluid, i.e. rhythmic.

2. The EVS's correspond to syntactic boundaries and are flexible with respect to the varying size of the processing unit. The size of the processing unit varies with context conditions of the written text; parsing activity varies according to the level of difficulty and sentential location. EVS's tend to narrow for example as the reader encounters the end of relatively longer sentences or the end of the final sentence in a paragraph. The initial scanning function of parsing which determines the limits of the processing segment undoubtedly accounts for the wider EVS's at sentence beginnings (new thought units).

3. The oral delivery of readers with characteristically longer (wider) EVS's are expressive and language-like, providing a "match" to the prosodic contour intended by the author of the written text. The latter finding confirms a relationship between effective parsing and prosodic reconstruction.

4. Regressive eye movements have distinctive patterns in good and poor readers. Poor readers tend to regress within words, indicating underdeveloped word recognition skills, overattentiveness to word detail and failure to use intraword levels of processing, including syntactic (parsing) cues. In contrast, good readers' regressions are more symptomatic of "backtracking" triggered by processing difficulties. The latter finding suggests that regressions in reading are deliberate and strategic efforts which, in certain instances, are likely to be metacognitively enlisted to correct specific processing errors and/or assist difficult processing. Moreover, backtracked segments typically fall within syntactic boundaries often at smaller units within the larger unit initially attempted. Such a finding suggests further that parsing works as well to alleviate processing "bogs" in mediation as it does to sustain efficiency in fluent reading (Hanes, 1984).

Vazquez, *et al.,* (1978) used EVS methodology to test the contribution of syntactic and semantic factors in unit segmentation (parsing). College-age readers read text under varying conditions of semantic and syntactic constraints. Results indicated findings consistent with those reported above, i.e. wider EVS's accompanied greater syntactic and semantic constraints. The most common site of processing under conditions of high constraint was at least at the clause level. This is in accord with the argument posed by Rode (1974–1975) and others.

Anomalous text and between-clause interruptions (via EVS procedure) resulted in significantly shorter EVS's. Implications for reading processing, with particular attention to segmentation, favored what Vazquez *et al.* refer to as the semantic integration model of reading. Semantic integration, according to the authors, recognizes the influences of semantic processing **along with** syntactic processing in the segmentation of text. Syntactic constraints are not diminished in this argument per se. Instead, parsing is proposed to be affected by the workings of both semantic and syntactic influences and, as a result, varies in intake of text according to the level of difficulty of the given linguistic material confronting the reader. For precisely this reason anomalous text insertions (within and between clauses, strategically placed in varying positions in the sentence) and within-clause interruptions (removal of text) imposed greater difficulty, and shorter EVS's accordingly were yielded.

The argument for the interrelationship between semantic and syntactic influences is consistent with psycholinguistic accounts of proficient reading. Much of the contention relates as well to the account of anticipation of a schedule of movements based on prior intent. It is here that the interplay of the linguistic correlates of rhythm — prosody and parsing — are best appreciated. Prosody with its distinctive attributes of constrastive stress is clearly influenced and shaped by the speaker's semantic intent; parsing is the syntactic execution of the schedule to meet the intent. As it had been earlier discussed in the production and reception of speech, prosody carries the heaviest load of information. Contrary to the lead prosody takes in speech, parsing is more of a syntactic product defined by the natural phrasing that consequently occurs. In written language, prosody is inaccessible via surface level conventions of text and awaits reconstruction by the skilled reader. In reading then, parsing predominates and emerges as both a critical decoding skill for breaking the run of continued text into manageable and meaningful units of processing and as a link to the rediscovery of the otherwise "silent" prosodic message which is a more direct link to comprehension. In fluent reading these interchanges appear to happen effortlessly and automatically (LaBerge and Samuels, 1974; Johnson, 1977; Schneider and Shiffrin, 1977). In mediation, parsing appears to be used advantageously by the reader when he/she actively regresses and backtracks to regain the relative phrasing or prosodic stress patterns in hopes of regaining meaning (Anastasiow, Levine-Hanes and Hanes, 1982; Hanes, 1984).

A final comment from the Vazquez, *et al.,* study of special interest to the discussion of rhythm in reading is the authors' description of the reader in instances of linguistic confusion. A "gating mechanism" was noted whereby readers were observed to pace themselves in preparation for difficult or potentially difficult text encounters. The gating mechanism is reminiscent of the timekeeping capability discussed earlier in the chapter as a constituent of rhythmic response (Shaffer, 1976, 1982; Martin, 1972). While such implications go beyond the scope of the Vazquez study, the analogy is compelling. Without loss to the relative timing between elements of a unit and without creating rhythmic dysjunctures between consecutive units of processing, the reader, like the copy typist, appears to be in control of the timekeeping capability (Vazquez, *et al.*, 1978; Willows, 1974). Such internal adjustments suggest automatic processing, the nature and onset of which most likely are not entirely conscious. It is intriguing, however, to what extent control might be made conscious so that the sense of timing could be strategically evoked for eventual self-enlistment in the mediation process. These notions raise questions of treatment possibilities for facilitating rhythmic reading. Studies do confirm that selected practice effects and techniques yield fluent reading performance, which, by definition, marks the achievement of relative timing and fluid coordination within and across segmented units. Such studies hold promise for the systematic learning of rhythmic reading. Methods of treatment include such practices as "neurological impress," repeated reading and teacher modeling. These methods share a common goal of accomplishing fluency. Other methods of treatment use rhythm related techniques to improve reading performance of learning disabled and aphasic populations. The collective findings of these studies bring direct testimony to the relationship of rhythm and reading.

Rhythm-Related Treatments

The Nature of Automaticity (Nonmediated Reading)

The common goal of instructional treatment designed for improving automaticity is fluency, the third correlate of rhythm in reading presented in this chapter. Reading with fluency is symptomatic of reading without the need for mediation, i.e. fluent reading signals automatic processing (LaBerge and Samuels, 1974; Johnson, 1977; Schneider and Shiffrin, 1977; Schreiber, 1980). As a construct, however, fluency is probably the least defined (perhaps the most difficult to define) reading phenomenon. As noted earlier, fluency is a state of notably smooth, fluid and expressive reading which the reader is able to sustain effortlessly (LaBerge and Samuels, 1974; Schreiber, 1980; Anderson, 1981; Allington, 1983). Fluency sometimes is measured in terms of accuracy and speed of oral delivery in studies that use it as an indicator of automaticity. However, it is thought to supercede either measure in isolation or the combined effect of such measures (LaBerge and Samuels, 1974). It is the bias of this author to interpret fluency as the acquisition of the intrinsic sense of timing in skilled rhythmic activity as noted in the previously mentioned works of Martin (1972), Shaffer (1976; 1982) and Fowler (1980), and as suggested by Vazquez, *et al.* (1978) in their notion of the skilled parser's ability to read with a self-pacing "gating mechanism."

The major difference between "proficiency" and "efficiency" in reading is the necessary acquisition of fluency in the latter. It may be more precise to say that the vital feature separating the proficient from the efficient reader is the acquisition of the timekeeping capability which, as in skilled motor performance, permits the pacing necessary to continue forward processing while maintaining both the relative timing within processing units and fluidity across consecutive units. This is not to say that the fluent reader never experiences difficulty which will require some slow down or mediation of some sort. But what distinguishes the fluent reader from the otherwise proficient reader (in addition to the speed with which the mediation is successfully accomplished) is the maintenance of the relative timing within groups of words (parsed units) so that even when reading is slowed down it is comparable to the natural phrasing that is characteristic of speech. Prosody, once encoded (reconstructed) by the reader, thus is readily sustained even when speed is momentarily slowed.

Proficient readers who are not as yet fluent achieve accuracy at what LaBerge and Samuels (1974) refer to as Stage Two. However, such readers may endure repeated mediation and "bogs" to easy processing; although with their noted acquisition of subskills, decoding is successful more often than not. Proficient readers may be methodical and in frequent need of mediation, but accuracy and comprehension are achieved with effort. Text coverage without loss of accuracy is less, and processing time is required in characteristically greater amounts. Comprehension is in jeopardy of disorganization if word mediation in particular is prolonged.

Fluent readers, at Stage Three, are automatic processors. The theory of automatic processing in reading posed by LaBerge and Samuels (1974) describes the fluent reader as one who is able to focus attention on the organization and reorganization of larger units (longer stretches) of the linguistic string and, consequently, to process larger units of meaningful information with relative ease. The fluent reader is virtually freed from overattention to isolated word detail and able to concentrate more on meaning, e.g. imagery, prediction and analysis, than surface-level decoding. The theory of automaticity contends that the reader is able to attend to no more than a single signal at any given time (although simultaneous processing is tolerant of several signals at once and will occur readily when processing is automatic and therefore not contingent on attention). If attention is limited to the reorganization of words into larger groups or "chunks" of information and accuracy is maintained, fluency sustains itself. If however attention is called upon repeatedly to focus on associations at the detail level, e.g. unfamiliar word encounters, morphological unknowns, etc., then automatic access to retrieval is laden and at risk of overload. The path to meaning is direct in automatic reading, i.e. in reading with fluency.

Particularly characteristic of fluent reading in terms of the processing model presented by LaBerge and Samuels (1974) is that what is being processed is well beyond the rapid recognition of word-by-word succession. Rather, the processing units are wholistic word groups in a direct path to the semantic (meaning) memory code. If the path to semantic is indirect, requiring activated attention to the visual memory, phonological memory or episodic memory codes (the latter supplies associative learning, often personal, to assist recall) then automaticity is precluded. The reader is bogged down in time, and fluidity of forward processing is disjointed or in essence, dysrhythmic. Direct access to meaning enables the organization of larger word groups to be recoded and stored into new meaning for ready recall and adjustment as the accumulation of meaning continues through the unfolding of text. Such new codings and re-codings are essential for stored recall; otherwise the primary memory is taxed and overloaded.

According to LaBerge and Samuels (1974),

> The fluent reader has presumably mastered each of the subskills at the automatic level. Even more important, he has made their integration automatic as well. What this implies is that he no longer clearly sees the dividing lines separating these skills under the demands of his day-to-day reading. In effect, this means that

> he is no longer aware of the component nature of the subskills as
> he was required to be when he was a beginning reader, learning
> skills one-by-one [Stage One]. Therefore, if you should ask a
> typically fluent reader how he perceives his reading process, he is
> likely to tell you that he views it as a wholistic one (p. 318).

Comprehension is assumed to exist together with fluency and automaticity.
The relationship between fluency and comprehension has been demonstrated repeatedly enough to warrant confidence that it is reliable, although
critics are quick to point out that comprehension is merely a by-product
and not a direct concern of research on the effects of increasing fluency
(Schreiber, 1980). Moreover, the reasons given for comprehension achievement in fluent states are somewhat speculative. In keeping with the
model of automaticity, LaBerge and Samuels explain that

> . . . for high-level comprehension of a passage, attention must be
> directed to organizing [the] meaning codes, and presumably this
> is where effort enters into the reading just as it does in understand-
> ing difficult spoken sentences.
> So long as word meanings are automatically processed, the focus
> of attention remains at the semantic level and does not need to be
> switched to the visual system for decoding nor to the phonological
> level for retrieving the semantic meanings . . . The model indi-
> cates that meanings of familiar words and word groups may be
> activated automatically, leaving attention free to wander to other
> matters, perhaps to recent personal episodes. If the reader gives
> little attention to organizing meaning into new codes for storage,
> it is not surprising that he later finds he cannot recall what he has
> been reading (p. 320).

Treatments and Treatment Effects on Automaticity

Various treatments and instructional approaches have been successfully used to increase fluency in reading. These include 1) repeated
reading, 2) teacher modeling, 3) neurological impress and 4) cloze
techniques. Of these methods, repeated readings employs repeated trials
of reading (most typically, oral reading) of the identical material until
fluency is achieved. The procedure is thought to be successful contingent upon the reader's increased attention to recoding word groups into
increasingly larger units of meaning. These are stored for ready access
when adjustments in processing are needed to accommodate the meaning of newly encountered information (LaBerge and Samuels, 1974). The

latter explanation is consistent with the model of automaticity which is largely concerned with the processing path and more specifically with the target of the reader's attention. The relationship between fluency and comprehension is for the most part demonstrated in this explanation as well. The recoding of word groups is itself contingent on meaning as the anticipated and only useful product of "chunking" information. As processing continues, reference to this stored meaning is critical to oncoming coordination and reorganization activity as the remaining text is encountered. Without the recoding of word groups into larger units of meaningful information, repeated trials accordingly will show no improvement in fluency and, consequently, comprehension. The benefits of successful practice in repeated readings apparently extend to improved word recognition performance as indicated by marked decreases in word errors with the rereading of passages in which the reader's initial performance approached ceiling or frustration level (Gonzales and Elijah, 1975).

Schreiber (1980) offers another rationale for the success of the repeated readings method in increased fluency. Schreiber poses that what the reader is in essence learning from repeated trials with a given passage is to compensate for the absence of prosody via the recognition of additional morphological and syntactic cues which, in turn, generate semantic information. The reader accomplishes this through increased phrasing skill, i.e., parsing ability, acquired through repeated exposures to the identical text. Schreiber states,

> As a result of reading and rereading a given passage, the Stage Two [accurate decoding ability] reader begins to recognize what kind of syntactic phrasing is necessary in order to make sense of the passage; this recognition comes about as he discovers and makes use of the syntactic, semantic, morphologic and contextual features which are found in the written form and which correspond to features that he can and does use to a greater or lesser extent in aural processing. But once this step takes place in the repeated readings of a given passage, the way toward fluent reading becomes less and less mysterious, as it becomes more and more obvious that, in order to discover the appropriate syntactic phrasing in the written signal, the reader must rely on cues other than the prosodic ones that play so large a role in the preception of phrasing in the oral signal (p. 182).

Skilled parsing, in turn, allows even greater attention to be given to the various morphological and syntactic cues that are available within a linguistic unit that is to be processed.

As a child learns (tacitly, of course) that the prosodic cues are not
systematically preserved in writing, he begins to make better use
of the other kinds of signals that are preserved such as function
words, inflectional endings, and other morphological signals, the
form-class membership of lexical items, as well as the various
perceptual strategies that may be based on the use of these formal
signalling devices (pp. 182–183).

The argument of parsing versus recoding is hardly a contest. In fact,
such skills are highly complementary. Indeed, the reorganization of the
linguistic string for the sake of processing larger chunks of information
is certainly dependent on parsing. Whatever the skill practiced in repeated
readings, be it parsing or recoding, it is apparently transferrable to novel
reading encounters and may serve therefore as the link that bridges Stage
Two and Stage Three (from accurate decoding to fluency, respectively)
according to automatic information processing theory (Schreiber, 1980;
LaBerge and Samuels, 1974; Anderson, 1981; Allington, 1983; Samuels,
1979; Kann, 1983).

Of particular interest to the discussion of rhythm and reading is the
notion that as remote to rhythm as an account of reading fluency methodology would appear to be, the rhythm correlates—prosody, parsing and
fluency—emerge quite matter-of-factly. The linkage of fluency in reading to prosody and parsing in speech reception and production is increasingly appropriate from this perspective. The acquisition and application
of the skills that underlie each of these correlates have been explained in
terms of the principles of relative timing which [as Martin (1972) and
Shaffer (1976, 1982) have suggested] is the vitality of skilled rhythmic
activity. This brings a firmer foundation to the linkage.

Other methods aimed at increasing fluency include neurological
impress, teacher modeling and cloze techniques. Neurological impress
employs simultaneous reading methodology whereby the teacher and
the student read in unison. The teacher is careful not to dominate the
oral delivery of the passage, keeping his or her voice modulated at a
quiet but natural language-like delivery. The fluency and proficiency of
the teacher allows for a "just noticeable" lead to insure the appropriate
pacing of the oral delivery, including the natural phrasing and prosodic
contour. In essence, the teacher supplies an "expressive" lead. The
developing reader is able to keep pace and thereby sustain his participation.
The developing reader imitates the phrasing and prosodic delivery of
the teacher who, sitting to the side of the reader, projects the voice into

the ear of the student as he follows along in unison. The eye of the reader is directed at the text. Often finger pointing is used to highlight the graphic array of the linguistic string as the oral reading proceeds. The method is thought to be successful in that the developing or remedial reader is focused beyond the limitations of word detail into word groups and phrasing units. Through the impress method such readers are receiving for the first time a fluent experience which would otherwise be unattainable via their habituated approach to print (Heckelman, 1966; Hollingsworth, 1978; Anderson, 1981; Cunningham, 1979; Kann, 1983).

Teacher modeling, sometimes referred to as echo reading, involves taking turns in reading—the teacher reads first, followed by the developing reader's independent attempt. The success of this method in research and clinical studies illustrates the benefits of the oral presentation by the teacher. More specifically, the preservation of the natural phrasing and rediscovery of the prosodic features modeled by the teacher are thought to provide substantial familiarity with the context and language usage of the text. This aids comprehension and word recognition so that subsequent trials by the reader successfully approximate simulated phrasing and rhythmic coordination across processing units. In effect this and related methods afford the reader entry into automaticity by freeing him from the demands of decoding and surface-level semantic processing. Fluency is the target of practice or drill, and much to the surprise of the reader, deeper comprehension is often derived with repeated practice on a given passage. These expectations are thought to transfer to new reading encounters with the effect of undoing habituated approaches to print and leaving the reader more responsive to instruction, particularly to modeling attempts. Some of the versions of teacher modeling or echo reading make deliberate use of repeated presentations of the text. Following the aural/graphic experience, the reader independently attempts to read without assistance. Oral reading is not necessarily the mode of continued practice; however, the reader is asked after repeated practice to demonstrate mastery, i.e., fluency, through oral presentation to the teacher (Smith, 1979; Schneeberg, 1977; Chomsky, 1976; Anderson, 1981; Cunningham, 1979; Anastasiow, Levine-Hanes, and Hanes, 1982; Hanes 1984).

The cloze technique is used to model fluency as well as to reinforce rapid word retrieval. The procedure is a verision of echo reading in that the teacher reads orally as the reader follows along silently in his copy of the passage. This is done however, with the prior understanding that the teacher will momentarily pause at varying points in the passage (usually within each sentence) at which time the reader is to supply the next word or phrase before the teacher resumes reading. The developing reader is encouraged to supply the missing words and phrases as rapidly as possible and with appropriate intonation so that the flow and prosody (rhythm) are not disrupted. This interchange continues until such time as the reader is able to assume the lead. Ample prereading, or, at the very least, ample exposure to the passage has occurred by the time a change of command takes place. The success of this technique is influenced largely by the combination of teacher modeling and practices in rapid word retrieval, as is the case with most rereading techniques (Hokisson, 1975; Anderson, 1981; Cunningham, 1979).

The use of semantic and contextual cues to aid word recognition is indirectly emphasized in the cloze technique, thus providing the reader experience with word approximation in accord with Smith's (1982) notion of reduction of uncertainty. While the technique is not employed to teach mediation, the incidental effect may be just that. The case in point, semantically-appropriate word approximation, is a key strategy in psycholinguistic mediation. Such a strategy enables the retrieval of the target word, or an approximation, without loss of meaning and with good potential for regaining fluency if fluent reading conditions had preceded the onset of mediation. Semantic (and syntactic) cueing, from a psycholinguistic perspective, is the best alternative when the level of word difficulty prohibits automatic retrieval.

A variation to the oral cloze procedure is the written cloze technique with passages within the developing reader's independent reading level. Words are partially deleted approximately every 20 words, with only initial consonants and consonant blends left intact. Readers are thereby given practice in combining word attack and context cues to aid word recognition (Cunningham, 1979).

Once again, a parallel to psycholinguistic orientation warrants mentioning. Combining context cues and word attack (i.e., semantic and syntactic cues) is a desirable approach from a psycholinguistic standpoint. A major concern of the early proponents of psycholinguistic reading theory, emerging at a time when phonics was emphasized as a primary developmental and remedial instructional tact to the teaching of reading, has been the overuse of phonic and graphic decoding strategies. The consequences of such over indulgence were thought to lead a reader further and further from the connection between reading and meaning.

It was a concern that indeed young readers who were otherwise normal processors were becoming habituated into a phonic/graphic approach to reading at the expense of acquiring the more critical semantic and syntactic strategies. These circumstances threatened a further separation of reading from its language foundation (Goodman and Goodman, 1977; Smith, 1977, 1982; Anastasiow, *et al.*, 1982).

None of the various treatments designed to achieve fluency employ direct instruction, e.g., correction, mediated assistance, etc. The reader experiences increasingly closer approximations to fluency until it is achieved, whether it is modeled prior to the reader's independent attempts or "teacher-paced" as in the case of impress and cloze conditions. In the case of repeated readings, the extent of indirect assistance apparently varies in practice. Repeated readings at times follow at least a single listening experience with the practice passage. Where they do not, the appropriate matching of the reader and material to be practiced is paramount (Rashotte and Torgesen, 1985). The level of difficulty must be easy enough to insure rapid word retrieval and a diminished need for mediation which would otherwise take attention away from reorganization and recoding (LaBerge and Samuels, 1974; Samuels, 1979).

Lastly, a treatment radically different from those discussed above is "visual speech rhythms." The procedure was developed by Martin and his associates (1976, 1978) who translated the notion of relative accent and timing theory of rhythmic activity in speech into the visual presentation of written text. They write,

> The basic methodological notion is very simple and consists of yoking the visual and auditory timing of syllables in synchrony so that a sentence could be presented visually but timed syllable-by-syllable with the same timing it has when spoken. This was accomplished by synchronizing the onset of each syllable as it appeared on the screen of a TV monitor with the onset of each syllable as it was heard through the speaker. The result was a sentence which "grew" left-to-right across the screen and which could be presented visually either by itself or in combination with the auditory channel . . . (p. 154, 1976).

Fluency and comprehension gains have reportedly been significant with groups of primary developmental readers receiving visual rhythm training (Martin and Meltzer, 1976; La Coultre and Carroll, 1981) as well as with groups of foreign language learners reading in their second language (Martin, Meltzer and Mills, 1978). Benefits for the deaf reader have also been posed (Martin and Meltzer, 1976). While fluency was markedly improved following training, long range and transfer effects have not been studied. The definition of fluency in these studies varied as well. Fluency was measured in the Martin studies by professional and lay judges. In the La Coultre and Carroll (1981) study, however, fluency was measured strictly in terms of speed and accuracy; and in this instance there were no substantial fluency gains with the visual rhythms treatment, although favorable effects on comprehension performance over other conditions were demonstrated. The discrepancies among studies may indeed support the notion presented earlier in the chapter that fluency supercedes measurement by the single or combined dimensions of speed and accuracy.

When reading is fluent it appears rhythmic. In other words, fluency is rhythm in behavioral terms. It may be well to propose further that what distinguishes proficient decoding from fluent reading is the internal workings of the very sense of timing attributed to skills motor performance (Martin, 1972; Shaffer, 1976, 1982). It may be that automatized reading is accomplished by this sense of timing which enables swift accommodations and adjustments without disrupting the rhythmic flow. It may be, too, that the judges in the Martin studies (1976, 1978) were responding intuitively to such attributes.

Rhythm and Mediation

The intrinsic sense of timing that links rhythm and automaticity may also serve to link rhythm to mediation. Although some degree of speculation may be enlisted to argue the point, it is the intent of this final discussion to hypothesize a legitimate role for rhythm in the developmental reading process—which for the most part entails the acquisition of mediation strategies.

As stated earlier, mediated and nonmediated reading often interchange during the course of a single reading encounter and are in these instances highly interdependent. It may be here in fact that rhythm plays its most important role in skilled reading.

The efficiency with which the reader accommodates the transition from nonmediated to mediated processing and back again may be solely attributed to the intrinsic sense of timing that keeps an otherwise fluent reader fluent, even through episodes of mediation. Fluency appears tolerant of occasional mediation as long as the results are successful and efficient in terms of time consumption. It is not the kind of mediation strategy per se that separates proficient and fluent readers (although some selected strategies are thought to be more beneficial than others), but their **efficiency** in employment. The facility of execution which rhythm brings to skilled motor functioning deserves due consideration in such a discussion of mediated activity.

In addition to its contribution to increased efficiency, rhythm in mediation is implicitly described by its organizational property. Whereas efficiency may separate merely proficient from fluent performance in reading, a seemingly organized or strategic approach to implementing mediation apparently separates proficient from disabled readers. Torgesen (1977, 1980) proposed that disabled learners are disorganized and non-strategic in their approach to task performance. Sustained performance required for task completion disintegrates rapidly as a result. Disabled learners may indeed be markedly dysrhythmic, but such deficiencies may not be limited to more apparent performances on motor and verbal tasks (Hantman, 1970; Sparks, *et al.*, 1974; Sparks, *et al.*, 1976). Instead the lack of rhythmicity may be reflected more subtly in approaches to task performance. Organized approach-to-task from a rhythmic perspective would require sustained control over anticipatory and adjustment activity which is critical to the coordination of mediation efforts.

Rhythm is evident as well in certain mediation strategies employed by skilled readers. Their examination promises insights into identifying methods for eliciting these strategies in developing readers and treating disabled readers who are symptomatically dysrhythmic (inefficient and disorganized) in their mediation efforts. Speech recoding in reading is an example of such a strategy. It refers to an "inner voice" which transforms automatic and often rapid accumulations of information into speech at the critical juncture between short- and long-term memory during difficult processing. As a strategy typically enlisted by the reader, speech recoding serves in effect to extend the time constraints of the working memory (Kleiman, 1975).

Parsed units of the text are internally vocalized (the "inner voice") as mediated processing continues. The positive effects of speech recoding are attributed to the acoustic feedback (independent of articulatory execution and audible sounding) and particularly to the recitation of rhythmic language within the parsed units. The rhythm of language is virtually echoed, as the processing of the next unit is attempted, awaiting resolution of the difficulty while keeping active both the place and tempo of the processing preceding the onset of mediation. Verbal rehearsal is another more direct attempt to achieve similar effects, differing from speech recoding primarily in that verbalization is articulated at audible levels. Remedial reading procedures often make use of verbal rehearsal techniques to achieve comparable results. Verbal rehearsal can be explicated and demonstrated through modeling. Both the disabled and young reader in development reportedly respond to such techniques (Flavell, 1979; Torgesen and Goldman, 1977). The technique is borrowed from metacognitively-able readers who report the deliberate self-selection of such strategies, as well as from clinical studies of observable task strategies and study behaviors of able readers (Kleiman, 1975; Torgesen, 1977, 1979; Torgesen and Goldman, 1977; Wagoner, 1983).

Finally, what may be the most intriguing of all linkages is the association of rhythm and metacognition which in itself is highly contingent on the delicate synchrony of multi-level processing (Flavell, 1979; Brown, 1980; Woods, 1980; Wagoner, 1983). Megacognition is defined as the overlying layer of mental operations which accompany the path of cognition and monitor its progress. Cognition, on the other hand, is more concerned with the decoding process and use of skills to gain meaning from text. The dual operations working simultaneously and synchronously (rhythmically) allow continual self-monitoring of the status of comprehension and the ongoing accumulation of text information. While processing is going well, cognitive mediation is dormant although metacognitive processing is ongoing. The moment difficulty arises however, metacognition elicits selected strategies for mediation which then are brought into the cognitive foreground. Metacognition continues to monitor progress and determines the point at which forward processing should resume, or, in the case of insurmountable difficulty, elicits additional strategies for assistance as necessary. Such intricate processing, which remains fluid and synchronized, is highly aligned with the qualities of rhythmic processing as presented in this chapter.

Summary

In summary, the salient properties of rhythmic structure and functioning in skilled motor performance and language (reception and production) as described in the works of Martin (1972) and Shaffer (1976, 1982) are readily identified in reading behaviors characteristic of developmental and skilled performance. Of particular importance to reading are the rhythmic properties inherent in its hierarchical organization, time keeping, anticipatory and accommodative capabilities. Comparable behaviors have been reliably predictive of reading in mediated and automatic processing, but without benefit of a broader recognition which would associate them with rhythmic principles and the acquisition of rhythmic skills as a natural consequence of reading development.

It is in large part for this reason that rhythm as a factor in reading acquisition has been virtually overlooked, even though its constituent properties are evident in the acquisition of mediation strategies, meta-cognition and automatized (fluent) reading. The primary purpose of this chapter was to establish such linkages between rhythm and its correlates in reading, although this represents, at best, a beginning. A promising consequence is the recognition of rhythm as a legitimate factor in reading and the appreciation of the potential insights that such recognition can bring to refining the theoretical understanding of reading and knowledge of treatment interaction.

Reading at its most skilled level of performance is rhythmic. Fluency as a correlate to rhythm in reading demonstrates the strongest and most immediate of linkages discussed in this chapter. Rhythm is a predominant factor in automatized or fluent reading, working to anticipate and adjust the flow of processing so that prosody—the direct link to comprehension—is sustained through difficult encounters. In this regard rhythmic skill is the ultimate aim of reading acquisition. Rhythm contributes significantly as well to successful mediation, which suggests the developmental nature of rhythmic skill acquisition. This contention is particularly defensible in those instances of speech recoding and verbal rehearsal. These rhythmic strategies extend the limitations of the primary memory by maintaining the tempo and rehearsing the meaning of parsed units while the reader attends to semantic approximation or decoding i.e., psycholinguistic mediation, as necessary. Considering that these strategies may be deliberately enlisted suggests further that metacognitive mediation and rhythm are linked and that mediation in general, and metacognition in particular may be contingent on rhythmic skill to ensure efficient and fluid interchange of psycholinguistic, metacognitive and automatized processing.

REFERENCES

Anastasiow, N. J., Hanes, M. L. & Hanes, M. L. *Language and reading for poverty children.* Baltimore, MD.: University Park Press, 1982.

Anderson, B. The missing ingredient: fluent oral reading. *The Elementary Schools Journal*, 1981, *81*, 173–177.

Allington, R. L. Fluency: the neglected reading goal. *Reading Teacher*, 1983, *36*, 556–561.

Bolinger, D. Accent is predictable (if you're a mind-reader). *Language*, 1972, *48*, 633–644.

Boomer, D. S. & Laver, J. D. Slips of the tongue. *British Journal of Disorders of Communication*, 1968, *3*, 1–12.

Brown, A. L. Metacognitive development and reading. In R.J. Spiro, B.C. Bertram & W. F. Brewer (Eds.), *Theoretical issues in reading comprehension*. Hillsdale, N.J.: Lawrence Erlbaum Associates, 1980, 453–481.

Buswell, G. T. An experimental study of the eye-voice span in reading. *Supplementary Educational Monographs No. 17*. Chicago: University of Chicago Press, 1920.

Chomsky, C. After decoding: What? *Language Arts*, 1976, *53*, 288–96.

Chomsky, N. & Halle, M. *The sound pattern of English*. New York: Harper & Row, 1968.

Clay, M. M. & Imlach, R. H. Juncture, pitch and stress as reading behavior variables. *Journal of Verbal Learning and Verbal Behavior*, 1971, *10*, 133–139.

Cunningham, J. W. An automatic pilot for decoding. *The Reading Teacher*, 1979, *32*, 420–424.

Dearborn, W. F., Johnston, P. W. & Carmichael, L. Oral stress and meaning in printed material. *Science*, 1949, *110*, 404.

Flavell, J. H. Metacognition and cognitive monitoring: a new area of cognitive-developmental inquiry. *American Psychologist*, 1979, *34*, 906–911.

Fowler, C. A. Coarticulation and theories of extrinsic timing. *Journal of Phonetics*, 1980, *8*, 113–133.

Fromkin, V. A. The non-anomalous nature of anomalous utterance. *Language*, 1971, *47*, 27–52.

Golinkoff, R. M. A comparison of reading comprehension processes in good and poor comprehenders. *Reading Research Quarterly*, 1975–1976, *11*, 623–659.

Gonzales, P. C. & Elijah, D. V. Rereading effect on error patterns and performance levels on the IRI. *Reading Teacher*, 1975, *28*, 647–52.

Goodman, K. S. Miscues: Windows on the reading process. In K. S. Goodman (Ed.), *Miscue analysis: applications to reading instruction*. Urbana, IL.: National Council of Teachers of English, ERIC Clearinghouse on Reading and Communication Skills, 1977.

Goodman, K. S. & Goodman, Y. M. Learning about psycholinguistic processes by analyzing oral reading. *Harvard Educational Review*, 1977, *47*, 317–333.

Goodman, Y. M. & Burke, C. *Reading miscue inventory: procedure for diagnosis and evaluation*. New York: Macmillan, 1972.

Hammill, B. W. A linguistic correlate of sentential rhythmic patterns. *Journal of Experimental Psychology*, 1976, *2*, 71–79.

Hanes, M. L. When children repeat . . . : oral reading repetitions that signal proficiency. *Florida Reading Quarterly*, 1984, *21*, 27–30.

Hantman, D. Reading comprehension and nonverbal aspects of spoken language. *Academic Therapy,* 1970, *5,* 281–293.

Heckelman, R. G. Using the neurological-impress remedial-reading technique. *Academic Therapy Quarterly,* 1966, *1,* 235–239.

Hollingsworth, P. M. An experimental approach to the impress method of teaching reading. *The Reading Teacher,* 1978, *31,* 624–626.

Hokisson, K. The many facets of assisted reading. *Elementary English,* 1975, *52,* 312–15.

Johnson, N. F. A pattern-unit model of word identification. In D. LaBerge & S. J. Samuels (Eds.), *Basic processes in reading: perception and comprehension.* Hillsdale, N.J.: Lawrence Erlbaum Associates, 1977.

Kann, R. The method of repeated readings: expanding the neurological impress method for use with disabled readers. *Journal of Learning Disabilities,* 1983, *16,* 90–92.

Kleiman, G. M. Speech recoding in reading. *Journal of Verbal Learning and Verbal Behavior,* 1975, *14,* 323–339.

Kleiman, G. M., Winograd, P. N. & Humphrey, M. H. Prosody and children's parsing of sentences. Technical report no. 123. Urbana, IL.: Center for the Study of Reading, University of Illinois, 1979.

Kolers, P. A. Eye-voice span or response bias? In D.L. Horton & J.J. Jenkins (Eds.), *The perception of Language.* Columbus, OH: Charles E. Merrill, 1971.

LaBerge, D. & Samuels, S. J. Toward a theory of information processing in reading. *Cognitive Psychology,* 1974, *6,* 293–323.

LaCoultre, E. & Carroll, M. The effect of visualizing speech rhythms on reading comprehension and fluency. *Journal of Reading Behavior,* 1981, *13,* 279–85.

Lashley, K. S. The problem of serial order in behavior. In L. A. Jeffress (Ed.), *Cerebral mechanisms in behavior.* New York: Wiley, 1951.

Lieberman, M. *The international system of English,* unpublished Doctoral dissertation, MIT, Cambridge, MA., 1975.

Lieberman, M. & Prince, A. On stress and linguistic rhythm. *Linguistic Inquiry,* 1977, *8,* 249–336.

Martin, J. G. Rhythm-induced judgments of word stress in sentences. *Journal of Verbal Learning and Verbal Behavior,* 1970, *9,* 627–633.

Martin, J. G. Rhythmic (hierarchical) versus serial structure in speech and other behavior. *Psychological Review,* 1972, *79,* 487–509.

Martin, J. G. & Meltzer, R. H. Visual rhythms: report on a method for facilitating the teaching of reading. *Journal of Reading Behavior,* 1976, *8,* 153–60.

Martin, J. G., Meltzer, R. H. & Mills, C. B. Visual rhythms: dynamic text display for learning to read a second language. *Visual Language,* 1978, *12,* 71–79.

Mosse, H. *The complete handbook of children's reading disorders* (Vol. 2). New York: Human Sciences Press, 1982.

Rashotte, C. A. & Torgesen, J. K. Repeated readings and reading fluency in learning disabled children. *Reading Research Quarterly,* 1985, *20,* 180–88.

Restle, F. Serial patterns: The role of phrasing. *Journal of Experimental Psychology,* 1972, *92,* 385–390.

Rode, S. S. Development of phrase and clause boundary reading in children. *Reading Research Quarterly,* 1974–1975, *10,* 125–142.

Samuels, S. J. The method of repeated readings. *Reading Teacher,* 1979, *32,* 403–408.

Schneeberg, H. Listening while reading a four year study. *Reading Teacher,* 1977, *30,* 629–35.

Schneider, W. & Shiffrin, R. M. Automatic and controlled information processing in vision. In D. LaBerge & S. J. Samuels (Eds.), *Basic processes in reading: perception and comprehension.* Hillsdale, N.J.: Lawrence Erlbaum Associates, Publishers, 1977.

Schreiber, P. A. On the acquisition of reading fluency. *Journal of Reading Behavior,* 1980, *12,* 177–186.

Selkirk, E. O. The role of prosodic categories in English word stress. *Linguistic Inquiry,* 1980, *11,* 563–605.

Shaffer, L. H. Intention and performance. *Psychological Review,* 1976, *83,* 275–293.

Shaffer, L. H. Rhythm and timing in skill. *Psychological Review,* 1982, *89,* 109–122.

Smith, D. D. The improvement of children's oral reading through the use of teacher modeling. *Journal of Learning Disabilities,* 1979, *12,* 39–43.

Smith, F. Making sense of reading—and of reading instruction. *Harvard Educational Review,* 1977, *47,* 386–395.

Smith, F. *Understanding reading.* New York: Holt, Rinehart and Winston, 1982.

Sparks, R., Helm, N. & Albert, M. Aphasia rehabilitation resulting from melodic intonation therapy. *Cortex,* 1974, *10,* 303–316.

Sparks, R. W. & Holland, A. L. Method: Melodic intonation therapy for aphasia. *Journal of Speech and Hearing Disorders,* 1976, *41,* 287–297.

Stice, C. K. The relationship between comprehension of oral constrastive stress and silent reading comprehension. *Journal of Learning Disabilities,* 1979, *12,* 39–42.

Torgesen, J. K. The role of nonspecific factors in the task performance of learning disabled children: A theoretical assessment. *Journal of Learning Disabilities,* 1977, *10,* 27–33.

Torgesen, J. K. Conceptual and educational implications of the use of efficient task strategies by learning disabled children. *Journal of Learning Disabilities,* 1980, *13,* 19–34.

Torgesen, J. K. & Goldman, T. Verbal rehearsal and short-term memory in reading disabled children. *Child Development,* 1977, *48,* 56–60.

Vazquez, C. A., Glucksberg, S. & Danks, J. H. Integration of clauses in oral reading: The effects of syntactic and semantic constraints on the eye-voice span. *Reading Research Quarterly,* 1977–1978, *13,* 174–185.

Wagoner, S. A. Comprehension monitoring: What it is and what we know about it. *Reading Research Quarterly,* 1983, *18,* 328–346.

Willows, D. M. Reading between the lines: Selective attention in good and poor readers. *Child Development,* 1974, *45,* 408–415.

Woods, W. A. Multiple theory formation in speech and reading. In R. J. Spiro, B. C. Bruce & W. Brewer (Eds.), *Theoretical issues in reading comprehension.* Hillsdale, NJ: Lawrence Erlbaum Associates, 1980, 59–82.

Chapter 7.

RHYTHM IN MUSIC

ALF GABRIELSSON

The concept of rhythm appears in a variety of different fields as evidenced by the contributions to this volume. Maybe music and dance are the fields which are the most inseparably connected with rhythm of them all. Rhythm is a basic characteristic of music in different cultures all over the world, and many consider it to be the most fundamental component of music. A book on rhythm without a treatment of rhythm in music would be incomplete indeed.

Before proceeding a word of warning must be said. The reader of this book will certainly note that the concept of rhythm is used in rather different ways in different contexts. The rhythm concept is both vast and complex. In some contexts certain properties of rhythm are emphasized, while other properties are more important in other contexts. This multidimensionality of rhythm is obvious also with regard to musical rhythm, as we shall see later. As a matter of fact, there is still no generally accepted definition of rhythm, although there have been hundreds of proposals from ancient Greece until our days. Due to the looseness of the concept, rhythm is sometimes simply used as a synonym for other, related concepts such as periodicity, recurrence, regularity, pattern, structure, change, and others. For more complete discussions of these problems, see Fraisse (1956; 1974; 1982), Bengtsson (1974), Bengtsson, Gabrielsson, and Thorsén (1969), Motte-Haber (1968).

Rhythm in music is an extremely large subject, which cannot be surveyed by a single author in a short chapter. Limitations are thus inevitable. The discussion in the following will mainly apply to rhythm in various types of Western music of today and some centuries back. Historical accounts of rhythm during different epochs of Western music may be found in Sachs (1953), Yeston (1976), and in the article on rhythm in **Grove's Dictionary of Music and Musicians** (1980). Rhythm in other music cultures is a large and fascinating field, in which a first orientation

131

may be gained by consulting the articles on various countries and cultures in **Grove's Dictionary;** these articles provide numerous references for further study.

It is also inevitable that the discussion will reflect the author's own background, which is research in experimental music psychology in close cooperation with musicologists. I will, therefore, concentrate on empirical investigations of rhythm and generally stress the importance of using empirical methods to approach the many unsettled questions about rhythm. In no way does this mean that other methods should be discarded. The problems concerning rhythm are so vast and so intricate that methodological pluralism is both desirable and necessary.

Rather than trying to be exhaustive (which anyhow would be impossible due to space limitations), I prefer to be selective and focus on certain themes, which will be apparent later. For some questions only hints are given, but they can be pursued further by the reader by means of the references.

Empirical Research on Rhythm Up To Around 1970

Most empirical research on rhythm has not directly dealt with musical rhythm, but rather more generally with **auditory rhythm.** There are at least two reasons for that. One is that it is much easier to generate and manipulate simple sound sequences than the complex stimuli found in real music. In many experiments the stimuli are thus sequences of short click sounds (like staccato in musical terms), which are varied with regard to durations, intensities, pitches (frequencies), etc. While this reason is mainly of technical nature, the second reason is more substantial. According to this, musical rhythm may be seen as an application of more general and fundamental principles common for all or many rhythmic phenomena in various fields. Hopefully these general principles would be easier to find in "simplified" situations, in which various confounding effects may be avoided.

Experimental research on rhythm started about 100 years ago in the then young experimental psychology. An impressive number of papers on rhythm appeared during the decades around 1900. Wilhelm Wundt, one of the fathers of the experimental psychology, discussed rhythm in his monumental **"Grundzüge der Physiologischen Psychologie"** (1911) far more extensively than in any later handbook of psychology. Like many other contemporary researchers (Bolton, 1894; Meumann,

1894; MacDougall, 1903; Woodrow, 1909) Wundt started by the perception of a **completely uniform sequence of sounds**, that is, identical sounds following each other at a certain speed. Although there were thus no physical dissimilarities between the sounds, the listeners typically reported that they perceived a **grouping** of the sounds. For instance, they grouped by four (́---- ́---- etc.) with an **accent** on the first member of the group (indicated by ́ here), and the interval between the successive groups seemed to be longer than the interval between the sounds within the group (also indicated in the illustration above). The number of elements in the group depended on the speed: the higher speed, the larger the group (six, eight, etc.), and conversely: the slower speed, the fewer members in the perceived group. To a certain extent this was dependent on the listener's attitude: in certain cases you may sometimes hear one type of grouping, sometimes another, and you may even deliberately change between these.

Already with a completely uniform sound sequence we may thus have so-called "subjective rhythmization." The next step was to introduce **systematic variations of physical variables:** to increase or decrease the duration of certain sounds (or rather of the intervals between the sounds), the intensity of the sounds, their pitch, etc. The purpose was, of course, to see how such changes would affect the perceived grouping, accentuation, and other phenomena. There were many possible combinations to investigate. The results from various investigations were not always consistent but indicated that any of the variables could affect the perceived grouping in different ways. Increased intensity on a certain sound tended to make this sound begin the group, while an increased duration tended to make the corresponding sound terminate the perceived group.

Generally the temporal factors were considered to be more important than intensity or pitch. Another important observation was that the grouping of successive sounds became more difficult, the slower the speed (the longer the intervals between sounds). You may easily verify that for yourself by clapping any rhythm pattern and successively make it slower and slower. When the interval between the sounds (claps) is about one second, grouping becomes somewhat strained, and when the interval is 1.5–2 seconds, grouping is almost impossible—the sounds become isolated from each other. In order for grouping to take place the total duration of the group must not exceed the upper limit for what William James (1890) called the **"specious present"** (another term is the "psychological present"). This is what we experience as "now" and usually extends for some few seconds; its upper limit depends on various factors but is roughly within 5–10 seconds.

If you measure the duration of a rhythmic grouping or the duration of a phrase in a melody, you will usually find that the duration is well below this limit. However, there is music in which the limit is exceeded and in which it is hard to experience the melody if you do not know it beforehand. For instance, the **cantus firmus** in many works for organ from the Baroque era proceeds so slowly that many listeners do not apprehend it. An example is given in Figure 1; try it yourself.

Figure 1. The beginning of Johann Pachelbel's chorale prelude "Gelobet seist du, Jesu Christ." The cantus firmus (c.f.) starts in the third bar. (Reproduced by permission from "Johann Pachelbel, Ausgewählte Orgelwerke II, BA 239," Bärenreiter-Verlag, Kassel und Basel, 1934.)

Wundt was the main representative for the so-called classical introspection, the attempt at finding the presumed basic elements (sensations and feelings) in immediate experience by means of specially trained subjects. Besides the auditory sensations, the subjects often reported about **kinaesthetic sensations** from various parts of the body and about **feelings** ("Gefühlselemente") like alternations between tension and release. Wundt's followers in the United States, Ruckmich (1913) and Titchener (1926), concluded that experience of rhythm usually included kinaesthetic sensations, and that perceived grouping and accent on certain elements was closely connected to periodically recurring kinaesthetic sensations, e.g., sensations of tension at accented elements.

Similar conclusions were also drawn by researchers in other psychological schools who studied the **spontaneous overt movements** in subjects listening to rhythm stimuli. These movements (tapping your feet, shaking your head, etc.) were usually synchronized with certain elements in the sound sequence and were stronger for louder sounds (Miner, 1903).

Stetson (1903, 1905) assumed that every sound caused a movement in the general musculature. The slower muscle-sets would adjust themselves to beats (sounds) at convenient time intervals, while the more mobile sets would be activated by the intervening sounds. These movements and the ensuing kinaesthetic sensations formed a basis for the experience of rhythm.

Wundt, MacDougall, and others emphasized the spontaneous and immediate character of rhythmic grouping which was considered as an example of "**Gestalt qualities.**" Each rhythm has its own specific individuality, which appears without any conscious knowledge about the single components in the pattern and their interrelations. These ideas were further elaborated by some Gestalt psychologists (Koffka, 1909; Werner, 1919; Sander, 1926). The well-known distinction between figure and ground was applied to rhythm patterns, e.g., the accented element was the figure and the other elements formed the background. There were also general discussions about how the Gestalt principles of proximity, similarity, good continuation, etc. would apply to perception of sound sequences, but these questions have been treated in more detail by later researchers.

A special problem discussed by Koffka, Werner, and Sander was the function of the **interval between successive groups.** In the "subjective rhythmization" (when all intervals are equally long and all sounds identical) the interval **between** the groups seems longer than the (equally long) intervals **within** the group. Sander called it a "Fugengestalt" equivalent to the perceived groups, and the experience of rhythm is thus "zweigestaltig," two Gestalts embedded in each other. Werner similarly talked about "Gestaltverkettung" (linking of Gestalts). This special function of the interval between groups is one of the things which distinguish experience of rhythm from experience of mere regularity.

Performance of rhythm patterns also was studied in many early investigations (Miyake, 1902; MacDougall, 1903; Brown, 1911; Schmidt, 1939). The subjects were usually instructed to tap groups of two, three, four, etc., either according to a verbally prescribed model (e.g., tap a sequence of trochees, dactyls, or the like), or to reproduce a given sound sequence. Among the results may be mentioned that elements intended to be accented were performed by lengthening the corresponding element (or the interval following it), and that the variability of the duration of the whole pattern was often smaller than the variability of the duration of the single elements within the pattern. Furthermore, the variability of the durations was smaller than the variability of the intensities of the taps, which may indicate that the temporal factors were more important than the intensity factor.

Many of the questions described above were investigated more thoroughly in the extensive rhythm research over several decades by Paul Fraisse and his co-workers in Paris. The numerous reports from this work are conveniently summarized by Fraisse (1956, 1974, 1978, 1981, 1982).

A long series of experiments was aimed at studying the **principles of rhythmic structuring**, especially with regard to temporal relations, which were considered as more important than intensity and pitch relations (however, these were studied as well). Production as well as reproduction techniques were used. A common result from many experiments was the existence of two separate regions of duration in the subjects' tappings called **"temps longs"** (long times) and **"temps courts"** (short times) in an approximate relation of 2:1 or higher. Furthermore, the subjects tended to reproduce given patterns in such a way that the distinction between the two classes of durations was clearer in the reproduction than in the original patterns. This is seen as an example of a striving towards as "pregnant" structures as possible in accordance with the Gestalt **"law of Prägnanz."** Another way of increasing the pregnance is to lengthen the interval between successive groups (cf. the above discussion on this question), especially for complex patterns, to better distinguish the groups from each other. Perceptually "temps courts" (roughly 150–300 milliseconds) correspond to a perception of "collection," while "temps longs" (roughly 450–900 milliseconds) correspond to **perception of "duration."** Thus rhythm perception is, temporally seen, a play between these two qualities, collection and duration.

Fraisse considers that these two distinct classes of time have their correspondence in the distinction between "long" and "short" syllables in prosody, and in the dashes and dots in the Morse alphabet. With regard to music, he points out that in musical scores most note values in many pieces of music belong to only two time classes in a 2:1 relation, e.g., half-note to quarter-note, or quarter-note to eighth-note. Examples of this, including 15 pieces of music, are given in Fraisse (1956, p. 107; or 1982, p. 172). However, he may go too far when he takes this as conclusive evidence for stating that "in reality a musical movement is based on only two notes—for example, the quaver and the crotchet, or the quaver and the pointed crochet, or two notes which are in a ratio of 2:3" (Fraisse,

1981, p. 237–238). He further says that the limitation to only two durations "seems to be related to our incapacity to discriminate in an absolute way more than two durations in the range of perceived durations (from 10 to 200 centiseconds)" (Fraisse, 1981, p. 219–220). This would seem incredible to most musicians.

Another group of the Paris studies dealt with the listener's **motor activities** during listening to sound sequences or music. As mentioned earlier, the movements were usually synchronized with certain elements, e.g., with the accented elements. However, the synchronization was not perfect in a physical sense: often the movement came somewhat before (say 30 milliseconds) the actual sound. Generally synchronization presupposes some kind of expectation about when the following sound(s) will come and gets more difficult for more complex or varying patterns. Synchronizing in ensemble music performance also builds on such expectations. Relevant to this, it has been noted (Rasch, 1979, 1981) that there is a slight asynchronization (30–50 milliseconds) between the tone onsets from different instruments when playing simultaneous tones according to the score. The asynchronization is not directly noticed but may contribute to separate the different instruments or parts from each other.

Fraisse, Oléron & Paillard (1953) and Paillard, Oléron & Fraisse (1953) studied motor activity during music listening, including electromyographic registrations. Some of the results were that the movements were stronger and more numerous for louder music, as well as for more "rhythmic" music (e.g., dances, marches), and that different parts of the body (hands, feet, legs, etc.) accompany different parts of the music (e.g., melody and accompaniment; cf. Stetson above). Oléron & Silver (1963) hypothesized that motor activity acts as a releaser of tension—and conversely that if the motor activity is made more difficult, e.g., by changes in tempo, frequent changes of meter, etc., this would result in an increased feeling of tension. Certainly this seems musically reasonable.

Fraisse repeatedly stresses the dependence of rhythm on our body movements: "La psychologie du rythme commence avec celle des mouvements humains ordonnés" (Fraisse, 1974, p. 10). The temporal structuring in rhythm originally goes back to pendular movements of our limbs and "variations" (doublings, halvings) of the corresponding intervals. Similar ideas are expressed by other authors, e.g., Wundt, who considered the pendular movements in walking as fundamental for rhythm.

Although most of the research described until now does not directly deal with rhythm in music, its relevance for musical rhythm should still be obvious. The phenomena and principles concerning grouping of sounds and its dependence on various factors, the limits put by the psychological present, the observations on overt movements and on kinaesthetics, etc. are also found in connection with real music, although often in much more complex and sometimes diffuse ways. Some of this can be seen in early investigations on the **characteristics of music performance.** Since registrations of music performances are technically very demanding, there are relatively few studies of this. Nevertheless, those which exist have shown interesting results. We will concentrate now on questions related to rhythm.

Sears (1902) succeeded in measuring the tone durations in organists' performance of five hymns. He used an electromechanical device which permitted the registration of the key depressions on a kymograph. Another technique used by Hartman (1932) was to make measurements on "player rolls," which were produced for reproduction by mechanical pianos. The original performance by a pianist was stored as a pattern of small apertures on a paper roll. The position and length of the apertures corresponded to the pitch (key) and duration of the tones, and thus measurements could be made directly on the roll. Both Sears and Hartmann found considerable variations in the durations of tones designated by the same note value in the score (in extreme cases a half-note performed "short" could be shorter than a quarter-note performed "long," etc.). They also discovered, not unexpectedly, that the presumed simple ratios like 2:1 (e.g., half-note to quarter note) or 3:1 (dotted half-note to quarter-note) rarely appeared in real performances.

Performance studies on a larger scale were undertaken by Carl Seashore and his co-workers at the Iowa University. Their numerous contributions, in fact the most comprehensive bulk of data on music performance even today, appear in several papers, especially in Seashore (1937) and in his textbook on music psychology (1938). They studied piano performance by filming the movements of the hammers and, like Hartmann, by measurements on player rolls. Singing and violin playing were studied by means of various phono-photographic techniques. With regard to rhythm their results amply confirmed the variability of durations and deviations from simple ratios found by Sears and Hartmann. Accents were shown to be complex functions of many variables (intensity, duration, pitch, melodic and harmonic factors) depending on the context. Chords on the piano were usually played asynchronously, for instance, with the melody or bass part leading.

Phrasing was made by temporal means, like retards toward the end of phrases and speeding up in the beginning of the next phrase, and also by various subpatterns of temporal deviations. Further dynamic means were used, e.g., by a crescendo starting from the beginning followed by a decrescendo during the latter part of the phrase.

Of course, these results cannot be isolated from many other results on intonation, dynamics, etc., but have to be considered in connection with these in the respective piece of music. There were considerable other inter-individual variations. A short survey of these early performance studies is given in Gabrielsson (1985).

A far more detailed account of empirical rhythm research was published earlier by the author (in Bengtsson, Gabrielsson, & Thorsén, 1969). This emphasized the dependence of this research on the ideas in the different psychological "schools" (structuralism, functionalism, behaviorism, Gestalt psychology) during the history of experimental psychology. A shorter version appeared in Gabrielsson (1979).

Different Aspects of Musical Rhythm

As stated earlier, rhythm is multidimensional. With regard to musical rhythm we may use the following simple descriptive model to clarify this (see Figure 2). To the left we have one or more musicians performing some music, in the middle we have the sound sequences generated by their instruments (a purely acoustical level), and to the right is the listener's rhythm response to this music. In this model rhythm thus may be defined as a **response to certain properties of the sound sequences** ("the music"). This response, in turn, can be conveniently sub-divided into **experiential, behavioral, and psycho-physiological aspects.**

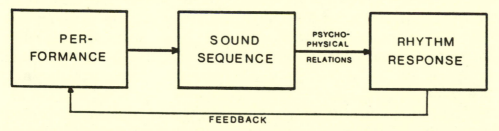

Figure 2. A general framework for empirical research on rhythm in music. (See further explanation in Gabrielsson, 1979, 1982.)

We may thus talk about different aspects of rhythm:

(1) **Rhythm as experience** refers to such things as perceived grouping, accents, pulse and tempo, various motion characters (such as swinging, dancing, walking, etc.), feelings of excitement, tension, calmness, release, etc.;

(2) **Rhythm as overt behavior** includes well-known things as tapping your feet, shaking your head, clapping your hands, and, of course, dancing (which has, in fact, been little treated in rhythm research);

(3) **Rhythm as psychophysiological response** refers to changes in breathing, heart rate, muscle activity, activity in the brain, etc.; that is, various physiological responses which may appear in connection with listening to music. Although this last type of response has been studied for quite a long time, there are few consistent results (see Dainow, 1977, for a short review and discussion of problems).

This division may be seen as one example of multidimensionality. It should be emphasized, however, that there are no strict limits between these categories: they are different aspects of the "same" phenomenon, the rhythm response, and are interrelated in extremely complex ways. The division may help us to analyze certain problems in a better way — but we shall not forget the spontaneous holistic nature of the rhythm response. Persons in it generally do not care about what should be considered as experience, behavior, or physiology.

Yet another example of the multidimensionality is the demonstration that experience of rhythm can be regarded as comprising **structural, motional, and emotional qualities** (Gabrielsson, 1973a, b, c; see also Gabrielsson, 1979, 1982, and Bengtsson & Gabrielsson, 1977). This result was obtained in a long series of experiments in which musicians (and non-musicians in some experiments) listened to different types of rhythm stimuli and judged them by various methods. The stimuli represented three categories: (a) monophonic stimuli performed on a drum (see Figure 3 for some examples); (b) polyphonic patterns generated by an electronic rhythm box which simulated dance rhythms as foxtrot, swing, samba, beguine, and others; and (c) real pieces of dance music taken from gramophone records (waltz, foxtrot, slowfox, swing, rock'n'roll, tango, samba, polska, hambo, and others — in all 20 pieces, also including a march).

The listeners judged the experienced rhythms with regard to their similarity with each other (the rhythms were presented in pairs, and the subjects rated their similarity on a certain scale), and in a large number

Figure 3. Examples of monophonic rhythm patterns used in one experiment in Gabrielsson (1973b). Metronomic tempo 108 quarter notes per minute, if not otherwise stated. (From *Scandinavian Journal of Psychology*, 1973, 14, p. 255.)

of adjective scales selected among hundreds of adjectives proposed by musicians in a previous study. The similarity ratings were analyzed according to a model for multidimensional scaling (Carroll & Chang, 1970), and the adjective ratings in a way similar to that used for the so-called semantic differential (see, for instance, Snider & Osgood, 1969). Both methods aim at discovering the dimensions (components) of a composite phenomenon—in this case, the dimensions within experience of rhythm.

The combined results of all experiments suggested a classification of the resulting dimensions into three categories:

(1) Dimensions related to the **experienced structure** of the rhythms, for example, meter, position and strength of accents, uniformity vs. variation, simplicity vs. complexity, and others. Similar structural dimensions were found by Motte-Haber (1968).

(2) Dimensions related to the **experienced motion character** of the rhythms,

such as overall rate (related to the density of all sound events), tempo (rate of the underlying beat), forward motion (e.g., in a galloping rhythm) and numerous other motion characters as swinging, dancing, walking, rocking, knocking, etc.

(3) Dimensions related to the **emotional character** of the rhythms, such as vital vs. dull, excited vs. calm, rigid vs. flexible, solemn vs. playful.

To get a closer understanding of the dimensions it is necessary to study the original papers (Gabrielsson, 1973 a–c). However, the main result is that **experience of musical rhythm includes structural, motional, and emotional aspects.** For any rhythm you may ask: How is this rhythm structured? What kind of motion character does it have? And how do you experience its emotional character? Again it must be emphasized that there are no strict limits between these categories; they are different, but interrelated, aspects of the rhythm experience. In a comment on this Fraisse (1974, p. 167; 1978, p. 246) noted that these three aspects agree with suggestions in some early discussions of rhythm (e.g., by Wundt). It is also interesting to see that the same three aspects resulted from a thorough survey of some 200 definitions of rhythm by various authors (Bengtsson, 1966).

It is obvious, however, that most research has concentrated on the structural aspects, especially on different types of grouping and the factors influencing them. The motional aspects have been studied with regard to overt movements (e.g., synchronization) and kinaesthetic sensations, but the experienced motion character and the emotional aspects of different rhythms have received relatively little attention from an empirical point of view. Some of these questions may appear in other investigations dealing with expressions in music, for instance, those by Hevner (1936). She presented two versions of the "same" piece of music, one with "firm" rhythm and the other with "flowing" rhythm. The results of her listeners' selection among given adjectives indicated that "firm rhythms are vigorous and dignified; flowing rhythms are happy, graceful, dreamy and tender . . . " (Hevner, 1936, p. 268). However, the definitions were vague and Hevner was well aware of the difficulties in arranging two versions so that they should differ with regard to only one variable at a time.

In the following sections we will look at more recent contributions (and some of their predecessors) to rhythm research, and use the distinction between structural and motional-emotional aspects for our disposition.

Research on Structural Aspects of Rhythm

The conditions for perceptual grouping of auditory sequences have continued to be a central question. The modern approaches are somewhat different, and the technical facilities are more sophisticated. Rhythm perception is considered as an example of **pattern perception**, and principles from Gestalt psychology often appear. The sound sequences are frequently composed of only two different elements (e.g., two different pitches, or two different intensities, durations, spectra, etc.), but the order of these elements is varied in many different ways. If the two elements are designated by 1 and 0, respectively, one sequence may be 11001100, another one 10110010, still another 01110010, etc. Each sequence is repeated many times in immediate succession, and the subjects indicate in some way the perceived patterning. One of the elements (say 1) may be perceived as figure, the other (0) as ground. Many results could be interpreted in terms of a "**run principle**," which says that the longest string of the figure element (1) begins the perceived pattern, and a "**gap principle**," according to which the longest string of ground elements (0) would terminate the pattern. Depending on the specific sequence, these principles may lead to the same result, or they may conflict, in which case other factors have to be taken into account. The patterning is perceived directly at higher rates. At slower rates, however, the listener's patterning is much more of a cognitive, intellectualized process (compare the "psychological present" mentioned earlier). Among many studies on these questions may be mentioned those by Garner & Gottwald (1968), Royer & Garner (1970), Preusser (1972), and Handel (1974). Reviews and discussions appear in Fraisse (1978, 1982) and Jones (1978).

Although these works do not at all deal with music, they reveal a lot about how many factors may affect the perceived grouping. A step towards music is taken in the studies by Handel & Oshinsky (1981) and Handel & Lawson (1983). They used polyrhythms, such as 2×3 (that is, one string of two, and another with three, equidistant sounds per pattern, the duration of both patterns is the same), 3×4, 2×5, and even with three strings as $3 \times 4 \times 5$, or $2 \times 3 \times 7$. They further varied rate, pitch, intensity, and duration in various constellations. The subjects were instructed to tap along with the perceived rhythm. Analysis of the tappings revealed that the perceived meter or beat may be affected by all factors varied, often in complex interactions. The results are thus intricate, and it is stressed that the listener's interpretation of the rhythm is highly dependent on the actual context of all relevant factors. It is also pointed out that, contrary to what many believe, rhythm does not remain invariant across changes in tempo.

Although such results may be disappointing with regard to the prospects of constructing a general theory of rhythm, they are no surprise to researchers trying to understand the complexities found in registrations of music performance (see Seashore above and later). In fact, Handel & Lawson (1983) generally stress the importance of using stimuli which permit the intricacies of rhythmic interpretation to emerge.

This point of view finds support among many musicologists, who often find the stimuli used in experiments too simple and uninteresting with regard to real music. In fact it is a well-known and perennial problem how to balance the requirements on careful experimental control on one hand against the desirability of using realistic stimuli on the other hand. An influential musicological text on rhythm is that by Cooper & Meyer (1960). It is clearly oriented towards the structural aspects, e.g., "to experience rhythm is to group separate sounds into structured patterns" (p. 1). They postulate that there are five basic rhythmic groupings, denoted by terms taken from prosody: iamb (⌣–), anapest (⌣ ⌣–), trochee (–⌣), dactyl (–⌣⌣) and amphibrach (⌣–⌣). These are certainly used in many other texts as well, but not as consistently as they are used by Cooper & Meyer to analyze rhythmic groupings in different meters and on different levels. Their method essentially means that they present the score of the music and add their analysis in terms of the above designations. The reader is supposed to be able to imagine how these examples sound and to judge the appropriateness of the proposed analyses for himself. A kind of systematic variation is introduced in the sense that they suggest certain changes in a given example, and proceed to analyze the consequences of such manipulations. This is made in a very pedagogical way, for instance, in their very first example "Twinkle Little Star," which is given in the original version and then in different variants intended to show the effects of changes in duration, melody, accompaniment, instrumentation, etc.

The examples range from simple tunes up to movements of a symphony, but the basic units (iamb, anapest, etc.) remain the same. However, the authors have to supplement them with other units (e.g., inverted trochee) and various qualifying conditions, so that their number of symbols in the analyses increases considerably. The obvious criticism of this approach is the attempt at reducing all groupings to the five mentioned above.

They are not enough to accurately discriminate between the many fine shades of rhythm (Yeston, 1976, p. 24; Clynes & Walker, 1982, p. 192), nor is the definition of these units and their designation unambiguous (Bengtsson, Gabrielsson, & Thorsén, 1969).

Another objection concerns their attempt at extending the use of these kinds of rhythmic groupings to much larger formats than usual. Consider, for instance, how they are applied (in one of the simplest examples) at successively higher levels (levels 1–4) (see Figure 4). Although this melody comprises only 16 bars, it is very doubtful that we experience a grouping like that indicated by level 4 in the figure. This exceeds the limit of the psychological present, and one would rather talk about "conceived rhythm," that is, "the rhythm is . . . inferred from a mental construction" (Fraisse, 1982, p. 150), or perhaps "rationalized perception" (Garner & Gottwald, 1968, p. 109). This is, of course, even more the case when similar analyses are made for still larger pieces, e.g., the "rhythmic analysis" of the first movement in Beethoven's Symphony No. 8 (Cooper & Meyer, p. 203). It seems much more reasonable to use concepts like "structure" or "form" for such purposes rather than add more to the already large confusion concerning the rhythm concept.

Figure 4. The analysis proposed for the tune "Au clair de la lune." (Reproduced by permission from G.W. Cooper & L.B. Meyer "The Rhythmic Structure of Music," University of Chicago Press, 1960. p. 144. Copyright 1960 by The University of Chicago.)

Despite these criticisms, this book is important reading for any researcher on musical rhythm. It provides many instructive examples of insightful analyses from which the experimentalist can both learn and get a fruitful challenge. This may also be said about the more recent book by Yeston (1976). His theoretical starting point is taken from the music theorist Henrich Schenker, a much cited authority nowadays, who developed a system for uncovering the structure of "deeper levels" underlying the structure of the notated piece of music. The notation represents a "foreground," and the analysis proceeds according to certain principles to discover "middlegrounds" and finally a fundamental "background" which constitutes the real core of the piece (see further, for instance, the article on Schenker in **Grove's Dictionary**). Yeston applies similar principles with regard to rhythm, describing **how the rhythmic "foregrounds" are products of deeper rhythmic strata** (levels) in interaction. He discusses concepts as meter and syncopation in terms of such interactions, and makes a distinction between "rhythmic consonance," in which the rate of any level can be expressed as a multiplication or division by an integer greater than 1 of the rate of any other level, and "rhythmic dissonance," in which this is not the case (e.g., in polyrhythms as those used by Handel & Lawson above).

Yeston provides instructive examples to explain these concepts (e.g., the beginning of Mozart's "Eine Kleine Nachtmusik" as illustrating "rhythmic consonance"—a term which may not be the most apt). Throughout he emphasizes the importance of pitch and melodic factors for rhythmic structuring, which are rather apparent in much music but have been little investigated in empirical work.

One fundamental point in rhythmic structuring is how we **perceive the beat or the meter** in music. This is sometimes apparent from overt behavior; for instance, how you tap your feet may indicate how you feel the beat. It should be noted, however, that the beat (pulse) can often be perceived at two, or even more, levels, e.g., one at a rapid rate (corresponding to, say, quarter notes in a score) and another at half this rate (half notes). Not being able to grasp the beat at all often causes much tension (cf. Oléron & Silver above), and the reader may have experienced what a release it is when one succeeds in getting hold of it.

However, little is known about this process, as pointed out by Longuet-Higgins and his co-workers (Longuet-Higgins, 1976, 1979; Steedman, 1977; Longuet-Higgins & Lee, 1982, 1983). Their approach in investigating these problems involves postulating various "rules," based on assumptions about the relevant perceptual processes, and implementing these rules in a computer program. This program then operates on musical scores (that is, lists of notes, not actual sounds) to see if the program succeeds in revealing the correct meter (as given in the score). The rules build on information provided by durational and/or melodic factors in the music, and have been applied, among many other examples, to the fugue subjects in J. S. Bach's "The Well-Tempered Clavier."

The listener, whose activity is simulated by the program, is seen as an active processor of the available information, starting to build hypotheses about the beat or meter already after the very first notes (the beginning is crucial, of course) and extending or revising this hypothesis in light of the following notes. The computer program often succeeds in finding the correct meter, thus confirming the rules and underlying assumptions, but the mistakes are also instructive in showing factors which have not been given enough attention. It is also pointed out that in real music performance the performer may use various available means (depending on which instrument) in articulation, phrasing, etc. to make the intended structure clear to the listener. This is especially important in ambiguous cases (see Bengtsson, 1974, for some examples). There are also examples in which the perceived meter may not agree with the notated meter, e.g., the well-known theme from the Finale of Schubert's Great C Major Symphony (see Figure 5).

Figure 5. Theme from the Finale of Schubert's Great C major Symphony. Most listeners who do not know about Schubert's notation (3) will probably perceive the grouping (bars) as indicated by alternatives Nos. 1 or 2. (Reproduced by permission from Bengtsson, 1974, in "Hamburger Jahrbuch für Musikwissenschaft, Band I," Verlag der Musikalienhandlung Karl Dieter Wagner, Hamburg.)

A related work is that by Povel (1981), who proposed a "beat-based" model for perception of temporal sequences. That is, the listener first achieves a segmentation of the sequence into equal intervals, and time intervals shorter than these beat intervals are expressed as sub-divisions of the beat interval. However, the number of sub-divisions may be limited to a few "simple" cases, as intervals in 1:1 or 1:2 relations.

Research on Motional and Emotional Aspects of Rhythm

Motional and emotional aspects of rhythm experience are by their very nature much more elusive to analysis and investigation than the structural aspects, and may also require other techniques in order to be properly studied—at least for certain questions. We will look at some different attempts in this direction.

Among the motional aspects **tempo** may be said to be the most familiar. For most pieces of music there is a more or less precise indication of the proper tempo like a metronomic value (e.g., $\quad$ = 100, that is, 100 quarter notes per minute) or a more general prescription like allegro, moderato, adagio, etc. or their equivalents in other languages and in the everyday conversation among musicians. The tempo is very important for the listener's impression of the music, and frequently the difference in tempo is what you notice first, when you compare different performances of the "same" piece of music.

However, there are problems of definition with this seemingly well-established concept. How rapidly you perceive the music to be is not a simple function of a given metronomic value or the like, but also depends on many other factors such as the density of the sound events (number of tones per unit of time), the specific structure of the rhythm pattern, melodic and harmonic progressions etc. These dependences are still little studied and present many problems for proper investigations (see Motte-Haber, 1968; Behne, 1972; Gabrielsson, 1973b,c). It seems preferable to make a distinction between (perceived) tempo and rate (rapidity, speed), so that tempo designates the perceived rate of the beat or pulse, while the latter terms refer to the "total" impression of speed (Bengtsson, Gabrielsson, & Thorsén, 1969); note also that **metronomic** tempo and **perceived** tempo may be different. The example given in Figure 6 illustrates a case in which one at the same time may perceive a slow tempo (the pulse in this "Adagio molto" movement may be felt at quarter note or eighth note level) and a very rapid motion due to the high density of tones in the upper part.

As long as one deals with stimuli like metronome clicks, short sound pulses and the like this distinction is less important. Madsen (1979) found that discrimination of rate of metronome clicks was better for decreases (slowing down) than for increases, and that the absolute identification of rate in number of clicks per minute was not especially good. Wapnik (1980), using metronome clicks as well as music, generally concluded that perception of change in rate was not very precise. When real music is used as stimulus, an important problem is how to vary its rate. This is especially discussed by Behne (1972) who used both a device for "mechanical" speeding up or slowing down of recorded pieces and real performances of the "same" piece in different tempi. This difference may

Figure 6. From the second movement, Adagio molto, of Beethoven's Piano Sonata Opus 10, No. 1, in C minor. (Reproduced by permission from "Beethoven, Klaviersonaten, Band I," G. Henle Verlag, München-Duisburg, 1952.)

be crucial because the way of performing rhythm may be different at different tempi (see some evidence below).

Behne also found that his listeners judged the tempo of certain pieces of music as adequate within a relatively wide tempo range (expressed in metronomic values), which suggests that the existence of a single "correct" tempo for a piece of music is probably an exception. Furthermore, the listeners' judgments of the tempo deviated from the composer's idea about tempo (the pieces were composed especially for the investigation); the listeners' tempo preferences tended towards a midway region in comparison with the composer's intentions.

With regard to the emotional aspects, older investigations by Hevner (1937) and Rigg (1940) indicated, not unexpectedly, that higher tempo was associated with judgments like "pleasant," "happy," "exciting," "restless," and slower tempi roughly with the opposite judgments. Partly similar results were also found by Motte-Haber (1968), Behne (1972), and Gabrielsson (1973b); but the question is complex for several reasons, among them the possible dependence on other factors in the music.

Stability or **variability in performed tempo** within and between perform-ances of the same piece may be influenced by many factors, from purely acoustical ones (reverberation, etc.) to subtle questions concerning the musical expression. Wagner's (1974) experiments indicated highly stable tempo in different renditions of the same piece in case of a highly competent musician, the conductor Herbert von Karajan (performing on the piano). He also demonstrated almost exact absolute judgments of tempo (compare above). Clynes and Walker (1982) showed that the total duration for the performance of the same piece of music can be very similar even over long periods of time (examples from Toscanini and Clynes); however, old data by Guttman (1932) seem to demonstrate the opposite as well. Clynes and Walker (1982) also found, that "mental performance" of a piece of music (thinking the music) was in most cases slower than a real performance.

Although the metronomic indication of tempo is very exact, there are often considerable deviations from this during the course of the music in a real performance. The extent and direction of the deviations depend on many factors. For instance, in Viennese waltzes there are marked changes of tempo. This was studied in detail in connection with a synthesis of an excerpt from the famous waltz in "Die Fledermaus" by Johann Strauss, Jr. (Bengtsson & Gabrielsson, 1983). As a consequence it was proposed to make distinctions between "(a) the abstract **mean tempo**, calculated as the total duration of a music section divided by the number of beats in the same section; (b) the **main tempo**, being the prevailing (and intended) tempo obtained when initial and final retardations as well as more amorphous caesurae are deleted; (c) **local tempi**, maintained only for short periods but perceptually differing; and (d) **beat rate** . . . for describing minor fluctuations, which may not be perceptible as such" (p. 50).

Besides tempo there are many other motion characters. The importance of giving the rhythm or music its **proper motion character** may be illustrated by what the famous jazz musician, Count Basie, once said: "All we do is to make this music swing." "Swing" in jazz and dance music is one of the best known examples of motion character. Each dance is associated with a specific motion character, sometimes hinted at by its name (e.g., rock'n'roll, twist). A march must have a special motion character, and so should a Viennese waltz as studied in many papers (Bengtsson, Gabrielsson, & Thorsén, 1969; Bengtsson, 1974; Bengtsson & Gabrielsson, 1977, 1983).

The motion character of a piece of music (not only dance music!) is often indicated in a very general way, e.g., by a title (waltz, march, minuet, alla turca, etc.) or by designations as andante, agitato, grazioso, precipitando, pesante, etc., to take but a few of the common Italian designations. The designations often refer to a mixture of motional and emotional characters, like appassionato, con brio, capriccioso, dolce, energico, furioso, maestoso, morendo, tranquillo, etc. The performer has to learn how to bring about these qualities, and that is a learning which depends much on listening to different kinds of music. The musical score does not tell him very much; and in some cases there may not even be a score at all.

Investigations on motion characters of rhythms by verbal means (adjective ratings) are found in Motte-Haber (1968) and Gabrielsson (1973b). For example, 20 pieces of dance music were used by Gabrielsson, and among the resulting dimensions were "vital-gay-rapid vs. dull" (contrasting, for instance, mambo and samba against slowfox), "rocking-graceful-flexible vs. knocking-stamping" (e.g., some waltzes versus a march), and "excited-intense-aggressive vs. calm-soft" (pop, rock vs. slow waltz, schottis). Obviously the results may depend very much on the specific sample of pieces, and verbal descriptions represent a kind of approximation to the investigated qualities.

Francès (1958, p. 320) selected some pieces of music whose titles indicated some kind of movement, and asked the listeners to describe the movement (if perceived) by words and in drawings. Practically all subjects described movements which could be related to certain structures in the music. A selection of the drawings is given, which seems to reflect various movements, but there are several difficulties in the interpretation of the drawings as discussed by Francès.

Recently Clynes & Walker (1982) proposed new methods for studying the motional-emotional qualities of rhythm. The methods are based on Clynes' earlier work on expression of emotion using a pressure measuring instrument he called a **sentograph** (Clynes, 1977; Clynes & Nettheim, 1982; and earlier papers). The subjects were instructed to press with a finger on a pressure transducer (the sentograph), which is sensitive to vertical and horizontal pressure. It was found that the "expression" of different emotions (joy, hate, anger, love, etc.) on the sentograph resulted in different and characteristic patterns for each emotion. Moreover they seemed to be cross-culturally valid, indicating a biological basis. The same technique is now used to study the "motor output" of auditory and musical rhythm. For instance, the subject listens to repeated two-pulse patterns with certain characteristics regarding durations and amplitudes and "follows" them by pressing on the sentograph. The resulting "motor pulses" for various cases differ in general form, in rise and fall time, etc.

In studies of rhythm in ethnic music, rock and blues, an attempt was first made to shape a sound pulse that should be representative for the rhythm in the respective type of music. The assumption was that there is a "specific (nonsound) time form . . . which gives rise to the character of the musical rhythm," and that "this time form can be represented as amplitude modulated tones of a single sinusoidal frequency, the sound pulse" (Clynes & Walker, 1982, p. 193). These sound pulses were stored on a separate track of a tape, and the sounding music on another track of the same tape. It is said that listening to the music together with the adequate sound pulse reinforced the musical experience, but a pairing with a wrong sound pulse detracted from it.

To test the adequacy in another way, listeners were instructed to press the sentograph when listening to the music alone and also to the sound pulses alone. The resulting motor pulses for the music and for the corresponding sound pulses seemed to agree reasonably well. The form of the motor pulses was then tentatively interpreted with regard to emotional expression, using the earlier results from sentographic registration of emotional expression.

Another original contribution by Clynes is the study of **composers' "inner pulse"** (Clynes, 1977, 1983; Clynes & Walker, 1982). This may be characterized as a kind of motional-emotional quality, which is specific for different composers—Mozart, Beethoven, Schubert, and others. Its meaning is, of course, difficult or impossible to convey by words, but experienced listeners will generally agree that there is something special in the "flow" of the music by different composers.

The idea is, in fact, not new. Clynes refers to a well-known and much discussed work by the German musicologist, Gustav Becking (1928) who, in turn, relied on earlier German contributions by Sievers, Rutz, and Nohl. Becking described how he wanted a method to bring forth diffusely felt characteristics of different composers, especially the difference between Mozart and Beethoven. He got the idea to use "accompanying movements" ("Mitbewegungen," "Begleitbewegungen") to the music using his hands and holding a small stick. It should not be like conducting the music—on the contrary, you must subordinate yourself to the music, let yourself be conducted by the music. By means of this method Becking was able to describe the down-beat, up-beat, and the complete "Taktfigur" for Mozart and Beethoven, as well as for many other composers. For instance, the down-beat for Mozart is "smooth and rapid" ("glatt und schnell"); for Beethoven, however, it is "vaulted/round" as suggested in Figure 7 (the thickness indicates the exerted pressure at different moments of the beat).

Clynes tried to study the "inner pulse" of composers "by thinking the music and expressing the pulse by 'conducting' on the sentograph with

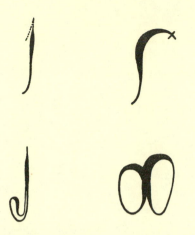

Figure 7. (Upper row) The down-beat ("Niederschlag") for Mozart (left) and Beethoven (right). (Lower row). The "Taktfigur" for Mozart (left) and Beethoven (right). (From G. Becking "Der musikalische Rhythmus als Erkenntnisquelle," Augsburg, Benno Filser, 1928.)

finger pressure" (Clynes, 1983, p. 92). Some results for Mozart and Beethoven are given in Figure 8, which show certain similarities with Becking's findings (although the ways of representation are different), e.g., earlier down-beat for Mozart than for Beethoven.

Clynes further attempted to translate the "inner pulse" into a sound pulse by generating sinusoidal tones with an amplitude envelope shaped to fit the respective composer's pulse. These are stored on a separate track of tape and may be presented together with the music. Numerous sound examples are given in Clynes (1983) and Clynes and Walker (1982), referring to Mozart, Beethoven, Schubert, Chopin, and Brahms. The "inner pulse" itself is not a sound; "it is a specific command configuration that directs . . . inner gesture, which affects the sound in a corresponding manner" (1983, p. 96).

These original measures of the pulse involved translations into movement reflecting its nature. But in recent work with computer controlled music shaping, Clynes (1983, 1985) has reported to have now determined for the first time how this musical pulse systematically affects each note of the music in detail: in terms of specific duration and amplitude deviations, combining their effect in a "pulse matrix." This work is described in the chapter by Clynes in this volume.

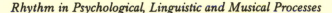

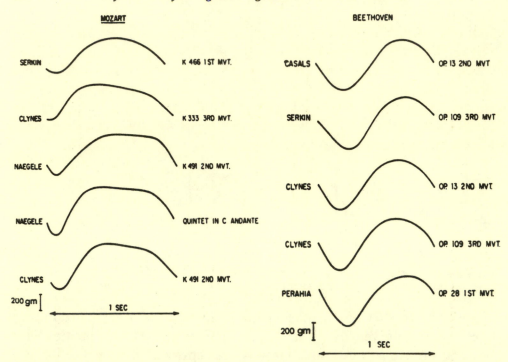

Figure 8. Essentic form of the "inner pulse" for Mozart (left) and Beethoven (right) resulting from "conducting" on the sentograph while thinking the music in real time without sound. (From Clynes, 1983, in J. Sundberg (Ed.) "Studies of Music Performance," Publications issued by the Royal Swedish Academy of Music, No. 39, Stockholm, 1983, p. 93–94.)

Recent Studies on Performance of Rhythm

Earlier described studies on performance of music revealed large variability in performance and various deviations from presumed properties according to the musical notation (e.g., deviations from simple ratios like 2:1, 3:1, etc., fluctuations in tempo, various dynamic deviations, and so on). To "explain" these facts, Seashore stated a principle concerning "deviations from the regular" as an art principle, e.g., "The unlimited resources for vocal and instrumental art lie in artistic deviation from the pure, the true, the exact, the perfect, the rigid, the even, and the precise. This deviation from the exact is, on the whole, the medium for the creation of the beautiful—for the conveying of emotion" (cited from H. Seashore, 1937, p. 155). Similar ideas were expressed in Germany by von Kries (1926) and Truslit (1938). They both stated that mathematical accuracy in performance results in dead and machine-like music, and that it is the deviations from such accuracy, which provides life to music: "Diese feinen Abstufungen in den Verhältnissen der Zeitdauer und der Stärke der Töne, die der Künstler durch die Tätigkeit seines Gestaltens hineinbringt, sind es vor allem, durch die er aus dem Ton lebendige Musik erstehen lässt" (Truslit, 1938, p. 29). Truslit generally meant that these phenomena in music performance are reflections of "inner motion" (cf. "inner gesture" above), and that "Bewegung ist das Urelement der Musik" (p. 53). He proposed three basic forms of musical motion and illustrated them by means of sound examples and measurements of durations and amplitudes in these.

A common idea for these authors is that "deviations" from constancy, exactness, etc. are necessary to give music life and expression. Rhythm is, of course, a central component in this context, and it seems that the above statements mainly refer to the motional and emotional aspects of rhythm, but they may apply to the structural aspects as well—there are complex inter-relations between them all. Recently the interest in the "microstructure" of music performance has increased very much, and the technical facilities for accurate registrations of performances are continuously improving. Bengtsson, Gabrielsson and Thorsén (1969), Bengtsson (1974), Bengtsson and Gabrielsson (1977, 1980, 1983), Gabrielsson (1974), Gabrielsson, Bengtsson and Gabrielsson (1983) have presented extensive registrations of music performed on different instruments, mainly monophonic but also polyphonic. The analysis is concentrated on various duration variables in the performance, especially the duration from the onset of a tone to the onset of the following tone, with a view to compare the durations in real performances with the corresponding durations in a purely mechanical performance (such as in music boxes and the like). The general hypothesis is that live music performance shows various deviations or systematic variations (SYVAR) in relation to a "mechanical norm." These variations are different in different types of music and may also be different for different performers.

The results reveal many SYVAR at all levels, from the within-beat level up to the phrase level. Patterns within beat as ♩♩ (mechanically 1:1), ♪.♩ (3:1), ♪.♩ (7:1) are performed with various deviations from the corresponding mechanical values. For instance, the ♩.♩ pattern may be performed "soft" (that is, with a ratio less than 3:1) or "sharp" (ratio higher than 3:1), depending on the musical context, and often the pattern becomes softer during the progression of the phrase. Double dottings are often performed with ratios much lower than the mechanical 7:1 ratio. Patterns as ♩ ♩ and ♩ ♪ in ¾ and ⁶⁄₈ meters are frequently performed with a ratio around 1.7:1 or 1.8:1 instead of 2:1. At the beat level, a well-known example of deviations is the performance of the accompaniment in Viennese waltzes such that the first beat is shortened and the second beat lengthened; another example may be lengthening of the third beat in "Oh my darling Clementine." The durations of the different bars in a phrase often reflect a performance type like slow start—accelerating—retarding towards the end. An illustration of deviations is given in Figure 9 for a favorite example in much music literature, the theme in Mozart's Piano Sonata in A major.

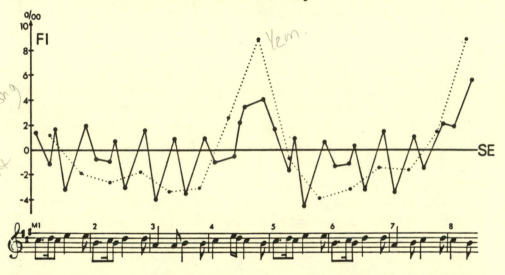

Figure 9. Deviations from mechanical performance in a pianist's performance of the theme in Mozart's Piano Sonata in A major, for each tone (black circles joined by the wholedrawn profile) and for half-measures (dotted profile). Mechanical performance is represented by the straight horizontal line at 0. The deviations are expressed in per mille of the total duration of the theme; a deviation upwards means lengthening, deviation downwards shortening, of the corresponding tone in relation to mechanical performance. Note the zig-zag pattern for sequences of quarter note + eighth note (= shortening of the quarter note, lengthening of the eighth note) and the retardations in the middle (bar no. 4) and towards the end. (From Gabrielsson, Bengtsson & Gabrielsson, 1983, Scandinavian Journal of Psychology, 1983, 24, p. 201.)

The deviations may relate to various structural aspects of the rhythm experience, e.g., they may help in clarifying the intended meter, accents, sub-divisions, etc. However, the main impression is that they essentially affect motional and emotional qualities. The perceived structure is often resistant to changes or deviations; for instance, a long-short relation like ♩ ♩ may vary as much as from 1.6:1 to 2.2:1 (depending on the context) without changing the perceived long-short relation. The change is rather noticed as a difference in the motion character (the "flow") and associated emotional quality. Another example is the "too early second beat" in the accompaniment in Viennese waltzes; it does not upset the basic tripartition of the bar, but it is of fundamental importance for the special motion character of such waltzes. Sound examples illustrating this are found in Bengtsson and Gabrielsson (1983). Generally the investigation of the relations between performance and experience may proceed in an interplay between analysis of live performances and synthesis of stimuli, which "imitate" different characteristics of the live performances and are judged by listeners regarding musical quality (Gabrielsson, 1985).

In Exeter in England very detailed studies of **piano performance** have been made possible by providing a Bechstein grand piano with photocell sensors and electronic circuits by which accurate registrations can be made of durations and intensities in performance. Shaffer (1980, 1981) has investigated various pianists' performances on this piano with special interest in the "motor programming" underlying the performance. Piano performance is thus studied as an example of highly skilled motor performance; another example of that, also studied by Shaffer, is typing. In the 1981 paper Shaffer reports three pianists' performances of a Chopin study (playing three in the right hand against four in the left), a Bach fugue, and a Bulgarian dance from Bartok's "Mikrokosmos," respectively. Detailed results on timing and dynamics are given for the Chopin study, in a form somewhat similar to that in Figure 9. The remaining two pieces are more generally surveyed, concentrating on certain questions. Numerous examples of "deviations" are discussed in relation to the score and especially in relation to the motor performance. With regard to the latter, the results revealed independence of the two hands in dynamics as well as in timing; that is, different dynamic levels can be maintained by each hand, and the timing of the hands (e.g., in the 3×4 polyrhythm) is at the same time both independent (e.g., the right hand can make excursions in time from the left hand) and coordinated in a flexible way. Although these facts may not be surprising to the experienced musician, they have not been observed enough in earlier motor research (often with unskilled subjects) and they necessitate new ideas about motor achievement and the underlying motor programming. This is, of course, of great interest for rhythm research.

Using the same piano Clarke (1982, 1985) studied the performance of piano music composed by Erik Satie. In the first paper dealing with

"Vexations" by Satie, a piece which shall be repeated over and over again for hours of playing, he demonstrated both the existence of "expressive deviations" from a mechanical interpretation of the score, and also that these were different for different tempi of the performance (cf. above on tempo). In the second paper Clarke reported a detailed study of a pianist's performance of Satie's "Gnossienne No. 5" with special emphasis on the many different and changing sub-divisions within beat which appear in this piece. The relative adherence to or deviation from the notated patterns is discussed in relation to the structure and provides an outline for a model on "expressive rhythmic performance." It seems that this concept relates to what has been called here the motional and emotional aspects of rhythm experience.

Also Sloboda (1983) used the Exeter piano to study which means pianists use to convey the proper impression of meter to the listener, thus concentrating on structural aspects. Notes carrying major stress were played louder or more legato (cf. similar results in Gabrielsson, 1974), and on the whole more advanced pianists used the available means of varying durations and intensities in a more pronounced way than less advanced pianists.

In the earlier mentioned study with von Karajan, Wagner (1974) also used direct registration from a grand piano by another technique. This study included a very interesting comparison between an intentionally "exact" performance and a musically adequate interpretation. The "exact" version showed smaller deviations and a certain acceleration in tempo. The "musical" version displayed much more expressive deviations, but nevertheless the mean tempo was practically constant. Povel (1977) used an oscilloscope to measure temporal relations in three performers' interpretation of the famous first prelude in C major in "The Well-Tempered Clavier" by J.S. Bach and found considerable individual differences with regard to patterns of deviations.

Unlike the foregoing studies, the works by Clynes (1983) and Sundberg, Frydén and Askenfelt (1983) generally are not directly founded on registrations of real performances. Rather they start from listening-based hypotheses regarding characteristics of good performances, and then synthesize examples in accordance with (or deviating from) the hypotheses to see whether they sound convincing or not. Clynes illustrates his ideas for many examples in Western art music, initially using only sinusoidals for timbre but varying amplitudes (in level as well as in envelope) and durations in accordance with various hypotheses. Spe-

cial care is taken with regard to the amplitude shapes, and the procedures include Clynes' findings regarding the "inner pulse" of different
composers. Several music sound examples are provided for the listener's
own judgment (see further in Clynes, this volume). Sundberg et al. also
state various hypotheses ("rules") concerning how the durations and
intensities of various units should be modified (in comparison with a
mechanical performance) depending on pitch level, melodic and harmonic progression, phrasing, etc. Syntheses are generated to illustrate
adequate performances according to the rules, as well as exaggerated
applications and purely mechanical performances. Sound examples are
given on the same record as for Clynes (1983) and Bengtsson & Gabrielsson
(1983).

It is evident that the micro-structure in music performance is considered to be extremely important for the listener's impression of the music,
not the least with regard to the various aspects of rhythm experience.

Some Other Questions

There are many other topics on rhythm in music, which could be
discussed. However, we will only give brief comments to some of them.

In **music education** rhythm is, of course, generally important. It is
especially emphasized in the eurhythmics school founded by Dalcroze
(1921, 1980), but also in other well-known systems in music pedagogy, as
the Orff school, the Kodaly system, the Carabo-Cone method, and others
(see Mark, 1978, for a survey). The very concrete dealing with rhythm in
these settings in terms of body movements to sound and music—walking,
jumping, running, bending, clapping hands, playing various games, etc.
—provides a fundamental sensori-motor understanding of many musical
concepts (tempo, pulse, accents, grouping, phrasing, dynamics, and, of
course, rhythm in general), even long before the verbal learning of such
concepts. It is tempting to believe that this also naturally contributes to
the understanding of the motional and emotional aspects of rhythm,
which tend to be suppressed in rhythm training which is solely based on
reading of notated patterns (see Rider and Eagle, this volume). In the
latter case mainly structural aspects are emphasized—correct meter, accents,
exactness in sub-divisions, etc.—which may lead to certainly very "exact"
but still lifeless and dull performance of rhythm. A proper balance
between structural and motional-emotional aspects seems to be the best
alternative for rhythm training. We may also note that most of so-called

rhythm tests included in various test batteries, from Seashore and onwards (see Shuter-Dyson & Gabriel, 1981, for a review), concentrate on structural properties and therefore may neglect other important aspects of rhythm.

With regard to **development** it has been shown that young babies are able to discriminate between different rhythm patterns (Demany, McKenzie, & Vurpillot, 1977; see Fraisse, 1982, p. 161 for further investigations). Various rhythmic movements may be observed in young children (rocking, foot kicking, head banging, etc.), and the repertoire of such movements is expanded. Some children move early in synchrony with the pulse or other events in music; but for most children, a consistent synchronization does not appear until relatively late in preschool age (Moog, 1968). On the other hand, Moog also observed that many young children adjusted their movements to the music in other ways, e.g., with regard to tempo and in various attempts to realize what they heard by movements, even as "expressive dance." In terms of our discussion here, this may indicate attentiveness to the motional-emotional aspects of the music (see also Condon, this volume).

In **music therapy** rhythm is usually considered as the fundamental component in music and as the most effective means in many treatments (see further the chapter by Rider & Eagle in this volume). One of the American pioneers in music therapy eloquently described the beneficial effects of rhythm and coined the expression "Rhythm: The Organizer and Energizer" (Gaston, 1968, p. 17). This seems to agree well with our distinction between structural ("organizer") and motional-emotional ("energizer") aspects of rhythm.

Regarding **theories of musical rhythm** we can briefly state that there is no comprehensive or generally accepted theory of rhythm, neither in music nor in other fields. What is sometimes called theories of rhythm in textbooks are in fact only rather loose hypotheses, and they refer only to limited parts of the whole complex. Considering the multidimensional character of rhythm, and the range of different phenomena to which the rhythm concept is applied (cf. the contributions to this volume), this state of affairs is not surprising. With regard to auditory-musical rhythm we have seen attempts at relating the structural aspects to principles from Gestalt psychology, but also to kinaesthetics and motor functioning. The "origin of rhythm" has been sought in the rate and regularity of the heart-beats (mother's heart-beats are felt by us even before birth), the breathing cycle, various electrophysiological processes in the nervous system, and not the least in the pendular movements of our limbs (e.g., in walking) or other body movements. All of these candidates are more or less plausible. For further comments see Fraisse (1956, 1974, 1982), Bengtsson, Gabrielsson, and Thorsén (1969), Lundin (1967), and Davies (1978).

That rhythm is somehow deeply rooted in the construction and functioning of the body seems beyond any doubt, and the apparent and multi-faceted connections between movements and rhythm speak very much for the movement alternative (which does not mean exclusion of other alternatives). Rhythm and music are sometimes seen as examples of "motion" in a general sense, also as "inner motion" or "inner gesture," and there are authors like Truslit (1938) who eloquently pleads for the intimate relation between music and motion. These questions are, of course, intricate (not the least in terms of definitions of the used concepts) and will have to await much discussion and investigation before approaching something like an answer.

In recent years there has been much interest in the possible **hemispheric specialization** of different components of music, including rhythm. Although many investigations seem to indicate left hemisphere connection with rhythm (e.g., Borchgrevink, 1982), the results are not unambiguous (see the reviews by Gates & Bradshaw, 1977; Bradshaw & Nettleton, 1981). The sometimes conflicting results may depend on many factors. One of them may be that rhythm often is taken as a unitary concept, which it is not. A more careful definition of the concept and observation of the different possible aspects of rhythm may prove to be of value in such investigations, as well as in many others.

Concluding Remarks

It is hoped that this survey, although incomplete, gives a feeling for the fascinating and intriguing phenomena of music rhythm. We are still far from an understanding of these phenomena, but rhythm research is now again in an active and exciting stage after a certain period of depression. New and unexpected ideas are launched, and there are bold revivals of some old speculations. We still need much more of interdisciplinary contacts between musicians, dancers, musicologists, psychologists, physiologists, educators, and therapists to name some of the disciplines involved. We need basic research on fundamental rhythm phenomena as well as research in concrete musical contexts—and above all we need much more of an interplay between different approaches and an unprejudiced methodological pluralism without losing the sense for critical judgment.

Rhythm cannot be isolated from other components in music. Music is not a simple sum of some "basic elements" as rhythm, melody, harmony, and timbre. There is a continuous and ever-changing interaction between these factors, and they are overlapping in meaning. In particular, the distinction between melody and rhythm is artificial: Is there a melody without rhythm? Is there rhythm without timbre, or what role does timbre play for rhythm? These questions are difficult, but at least we should be aware of them in planning what to investigate and how. Much thinking on music is "rationalized" and may look good on paper (this statement may include our conventional musical notation) but has limited relevance for our **experience** of the sounding music.

So perhaps the reader may wish to stop reading now and turn instead to the experiences of listening to some favorite music, moving and dancing, perhaps trying some quite different types of music—and so on. After all, that is the most natural and efficient way of learning about the diversity and multidimensionality of rhythm in music.

ACKNOWLEDGMENTS

I want to express my sincere gratitude to Ingmar Bengtsson and the other members of our rhythm research group for many years of fruitful cooperation in discussions and investigations. Economical support was provided by The Bank of Sweden Tercentenary Foundation and by Uppsala University.

REFERENCES

Becking, G. *Der musikalische Rhythmus als Erkenntnisquelle.* Augsburg: Benno Filser, 1928.

Behne, K. E. Der Einfluss des Tempos auf die Beurteilung von Musik. Köln: Arno Volk, 1972.

Bengtsson, I. Anteckningar om rytm och rytmiskt beteende. Uppsala University, Department of Musicology, 1966–1967. (Unpublished)

Bengtsson, I. Empirische Rhythmusforschung in Uppsala. *Hamburger Jahrbuch für Musikwissenschaft,* 1974, *1,* 195–220.

Bengtsson, I., & Gabrielsson, A. Rhythm research in Uppsala. *Music, Room, and Acoustics, Publications issued by the Royal Swedish Academy of Music.* Stockholm: 1977, No. 17, 19–56.

Bengtsson, I., & Gabrielsson, A. Methods for analyzing performance of musical rhythm. *Scandinavian Journal of Psychology,* 1980, *21,* 257–268.

Bengtsson, I., & Gabrielsson, A. Analysis and synthesis of musical rhythm. In J. Sundberg (Ed.), *Studies of Music Performance, Publications issued by the Royal Swedish Academy of Music.* Stockholm: 1983, No. 39, 27–60.

Bengtsson, I., Gabrielsson, A., & Thorsén, S. M. Empirisk rytmforskning (Empirical rhythm research), *Swedish Journal of Musicology*, 1969, *51*, 49–118.

Bolton, T. L. Rhythm. *American Journal of Psychology*, 1894, *6*, 145–238.

Borchgrevink, H. M. Prosody and musical rhythm are controlled by the speech hemisphere. In M. Clynes (Ed.), *Music, Mind, and Brain. The Neuropsychology of Music.* New York: Plenum Press, 1982.

Bradshaw, J. L., & Nettleton, N. C. The nature of hemispheric specialization in man. *The Behavioral and Brain Sciences*, 1981, *4*, 51–91.

Brown, W. Temporal and accentual rhythm. *Psychological Review*, 1911, *18*, 336–346.

Carroll, J. D., & Chang, J. J. Analysis of individual differences in multidimensional scaling via an N-way generalization of "Eckart-Young" decomposition. *Psychometrika*, 1970, *35*, 283–319.

Clarke, E. F. Timing in the performance of Erik Satie's 'Vexations.' *Acta Psychologica*, 1982, *50*, 1–19.

Clarke, E. F. Some aspects of rhythm and expression in performances of Erik Satie's "Gnossienne No. 5." *Music Perception*, 1985, *2*, 299–328.

Clynes, M. *Sentics, the touch of emotions.* New York: Anchor press/Doubleday, 1977.

Clynes, M. Expressive microstructure in music. In J. Sundberg (Ed.), *Studies of Music Performance, Publications issued by the Royal Swedish Academy of Music.* Stockholm: 1983, No. 39, 76–181.

Clynes, M. Music beyond the score. *Communication and Cognition*, 1985 (a), *18* (4).

Clynes, M. Secrets of life in music. *Analytica-Studies in the Description and Analysis of Music in Honor of Ingmar Bengtsson.* Publications issued by Royal Swedish Academy of Music. Stockholm: 1985, No. 47.

Clynes, M. & Nettheim, N. The living quality of music: Neurobiologic basis of communicating feeling. In M. Clynes (Ed.) *Music, Mind and Brain. The Neuropsychology of Music.* New York: Plenum Press, 1982.

Clynes, M., & Walker, J. Neurobiologic functions of rhythm, time, and pulse in music. In M. Clynes (Ed.), *Music, Mind, and Brain. The Neuropsychology of Music.* New York: Plenum Press, 1982.

Cooper, G. W., & Meyer, L. B. *The rhythmic structure of music.* Chicago: The University of Chicago Press, 1960.

Dainow, E. Physical effects and motor responses to music. *Journal of Research in Music Education*, 1977, *25*, 211–221.

Dalcroze, E. J. *Rhythm, music, and education.* London: The Dalcroze Society, 1980 (first published 1921).

Davies, J. B. *The psychology of music.* London: Hutchinson, 1978.

Demany, L., McKenzie, N., & Vurpillot, E. Rhythm perception in early infancy. *Nature*, 1977, *266*, 718–719.

Fraisse, P. *Les structures rythmiques.* Louvain: Editions Universitaires, 1956.

Fraisse, P. *Psychologie du rythme.* Paris: Presses Universitaires de France, 1974.

Fraisse, P. Time and rhythm perception. In E. C. Carterette, and M. P. Friedman (Eds.), *Handbook of perception*, Volume 8, 203–253. New York: Academic Press, 1978.

Fraisse, P. Multisensory aspects of rhythm. In R. D. Walk, and H. L. Pick (Eds.), *Intersensory perception and sensory integration (217-248)*. New York: Plenum Publishing Corporation, 1981.

Fraisse, P. Rhythm and tempo. In D. Deutsch (Ed.), *The psychology of music*. New York: Academic Press, 1982.

Fraisse, P., Oléron, G., & Paillard, J. Les effets dynamogéniques de la musique. *L'Année Psychologique*, 1953, *53*, 1–34.

Francès, R. *Le perception de la musique*. Paris: J. Vrin, 1958.

Gabrielsson, A. Similarity ratings and dimension analyses of auditory rhythm patterns. I and II. *Scandinavian Journal of Psychology*, 1973, *14*, 138–160, 161–176 (a).

Gabrielsson, A. Adjective ratings and dimension analyses of auditory rhythm patterns. *Scandinavian Journal of Psychology*, 1973, *14*, 244–260 (b).

Gabrielsson, A. Studies in rhythm. *Acta Universitatis Upsaliensis: Abstract of Uppsala Dissertations from the Faculty of Social Sciences*, 1973, No. 7 (c).

Gabrielsson, A. Performance of rhythm patterns. *Scandinavian Journal of Psychology*, 1974, *15*, 63–72.

Gabrielsson, A. Experimental research on rhythm. *Humanities Association Review*, 1979, *30*, 69–92.

Gabrielsson, A. Perception and performance of musical rhythm. In M. Clynes (Ed.), *Music, Mind, and Brain. The Neuropsychology of Music*. New York: Plenum Press, 1982.

Gabrielsson, A. Interplay between analysis and synthesis in studies of performance and experience of music. *Music Perception*, 1985, *3*, 59–86.

Gabrielsson, A., Bengtsson, I., & Gabrielsson, B. Performance of musical rhythm in ¾ and 6/8 meter. *Scandinavian Journal of Psychology*, 1983, *24*, 193–213.

Garner, W. R., & Gottwald, R. L. The perception and learning of temporal patterns. *Quarterly Journal of Experimental Psychology*, 1968, *20*, 97–109.

Gaston, E. Man and music. In E. T. Gaston (Ed.), *Music in therapy*. New York: MacMillan, 1968.

Gates, A., & Bradshaw, J. L. The role of the cerebral hemispheres in music. *Brain and Language*, 1977, *4*, 403–431.

Grove New Dictionary of Music and Musicians, London: MacMillan Publishers Limited, 1980.

Guttman, A. Das Tempo und seine Variationsbeite. *Archiv für die gesamte Psychologie*, 1932, *85*, 331–350.

Handel, S. Perceiving melodic and rhythmic auditory patterns. *Journal of Experimental Psychology*, 1974, *103*, 922–933.

Handel, S., & Lawson, G. R. The contextual nature of rhythmic interpretation. *Perception & Psychophysics*, 1983, *34*, 103–120.

Handel, S., & Oshinsky, J. S. The meter of syncopated auditory polyrhythms. *Perception & Psychophysics*, 1981, *30*, 1–9.

Hartman, A. Untersuchungen über metrisches Verhalten in musikalischen Interpretationsvarianten. *Archiv für die gesamte Psychologie,* 1932, *84,* 103–192.

Hevner, K. Experimental studies of the elements of expression in music. *American Journal of Psychology,* 1936, *48,* 246–268.

Hevner, K. The affective value of pitch and tempo in music. *American Journal of Psychology, 1937, 49,* 621–630.

James, W. *The principles of psychology,* I. New York: Holt, 1890.

Jones, M. R. Auditory patterns: Studies in the perception of structure. In E. C. Carterette, and M. P. Friedman (Eds.), *Handbook of perception,* Volume, *8,* 256–288. New York: Academic Press, 1978.

Koffka, K. Experimentaluntersuchungen zur Lehre von Rhythmus. *Zeitschrift für Psychologie,* 1909, *52,* 1–109.

von Kries, J. *Wer ist musikalisch? Gedanken zur Psychologie der Tonkunst.* Berlin: Julius Springer, 1926.

Longuet-Higgins, H. C. Perception of melodies. *Nature,* 1976, *263,* 646–653.

Longuet-Higgins, H. C. The perception of music. *Proceedings of the Royal Society of London,* 1979, *B 205,* 307–322.

Longuet-Higgins, H. C., & Lee, C. S. The perception of musical rhythms. *Perception,* 1982, *11,* 115–128.

Longuet-Higgins, H. C., & Lee, C. S. The rhythmic interpretation of monophonic music. In J. Sundberg (Ed.), *Studies of Music Performance, Publications issued by the Royal Swedish Academy of Music.* Stockholm, 1983, No. 39, 7–26.

Lundin, R. W. *An objective psychology of music* (2nd ed.). New York: Ronald Press, 1967.

MacDougall, R. The structure of simple rhythm forms. *Psychological Review Monograph Supplement 4,* 1903, 309–411.

Madsen, C. K. Modulated beat discrimination among musicians and nonmusicians. *Journal of Research in Music Education,* 1979, *27,* 57–67.

Mark, M. L. *Contemporary Music Education.* New York: Schirmer Books, 1978.

Meumann, E. Untersuchungen zur Psychologie und Aesthetik des Rhythmus. *Philosophische Studien,* 1894, *10,* 249–322, 393–430.

Miner, J. B. Motor, visual, and applied rhythms. *Psychological Review Monograph Supplement,* 1903, *5,* No. 21, 1–106.

Miyake, I. Researches on rhythmic action. *Studies from Yale Psychological Laboratory,* 1902, *10,* 1–48.

Moog, H. *Das Musikerleben des vorschulpflichtigen Kindes.* Mainz: B. Schott's Söhne, 1968.

de la Motte-Haber, H. Ein Beitrag zur Klassifikation musikalischer Rhythmen. Köln: Arno Volk, 1968.

Oléron, G., & Silver, S. E. Tension affective et effets dynamogéniques dus à la musique. *L'Année Psychologique,* 1963, *63,* 293–308.

Paillard, J., Oléron, G., & Fraisse, P. Influence des attitudes posturales sur l'accompagnement moteur spontané d'un rythme musical. *L'Année Psychologique,* 1953, *53,* 405–413.

Povel, D. J. Temporal structure of performed music. Some preliminary observations. *Acta Psychologica,* 1977, *41,* 309–320.

Povel, D. J. Internal representation of simple temporal patterns. *Journal of Experimental Psychology: Human Perception and Performance,* 1981, *7,* 3–18.

Preusser, D. The effect of structure and rate on the recognition and description of auditory temporal patterns. *Perception & Psychophysics,* 1972, *11,* 233–240.

Rasch, R. A. Synchronization in performed ensemble music. *Acustica,* 1979, *43,* 121–131.

Rasch, R. A. *Aspects of the perception and performance of polyphonic music.* Utrecht: Drukkerij Elinkwijk BV, 1981.

Rigg, M. G. Speed as a determiner of musical mood. *Journal of Experimental Psychology,* 1940, *27,* 566–571.

Royer, F. L., & Garner, W. R. Perceptual organization of nine-element auditory temporal patterns. *Perception & Psychophysics,* 1970, *7,* 115–120.

Ruckmich, C. A. The role of kinaesthesis in the perception of rhythm. *American Journal of Psychology,* 1913, *24,* 305–359.

Sachs, C. *Rhythm and tempo.* London: J. M. Dent & Sons, 1953.

Sander, F. Ueber räumliche Rhythmik. *Neue Psychologische Studien,* 1926, *1,* 123–158.

Schmidt, E. Ueber den Aufbau rhythmischer Gestalten. *Neue Psychogische Studien,* 1939, *14,* 1–98.

Sears, C. H. A contribution to the psychology of rhythm. *American Journal of Psychology,* 1902, *13,* 28–61.

Seashore, C. E. (Ed.). *Objective Analysis of Musical Performance. University of Iowa Studies in the Psychology of Music,* Volume IV, 1937.

Seashore, C. E. *Psychology of music.* New York: McGraw-Hill, 1938.

Seashore, H. G. An objective analysis of artistic singing. In C. E. Seashore (Ed.), *Objective Analysis of musical performance. University of Iowa Studies in the Psychology of Music.* 1937, Volume IV, 12–157.

Shaffer, L. H. Analyzing piano performance: A study of concert pianists. In G. E. Stelmach, and J. Requin (Eds.), *Tutorials in Motor Behavior.* Amsterdam: North-Holland Publishing Company, 1980.

Shaffer, L. H. Performances of Chopin, Bach, and Bartok: Studies in motor programming. *Cognitive Psychology,* 1981, *13,* 326–376.

Shuter-Dyson, R., & Gabriel, C. *The psychology of musical ability* (2nd ed.). London: Methuen, 1981.

Sloboda, J. A. The communication of musical metre in piano performance. *Quarterly Journal of Experimental Psychology,* 1983, *35A,* 377–396.

Snider, J. G., & Osgood, C. E. (Eds.). *Semantic Differential Technique.* Chicago: Aldine Publishing Company, 1969.

Steedman, M. J. The perception of musical rhythm and metre. *Perception,* 1977, *6,* 555–569.

Stetson, R. H. Rhythm and rhyme. *Psychological Review Monograph Supplement, 4,* 1903, 413–466.

Stetson, R. H. A motor theory of rhythm and discrete succession. *Psychological Review,* 1905, *12,* 250–270, 293–350.

Sundberg, J., Frydén, L., & Askenfelt, A. What tells you the player is musical? An analysis-by-synthesis study of music performance. In J. Sundberg (Ed.), *Studies of Music Performance, Publications issued by the Royal Swedish Academy of Music.* Stockholm: 1983, No. 39, 61–75.

Titchener, E. B. *Lehrbuch der Psychologie* (2:e Aufl.). Leipzig: Johann Ambrosius Barth, 1926.

Truslit, A. *Gestaltung und Bewegung in der Musik.* Berlin-Lichterfelde: Chr. Friedrich Vieweg, 1938.

Wagner, C. Experimentelle Untersuchungen über das Tempo. *Österreichische Musikzeitschrift,* 1974, *29,* 589–604.

Wapnik, J. The perception of musical and metronomic tempo change in musicians. *Psychology of Music,* 1980, *8:1,* 3–12.

Werner, H. Rhythmik, eine mehrwertige Gestaltenverkettung. *Zeitschrift für Psychologie,* 1919, *82,* 198–218.

Woodrow, H. A quantitative study of rhythm. *Archives of Psychology,* 1909, *14,* 1–66.

Wundt, W. *Grundzüge der Physiologischen Psychologie,* Dritter Band. (Sechste Auflage). Leipzig: Wilhelm Engelmann, 1911.

Yeston, M. *The stratification of musical rhythm.* New Haven and London: Yale University Press, 1976.

Chapter 8

WHEN TIME IS MUSIC

MANFRED CLYNES

INTRODUCTION

This chapter[1] is in three sections, each dealing with different aspects of the relation between time and music. The first section deals with music and meaning-mediated by subtle time deviations from arithmetic time ratios due to the pulse structure, and by temporal amplitude relations among tones. It shows how the musical pulse combines amplitude relations among tones with specific timing deviations as a master plan for various rhythms that yet have an underlying identity—the personal signature of the composer.

The second section is concerned with aspects of rhythms of the mind and of music; of musical thought and musical action.

The third section is concerned with the stability of mental clocks and how time is metered by music, as experience—the inverse of our habitual way of regarding the relation between time and music.

The perception of music and rhythm involves time consciousness. The rate at which we perceive the passage of time is a property of our human nature, our human brain, and is in no way absolute. One can imagine for example a living being for whom night and day could appear like a flicker. Beings in different planetary systems, in other galaxies, and even here on earth are likely to have highly different innate rates of experience of the flow of time—rates of psychobiologic clocks. (There is no concept of physics that governs or corresponds to this biologic relativity of "rate of flow of time." Relativistic changes in time of physics are superimposed on the effects discussed here.)

We may gain some indication of the rate of time consciousness from the time it takes a particular organism to make a simple decision involving motor behaviour. Insects such as flies can abruptly change their directions of movement about an order of magnitude quicker than a human is able to respond even with an eye blink. There is no reason to suppose that the rate at which time is experienced is not capable of variation from species to species.

Recently the gene controlling the diurnal biologic clock in Drosophila has been isolated and mapped out (Konopka and Benzer, 1971; Kyriacou and Hall, 1980; Bargiello and Young, 1984). Surprisingly it turned out that two mutations of this gene caused the diurnal clock rate to be substantially altered (increased to 29 hours and decreased to 19 hours) and governed certain periodicities of their mating "song" in a like direction. Thus we have the beginning of the story of how the genetic configuration may control the experience of the passage of time.

That rate sets the canvas on which the experience of a particular rhythm is depicted. The same rhythm at different time scales is no longer the same, experientially. The rate at which time flow is innately experienced sets the bench mark against which the experience of rhythm derives its significance and meaning for a particular species.

The basic sense of time flow may appear to deviate in a particular person under various social, diurnal and possibly other environmental influences, but rhythm in relation to music can be seen to have a high degree of stability derived from musical meaning and concepts (Clynes 1969, Clynes and Walker 1982, Clynes 1985). The stability of musical rhythm appears to be a good guide to the fundamental stability of the human sense of the rate of passage of time. Music can be a measure of time, perhaps the best psychic measure we have.

In the first part of this chapter we look at musical significance of subtle inflections in the temporal proportions of tones that constitute a musical pulse and other aspects of the code of musicality that have been unraveled. In the later parts we are concerned with the ability of the nervous system to produce highly precise temporal patterns guided by unconscious thought and describe remarkable stabilities of the psychobiologic clocks involved. In both, the findings relate to unconscious thought processes of musical thought. Musical thought employs memory functions at various levels of discernment, as does thought itself. Discovering more about these unconscious thought processes is of interest also to the development of artificial intelligence: the thought world of music models itself on a larger perspective of the world, and, framed in time, lends itself to precise observation.

MUSIC BEYOND THE SCORE

Musical Microstructure

Music has meaning. How does this meaning reside in the music? To examine this question it is not sufficient to look at music as a score. The music needs to be looked at for what it actually is: musical thought and performed musical sounds. Both musical thought and performance differ considerably from what is written in the musical score. Much of the meaning of music resides in such unnotated musical forms. Probably it is not too much to say that it is even impossible for musical meaning to exist without these differential forms which we shall call musical microstructure. If one were to be forced to think music exactly as a score is written, such thought, and corresponding performance would be practically meaningless (Sundberg 1983; Gabriellson 1983). The musical microstructure is read into it, both in thought and in performance.

Musical meaning (Meyer, 1973; Imberty, 1979; Cooke, 1959) of course is not a property of the microstructure itself. But music comes alive in organic wholes where musical structure and microstructure coexist (Clynes 1983).

We cannot look for musical meaning in the literal score. Perhaps this is why so many music theorists have found no musical emotional meaning. If you consider only relationships between the notes (mainly, in practice the pitches) of a musical score you have in fact unwittingly thrown out the possibility of full musical meaning. The relationships between pitches and corresponding harmonic progressions at best lead to descriptions of "tension and relaxation." This is where many music theorists have left musical meaning (Schenker, 1935; Bernstein, 1976).

That music expresses more than tension and its resolution is clear to most musical people, but many music theorists appear to have fallen into this trap by confining themselves to the study of musical score, rather than of musical thought—admittedly a more difficult process for study.

However, recently discovered laws of musical microstructure tell us about how musical meaning is formed and found in the living forms of musical sound (Clynes 1983). This meaningful sound is a reflection of the subtlety of our own natures. As we study this subtlety, we become increasingly amazed at the seemingly unlimited ability to evoke meaningful qualities (through sound) in their pure form. This wealth to be unearthed is in fact the secret of art and is also its power to suffuse our state with transcendent experience.

Meaning in music and subtlety of spatio-temporal form are of course inseparable.[2] Here modern technology comes to our aid in providing new understanding. It allows us to create the most subtle musical forms in time with discrimination, stability and repeatability far in excess of that of the power of any living musician. Musical forms now become like sculpture—time becomes the ally of the artist rather than his inexorable master. He can take his time, listening inwardly and outwardly; he does not have to give it with his body. Like a painter who works for many years on a painting to perfect every aspect, he has the potential to shape music's forms in time with a subtlety that no human real-time executant can match.

Pulse Microstructure

The first and most important of these laws of microstructure is the nature of the musical pulse and how it is embodied in the notes of the music. To understand the nature of the pulse we need to be aware of the property of the central nervous system called Time Form Printing (Clynes and Walker 1982, Clynes 1975). This function makes it possible to execute repeated movements with only one initial command requiring specific attention. The initial command determines the shape and rate of the repetitive movement such as, for example, a repetitive beat executed by an arm and hand. Full attention is required in initially establishing the shape and rate of the pattern. Repetitions conserve both the rate and shape of such movements without requiring special attention, so that other activities can be carried out simultaneously with such a repetitive beat pattern.

This short term memory function of the central nervous system is also used in the musical pulse, whether it is manifested by actual repetitive movement or occurs in thought only. In thinking the musical pulse, subliminal motor actions take place in a manner similar to those which occur when the sounds of speech are thought. The pattern of the musical pulse once taken tends to conserve itself throughout the piece. But it is crucial that the pulse be established initially in its appropriate form with all its subtlety. The mental shape of the musical pulse as a spatio-temporal form determines to a large extent the subtle character of the music. We now know that it does this specifically in two ways. The loudness of individual tones of melodies is moulded according to the character of the pulse, and secondly the duration deviations of the tones from the arithmetic ratios given in the score (e.g. a quarter, half, eighths, triplets, sixteenths) are also systematically moulded by the pulse (Clynes 1983). Introducing the pulse to a naked score already provides a considerable amount of enlivening.

Different music has in general different pulse forms (Becking, 1928; Michon, 1974; Cooper and Meyer, 1960; Clynes and Walker, 1982). But it is found that composers of Western music in the period 1750–1900 have evolved an intimate, personal pulse of their own which imbues all their music. We can thus speak of Mozart pulse, a Beethoven pulse, a Schubert pulse, a Brahms pulse and so on. We have in fact now determined the precise character of the Mozart, Beethoven and Schubert pulse forms (and most recently those of Schumann and Haydn and Mendelssohn) and how the pulse form affects the duration and loudness of the individual tones that from a pulse group (Clynes, 1983). These pulse forms appear to apply to the entire ouevre of the composer, to both slow and fast movements, and different meters, somewhat like a personal signature of the composer. As can handwriting, or a brush stroke of a painter, the pulse reveals aspects of the intimate, personal nature of the composer, his unique point of view. A Mozart piece played with a Beethoven pulse or vice versa sounds bizarre. But it is not a matter of style—Haydn and Mozart have quite different pulse forms, as do Debussy and Ravel. In the absence of the composer's characteristic pulse any of his compositions sound unauthentic and unconvincing. It is as if the presence of the composer has been withdrawn.

The pulse affects the microstructure of tones with a high degree of discrimination and sensitivity. In the temporal dimension the resolution is of the order of one millisecond, the amplitude of the order of one percent.

Musical pulses of course apply to ethnic music and baroque music and to any music in which there is a repetitive beat, including Jazz and Rock. It shall be emphasized particularly that the relative loudness of components of a melody partakes of the beat (pulse) just as much as the percussive accompaniment figures. This law of musical microstructure thus tends to negate the false idea that only rhythmic accompaniment figures are to have appropriate subtle dynamic rhythmic character, while the melodic line is essentially unmodulated in intensity by the pulse (as is prevalent with most synthesizers, and much performed music). We see that the pulse affects both the melody and rhythmic accompaniment figures in an integral way — only when both are appropriately modulated by the pulse is the living character fully realised.

Sensitivity to Pulse Parameter Values

Quite a small change of a single amplitude modifier parameter may change the character of the pulse considerably. A one percent change in a single lower level amplitude parameter is generally quite noticeable, while a 3–4% change may suffice to change the character from "light" to "heavy," or some other quite marked change in character for which words may not readily be found. A small difference in the pulse structure can have a large effect on its psychologic character. As an illustration, Fig. 1, we reproduce here the pulse matrix for Beethoven, Mozart and Schubert for a 4/4 meter. (Figures 1a, 1b, 1c illustrate the sentographic pulse forms measured earlier.)

Operation of the Pulse

The pulse is not altered by the varying musical content as the piece unfolds. The pulse may be momentarily suspended as in a fermata, or slow down or accelerate on occasion, but it does not therefore lose its internal structure and character.

The pulse operates on the tones of the music at several hierarchical levels (Clynes 1983, 1985). We will describe the function and structure of the pulse first for its lowest hierarchical level. This level takes as its unit the fastest notes of the music (not considering ornaments). These may generally be grouped as 2, 3 or 4. For example they may consist of four sixteenth notes in an allegro movement in 3/4 time. Microstructure for that level may be written as:

$$110, \qquad 92, \qquad 100, \qquad 96$$
$$\text{Level 1}$$
$$1 \qquad .53 \qquad .75 \qquad .87$$

where the numbers in the upper row indicate the relative duration modification of four tones (100 being perfectly even), and the lower row indicates the relative loudness (amplitude) modification of these tones — given on a linear scale here, referred to 1 as the first tone of the group.

If in the music the notes are not all sixteenth notes, and so are notated

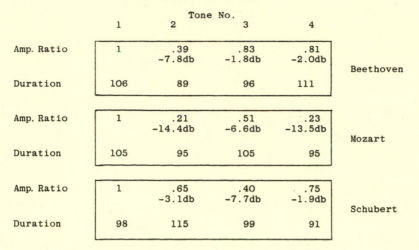

Figure 1. Pulse matrix for quadruple time — four component tones per pulse — for Beethoven, Mozart and Schubert.

Of the matrix elements, top rows across in each box give the relative loudness of tones 1, 2, 3, 4, with the loudness of tone 1 taken as 1 for comparison. Relativeness loudness is also given in db, immediately below the linear figures.

The second horizontal row indicates the relative duration of the tones, referred to 100. (Perfectly even duration would be 100 for all four tones.) The deviations given here are, of course, not experienced as unevenness but as characteristic personal "flavor." Note for example the slightly extended duration for tone 4 for Beethoven (111). For Schubert, on the other hand, tone 2 is characteristically extended (115).

The duration of tones longer than component tones is given by the duration of the sum of the constituent component tones. Loudness of such tones is determined by the loudness of the component tone corresponding to the beginning of the longer tone. Microstructure matrices of compound meters can be derived from the matrices of quadruple and triple meters according to rules given in Clynes, 1983. The pulse microstructure is applied to the entire piece. (Reprinted from Clynes, 1983.)

longer (as is generally the case), the duration of such a note is given by the sum of the duration of its component sixteenth notes. The loudness of such a note, however, is given by the loudness of its **first** sixteenth note component.

In our example the four sixteenth notes of the lowest level of the pulse together constitute a quarter note. The next level of the pulse may then consist of three such quarter notes. This second level then may comprise a bar in 3/4 meter. It may be written as:

$$103 \quad 97 \quad 102$$
Level 2
$$1 \quad .65 \quad .92$$

This means that the four sixteenth notes of each of the three quarter notes are all modified, i.e., **multiplied** by these parameters: the four

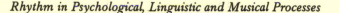

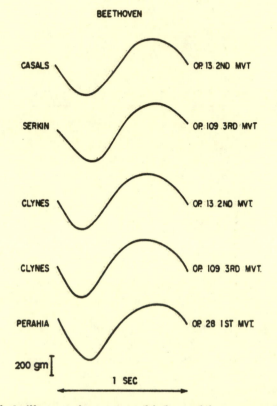

Figure 1a. Figs. 1a, 1b, 1c illustrate the sentographic form of the composer's pulse, as measured years before the pulse matrix was determined. Aspects of the sentographic form can be related to the pulse matrix, although the latter is much more precise, and shows how the pulse affects each tone of the music.

Essentic form of the inner pulse of Beethoven as produced by a number of artists. Different movements are compared, as well as the same movement for different interpreters. The forms are sentographic measures of the artist "conducting" the pieces with finger pressure on the sentograph while thinking the music in real time, without sound. The sentograph measures finger pressure as a function of time. (Average of 50 pulses.) (Figs. 1a, 1b and 1c are reprinted from *Information Processing in the Nervous System*, (Leibovic and Eccles, Eds., Springer-Verlag, 1969.)

durations of the sixteenth notes of the first quarter are multiplied by 103 percent, those the second quarter by 97 percent, and those of the third quarter by 102 percent.

The loudnesses of the first four sixteenth notes are multiplied by 1, notes in the second group of four sixteenth notes are multiplied by .65, and those of the third group are multiplied by .92. Thus the second level microstructure modifies the lowest level by deviating each group in duration and in amplitude, taking each **group** as an element.

Similarly, the highest level acts multiplicatively on all the elements

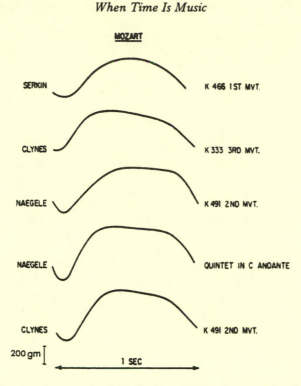

Figure 1b. The Mozart pulse, measured similarly as the Beethoven pulse shown earlier. Note the different shape; lighter and more buoyant in character.

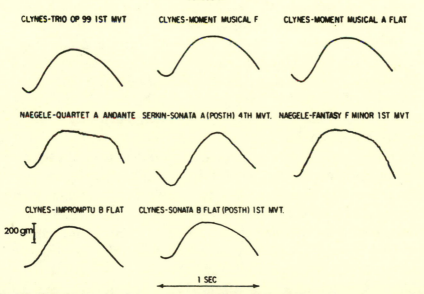

Figure 1c. The Schubert pulse shows a very early down peak. There is a characteristic upward deflection related to elements of hope and longing. The initially free beat tends to experience increased resistance and tension in this phase—a feeling of being pulled upwards.

of the lower groups. The microstructure of this level may be, for example,

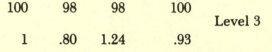

and represents **four bars** of the music in this example. Each element of this microstructure level modifies a group of twelve sixteenth notes in this example.

The entire pulse in this example comprises 4 × 3 × 4 **or 48 sixteenth notes,** all of which have individual durations and amplitudes.

The lowest two levels determine the general character of the pulse. The highest level allows the phrases to relate to each other in a musically compelling way. In general this level is too slow to be felt as a rhythmic factor—it is felt more as contributing to musical "logic," balance, and naturalness.

Composer's Pulse

The composer's characteristic pulse as described initially for a single level (Clynes 1983) operates, we find, on **both** of the two lower hierarchical levels. Depending on the tempo and the construction of the piece, an attenuation factor may be required which can soften the influence of the pulse from one level to another to a required degree, producing a partial hierarchy. This attenuation factor (one each for duration and for amplitude) operates equally on all component tones, and is useful to avoid exaggerated effects which may sometimes be produced through a full hierarchy. The composer's pulse as determined for 2, 3, 4, or even 5, groups is entered on both lower levels.

The highest level contains small duration deviations only, but considerable amplitude modifications. Of quite a different nature from the composer's pulse entered on the two lower levels, it is at our present stage separately determined for each piece; although it may be that further experience will reveal characteristic patterns for different composers also. These patterns however would not be expected to have a numerical relation to the pulse entered on the lower two levels.

In applying the pulse, the appropriate metrical durations need to be chosen for each level. There often is a choice between 2 or 4 as the grouping of the lowest level. This choice then influences the choice at the next highest level; and this in turn affects the metrical duration of the highest level. **It is part of the composition process that in fact only one solution is musically acceptable.** This solution does not necessarily lead to the bar as a unit of the highest level. It may be half a bar, or in fast tempos, even two bars.

The Pulse and Bar Structure

The three level pulse pattern may comprise 4 bars or some multiple or submultiple of this. However a composition may have a group or groups of 3 bars, or 2 bars inserted between the more usual 4 bar sequences.

Accordingly, in using the microstructure program in larger pieces it is necessary only to indicate places or bar numbers where the pulse is to "reset" its highest level.

Amplitude Shapes of Melodic Tones in Relation to Melodic Structure

The second law or rule of microstructure concerns the relation between the amplitude shapes of individual notes of a melody and the melodic structure. In a given melody, for a wholly expressive performance, each melodic tone needs to have its own distinct amplitude shape, and these shapes will vary considerably from one tone to the next. While many instruments cannot effectively produce varying amplitude shapes for different tones of a melody (such as the organ, harpsichord, or piano (even though the last named can readily produce varying amplitude sizes), performers on other instruments such as bowed string instruments and woodwinds, and singers of course can and do shape individual tone according to the musical requirements of the melody with greater and lesser success. Where an instrument is incapable of modulating the amplitude shapes we excuse the shortcoming and imagine these amplitude shapes in our minds even if they do not actually exist.

Musical thought necessarily includes individual tone amplitude shapes. And when the tone amplitude shapes produced by the musical instrument or singer correspond to those of musical thought a particular delight is experienced.

Accordingly, a computer can be used to good purpose to provide appropriately customised amplitude shapes for individual tones of a melody; even if this music be composed for instruments incapable of such a modulation. Further, the structure of the melody itself provides clues to the shaping of its individual tones, and a computer can also use these clues and in that sense produce musical thought.

What are these clues? The clue provided by the melody that governs the changes in shape of one tone to the next within a melody is the slope of the pitch-time curve (which includes both time and changes of pitch). The amplitude shape of a particular tone is influenced as a deviation from a basic shape as follows: If the time slope of the pitch-time curve is upward the shape is skewed forward, if the slope of the pitch-time curve is downward, it is skewed backwards—in both cases in proportion to the slope. This function has a singularly powerful property that **the shape of the present tone is governed by the nature (viz. pitch and time) of the tone to follow.** The shape of the present tone thus provides a clue to the listener to the tone to follow! This property is a significant property of musical thought, an important element of musicality. It helps to engender both a feeling of continuity and continuity of feeling.

More precisely, shapes of individual tones corresponding to this musical function are calculated in terms of Beta functions (Clynes, 1983). These functions are of great convenience and usefulness in providing a large range of shapes encountered in musical tone production.

Micropauses

A third aspect of microstructure involved in musical meaning is the insertion of micropauses appropriately placed in the musical fabric. Micropauses are very short, typically of the order of 30 milliseconds, and often are placed between musical phrases, often at the end of four or eight bar sections. They are not noticeable as pauses yet function to group sounds together according to the meaning of the musical phrase, representing musical punctuation. They are much shorter than the so called "Luftpauses," which are placed at certain major structural places in the music.

The elements of microstructure described can now be written as a microscore (Fig 2a) and also may be graphed (Fig. 2b).

Microstructure, Musical Thought and Meaning

The above rules are part of a grammar of musical thought. They are brought into effect unconsciously by the musician as an integral part of musical thought, of musicality. It is not possible to think music without

MOZART: QUINTET IN G MINOR, 1ST MOVEMENT

```
Duration  (sec)           :     8.58
MM (100 pt tones/min)     :   221.00
Base P₁,  P₂ :       0.88      1.12
```

T#	NOTE	DUR (PTS)	AMPL	P1	P2
1	D4	96(77)	168	1.47	0.67
2	G4	106	910	1.18	0.83
3	B4b	95	196	1.34	0.73
4	D5	105(70)	580	0.88	1.12
5	D5	96(68)	263	0.88	1.12
6	D5	201	850	0.88	1.12
7	R	105	0	1.44	0.68
8	G5	96	337	0.88	1.12
9	G5	120	1618	0.80	1.24
10	F5#	95	290	0.79	1.24
11	F5	105(70)	672	0.88	1.12
12	F5	96(68)	305	0.79	1.24
13	E5	201	540	0.88	1.12
14	R	105	0	0.80	1.24
15	E5b	96	276	0.88	1.12
16	E5b	132	1300	0.80	1.24
17	D5	95	238	0.88	1.12
18	D5	105	580	0.97	1.01
19	E5b	96	276	0.88	1.12
20	E5b	113	670	0.80	1.24
21	D5	95	238	0.88	1.12
22	D5	106	420	0.72	1.36
23	C5	96	170	0.88	1.12
24	C5	201	300	0.79	1.24
25	B4b,C,Bb	50,52,51	209	0.82	1.20
26	A4,B4b	23,25	84	0.88	1.12
27	A4	201	160	0.88	1.12

Figure 2a. Microscore of the first four bars of the Violin I part of Mozart's G minor Quintet K516, specifying duration deviations and shapes of each note. For each note the following is given, horizontally across.

1. Tone name; 2. The duration of the tone, or rest, in points; 3. Amplitude size; 4. Amplitude shape (p_1, p_2) (Beta function parameters); Rest is indicated as R; () = staccato tone duration.

Metronome mark per 100 points is also given. (Reprinted from Clynes, 1983.)

musical microstructure. Yet in thinking music one is not consciously aware of the microstructure as a separate process. Instead it issues from the livingness (Langer, 1953) of the musical thought. This living quality is essential to the musical meaning. The microstructure and structure form an indissoluble unity and it is only conventions of musical notation that have forced us to separate them.

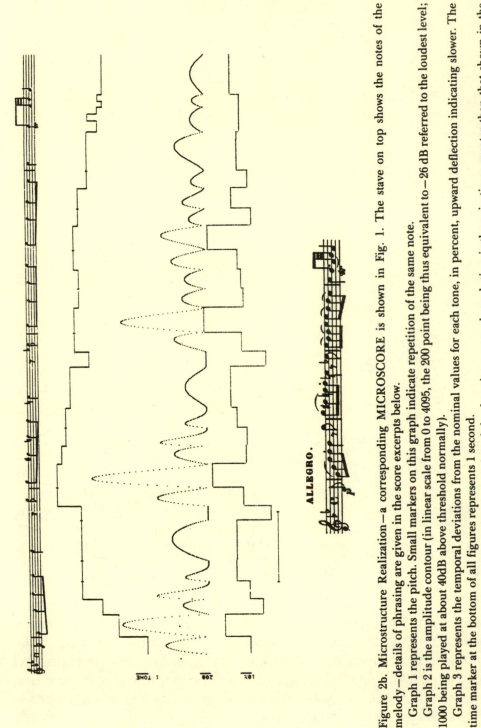

Figure 2b. Microstructure Realization—a corresponding MICROSCORE is shown in Fig. 1. The stave on top shows the notes of the melody—details of phrasing are given in the score excerpts below.

Graph 1 represents the pitch. Small markers on this graph indicate repetition of the same note.

Graph 2 is the amplitude contour (in linear scale from 0 to 4095, the 200 point being thus equivalent to −26 dB referred to the loudest level; 1000 being played at about 40dB above threshold normally).

Graph 3 represents the temporal deviations from the nominal values for each tone, in percent, upward deflection indicating slower. The time marker at the bottom of all figures represents 1 second.

The digital printout prints only every sixth point of the functions—actual resolution is thus six times greater than that shown in the illustrations. The computer performs the piece as shown, as a realisation of the MICROSCORE. (Reprinted from Clynes, 1983.)

The rules described represent aspects of subconscious musical thought. They happen on too short a time scale to be individually controllable. We control microstructure mainly by thinking music in the appropriately meaningful way rather than by selfconsciously trying, according to its dictate, to control the temporal feature of each tone separately. By thinking the appropriate pulse form, with one thought we establish an entire microstructure pattern which then is reproduced throughout the piece. The form of this microstructure pattern is imbued with meaning.

Likewise, the shape of individual tones affects the meaning both in terms of the specific note and its relation to other tones. This is a function independent of the repeated microstructure of the pulse. It derives only from the melodic structure, and is also directly linked to its meaning.

A further important aspect of microstructure results from the ability of the central nervous system to detect very small differences when hearing a musical phrase or motive more than once. These small differences in emphasis or shape of phrases are integral to the meaning of the music. These differences may be extremely small and may effect even only one note.

It is somewhat curious, and in a way quite remarkable, that a musical phrase, even if perfectly beautifully executed the first time (i.e. with fully appropriate meaning), is not perceived as perfect when it is heard the second time, even though it is played exactly the same way (as can now be done readily by computer performance). The second playing needs to be very slightly different to escape an impression of a certain deadness (dullness). (We are, of course, not talking here of major changes such as an echo effect and so on but small subtle, almost imperceptible changes in form.) How the second shape differs from the first often indicates, in a larger sense, the composer's point of view. Thus, for example, in the theme of the third movement of Beethoven's violin concerto the first five notes are repeated and here the repetition (notes six to ten) needs to have a very slightly more emphatic statement (Fig. 3). A lesser emphasis detracts from the energy of the theme and is too relaxed, while an equal emphasis to the first statement would be dull. A two percent difference in amplitude only of certain tones is quite sufficient to articulate the difference in emphasis between the first and second repetition to make the point. The theme is thus perceived as one of increasing energy at this stage, with Dionysian character. However, in a composition by Mozart, say, it is often required to play the repetition of a phrase with very slightly less emphasis on certain tones—providing a point of view of detachment, a "considered" view of the music, from what may appear to be a point of view of eternity rather than that of an ego function. In this way such slight differences give rise to larger differences of spiritual meaning; we may say that at the very least they are necessary to achieve such meaning.

Figure 3. Beethoven Violin Concerto, Op. 61, 3rd Movement.

Emotional Qualities and Musical Meaning

Emotional qualities are expressed temporally through essentic form. For details of the essentic forms of joy, anger, love, sex, hate, grief, and reverence as determined through experiments involving many hundreds of subjects in various cultures see Clynes (1969; 1973; 1977; 1980). Essentic form is a property of the central nervous system for the production and perception of expressions of emotional qualities—that is, for their communication and generation (Klages, 1950). It is common to various sensory modes, and in a sense more primary than any of them. Simple transforms of essentic forms expressed by touch into sound forms that express the same emotional quality have been determined (Clynes and Nettheim, 1982).

Essentic form is biologically given and appears to be genetically preserved. In music, dance and art, essentic form may be represented through various parameters in culturally determined modes. In Western music, essentic form is embodied in the sound mainly through the frequency and amplitude of musical tones.

In such music, essentic form is in the first instance present as the melodic pitch contour (Clynes and Nettheim 1982). In producing a melody, a composer places the notes so that they in effect fit the outline of the appropriate essentic form. The musical thought uses the template of essentic form to fill the notes. Musical tones are placed at suitable points along the path of an essentic form so that internally they can act as markers in the generation of the form. That is to say the musical tones engender internally the motor pattern of essentic form corresponding also to program points of a touch expression of the same quality. These program points suffice to extrapolate the shape. Thus a caress may be defined (represented) by two or three points along the pitch continuum. The essentic form of various emotions thus may be seen in the melodic outline constituted by a number of cardinal points (Clynes and Nettheim, 1982).

The amplitude contours permit the essentic form to be realized with a further parameter in a more detailed way. Either the outline of the peak amplitude of a number of tones, or the amplitude shape of individual slower tones can represent essentic form in terms of amplitude. The combined effect of frequency and amplitude contours is unmistakably more powerful as a clue to the nature of the essentic from than either alone. Thus a melody becomes fully expressive only when its tones are appropriately amplitude shaped. The expression of joy, sadness or love requires not only a pattern of tones, suitably spaced in time and pitch space, but also that these tones be organized in terms of amplitudes to correspond to the appropriate essentic form (Clynes, 1983; Clynes and Nettheim, 1982). And the more purely the essentic form is realized, the greater its power to move.

In this way a melody has direct access to engender the emotional quality in the listener without the need of auxillary symbolism. It can touch the heart as directly as can a physical touch. A caress or an exclamation of joy in music needs not to be consciously translated into a touch caress, or a physical "jump for joy" to be perceived as of such a quality (cf. Langer, 1953). It does so directly through perception of essentic form.

The perception of emotional qualities in music depends on being attuned to the language in which they are embodied. Although the tone of voice in speech is readily understood by practically all members of a culture and also reflects essentic form, the particular way in which essentic form is embodied in the musical fabric needs to be learned if that musical language is to be followed. Once tuned into that mode the listener can perceive the continuing changes in essentic form which, by subtlety or by contrast, tell the story of the piece.

The meaning of this kind of music[3] then unfolds on a double, hierarchical level. On one level there is the sentic story, a chain of essentic forms each having a clear beginning, middle and end, that constitute the elements of communication of emotional qualities. These tell the story. On another level is the musical pulse which also communicates the point of view, the identity of who tells the story. The pulse reveals the presence of the composer—a unique person, in an intimate revelation of a point of view, a basic Weltanschauung. Everything in the story is told from that perspective.

The musical logic thus combines these two hierarchical levels. The meaning is achieved combining the point of view, the intimate identity of the composer, with the particular story he tells. In this way the experience is much larger than just the elements of the story. It includes empathy with the being of the composer, and, by extension with all beings, a proof that the most intimately personal is also the most universal. When Kierkegaard said "thank you, immortal Mozart, without you I would not have known love," he was also telling us something important about the nature of music.

Emotions and Cognition—Generalised Emotions

A crucial but neglected aspect of musical meaning comes about through the inherent cognitive embodiments of generalised emotions.[4] Emotions enjoin cognitive fields that may comprise world views. By generating a sequence of generalised emotions music also potentially traverses and touches upon all facets of life. It can enlarge our horizon by engendering emotional qualities and corresponding cognitive fields previously beyond the experience of the individual. When Beethoven wrote that music was better than all philosophy this was not because he did not appreciate the attempts of philosophers but because he realized that music at its best could contain more wisdom and more effectively present the condition of life than could philosophers.

These cognitive embodiments are not to be confused with specific associations from one's personal life. To explain this further we refer to a recent series of experiments by which we were able to demonstrate an inherent link between love and trust (Clynes, Jurisevic, & Rynn, 1986). In these experiments, with a repeated sequence of expressions of love and also of anger, it is found that even a small insignificant lie temporarily tends to block the experience of love, while the same lie does not affect anger and in some instances even enhances it. These and other experiments show that there are cognitive embodiments attached to generalised emotions independently of personal associations. Thus a sequence of generalised emotional qualities portrayed in music can produce not merely a cathartic wringing out of one's emotional suppressions and needs but also insight into the nature of being. Apollonian rather than Dionysian views of emotional qualities become possible in music—a different mode of integration of the cognitive embodiments of the emotions, developing the powers of empathy rather than of sympathy. This higher function of music is fulfilled by the greatest works of Bach, Mozart and Beethoven.

Microstructure Memory Functions and Musical Experience

We have seen the importance of short term memory with respect to microstructure in two aspects. First the ability to create the repetitive pulse which maintains itself throughout the piece. This pulse is created from the single, original thought and command which determines its spatiotemporal and qualitative character.

Secondly we have seen that short term memory is involved in the perception of slight differences between musical statement and its repetition. In this function of short term memory there is no question of merely recognizing that the repetition repeats something heard before, it is rather the detection of the difference between the repetition and the original that is particularly noticed. These differences have an important role in the unfolding of meaning involving the larger structures. As the piece unfolds, the shorter term memory functions merge into somewhat longer term memory functions of recognizing similarities and differences a good many minutes apart and the recollection of entire sequences, phrases and larger sections (Deutsch, 1982; Sorantin, 1932). Symmetry, thesis and antithesis, balance in the musical experience includes the perception of larger temporal proportions (as also the golden section), by which more recent and less recent portions of the music are related to what is to follow. In this way memory and time perception are closely linked in the musical experience both in terms of structure and microstructure.

The time of an entire piece is even experienced as a unit specifically for that piece, and changes in interpretation tend to leave the overall length of time unchanged (Clynes and Walker, 1982; Clynes and Walker, 1986).

A piece of music, as well as smaller sections within it, are expected to have a beginning, middle and an end—in fact each musical phrase and emotional quality sets up expectation. A partially complete essentic form requires its completion. A complete essentic form sets up an expectation of a similar one to follow. Expectation may be fulfilled or not—

there may be a subtle change, or a strong contrast—a mix of satisfaction and surprise, giving rise to continuing interest.

Memory and expectation functions must be considered part of musical logic and grammar (Minsky, 1982; Pribram, 1982). In any language the interaction between expectation and what actually occurs is crucial to interpretation. The structure of an essentic form sets up such expectation. This is reinforced by the inertia of its corresponding generalised emotional state: one cannot readily follow too many short term, large and abrupt emotional changes. Each essentic form is usually repeated with variations a sufficient number of times for the mood to be established. It is likely that temporal characteristics of biochemical processes in the brain (neurohormonal processes, peptides; we do not speak of hormonal changes here, e.g., adrenalin) are of such a nature that a particular emotional quality can be effectively savoured only if given a time period equal to at least several essentic forms. (Some music may deliberately desire not to establish each mood to a substantive degree, and rather to "quote" such qualities in a more intellectual manner.)

The musical pulse sets up an expectation—an expectation of continuing identity. As we have seen, the shape of an individual tone of a melody sets up an expectation of the next melodic tone. These expectations of feeling and of form clothed in microstructure create the flow of music, transporting us, always surprised, into a state where joy and sorrow, love and death can exist in us—so real we sit motionless, transfixed, and know we are not dreaming.

In sum, in this first section we have considered meaning in music and musical thought as part of the anatomy of the largely unconscious thought processes that comprise what is loosely called musical logic and grammar, and is manifested as musicality. This meaning is generated by the following means:

> (1) The pulse, and its influence on relative loudness and durations of component tones.
> (2) The amplitude shape of individual tones and their relation to melodic structure.
> (3) Essentic forms as elements of expressive emotional communication.
> (4) Musical punctuation in terms of micropauses.
> (5) Subtle differences in repeated phrases and motives in relation to personality aspects, expectation and recognition.

Knowing these elements and principles in terms of microstructure and spatiotemporal forms—a substantial part of the code of musicality—

has also made it possible for the first time through synthesis to create a computer program that using them, gives expressive, authentic and moving performances of the themes of Beethoven, Mozart and Schubert (Clynes, 1983), and indeed of entire pieces (Clynes, 1985).

The above elements of musical language and musicality appear to be to a large degree common to musical languages of various cultures (in contrast to harmonic progressions and contrapuntal devices which we have not considered). Their power to communicate qualities of feeling and evoke continuing interest are functions of the mind relevant also to the field of artificial intelligence. Indeed it appears that deepening our understanding of how we think musically helps us to understand human nature, as well as the nature of music.

ASPECTS OF RHYTHM

Rhythm in Nature

In the physical world rhythm is fundamental to existence. A photon cannot exist without its frequency; an electron cannot abjure its orbital rhythm around a nucleus. Both of these rhythms or frequencies involve space as well as time. The photon has a wavelength, the orbit of the electron a particular shell size.

Curiously, however, nature treats these two frequencies differently: with the expansion of the universe the frequency of the photon decreases, its wavelength lengthens—as may be seen from the photons remaining from the initial Big Bang—while the frequencies and orbital distances associated with other particles, which do not move at the velocity of light, do not change with the expansion of the universe. On a very fundamental scale, the universe thus provides an interplay of rhythm— the changing rhythms of the free photons and the unchanging rhythm of the electrons in captivity.

The rhythms of the planets, stars and galaxies are, in part, reflected in our experience on earth: ice ages, summer and winter, day and night. To some of these we have entrained bodily functions—for example the sleep and wakefulness cycle. But none of these rhythms have the infinite precision of those of the elementary particles.

In rhythms we can observe directly, such as the waves of the ocean, and of the organic rhythm of flying wings, of breathing, of running and walking, of the beating of the heart and of speech; and of music we find interaction between dynamic elements that create the rhythm, and slower, non-rhythmic (or sometimes rhythmic) agencies that modulate the rhythm.

Rhythms of the Mind

In that region of time where the nature of our nervous system and neurobiologic function permit us to recognize individual events, as well as their immediate temporal relationship with neighbouring temporal events, we find the phenomena of musical rhythm. This region is approximately from 0.1 Hz to 8 Hz. In this region, human perception **involuntarily** includes temporal relationships. Slower temporal relationships are viewed through voluntary acts of comparison in which imagination, or deliberately evoked memory, must come to our help. But within this region of frequencies perception of rhythm is immediate, involuntary. (Similarly, on a clock, we see the second hand moving, but the minute and hour hands are known to move only through memory.)

In musical rhythms there is a hierarchical organization of frequency: the frequency of the tones, experienced as imperfect integrals of their frequencies (i.e., pitch), and the superimposed frequencies (durations) of the organisation of the tones. The latter has its own hierarchy.

Imaging Rhythm

Conscious perception of rhythm in this bandwidth seems largely to relate to the ability to conceive of voluntarily initiated alternating movement. But it is possible to imagine rhythms that contain no movement at all, such as rhythmic alternation of colors on a particular spot, or alternation of hot and cold at a particular place on our body, One can even imagine a rhythm devoid of any sensory quality such as mental alternation of "yes, no"; of "more alert, less alert"; "more hopeful, less hopeful"; and so on.

Note how remarkable this property is that we have: our faculty to be able to **imagine** rhythm! We can imagine rhythm in many different sensory modes. But can we imagine rhythms without sensory attributes? And how **precisely** (reproducibly) can we imagine rhythms?

In imagining a rhythm we mostly image some motor pattern—at times in a subliminal way, perhaps, as silently thought, words can subliminally activate the vocal apparatus. However, it is possible to think words faster than spoken rhythms without corresponding subliminal muscular motivation, as for example in speed reading, and it is also possible to image musical rhythms without the use of real time motor images.

But in most of our rhythmic experience of sound, we sense we are driven by it, involuntarily urged to move with it—and it would be good to know how!

Aspects of Time-Form Printing by the Central Nervous System

Expressed rhythm involves movement; agonist and antagonist muscle groups. Does this expression involve alternation between a period of muscular activity, and an interval of rest, like the action of a marker pen on a moving strip chart?

In our earlier studies of some aspects of rhythm (Clynes, 1969a) we implicitly considered it to be like this. We measured properties of rates of repeated tapping, with the implication that the tapping events were like marked points on a linear time scale and that an intervening period of rest occurred between successive taps. This conception turned out to be wrong, however. It has become clear (Clynes, 1977, 1980; Clynes and Walker, 1982) that the iteration of a rhythmic pulse is a unitary event preprogrammed not as an alternation of activity and rest, as musical notation implies, but as a replication of a single dynamic form stored in memory.

We understand now that the memory function which conserves the rate of tapping also conserves the "wave shape" of the iteration (which may be quite complex). The initial mental command which begins a train of repetitions specifies not only the time period but also the form of the repeated pattern. Thus, for example, in a repeated movement of the hand one may decide to move in an approximately elliptic path, triangular path, square path or in a rectilinear path at a given angle. The initially chosen shape will tend to maintain itself throughout the repetitions without further command or specific attention.

The repetitions are then performed "automatically" until further notice—that is until a specific command to stop, or to modify, is given. This ability of the brain is called Time Form Printing. The form and rate may exhibit a long term gradual drift over several hundred repetitions, along with self correcting short term fluctuations, or "errors." But there is a stabilizing effect on both rate and form if this form becomes a musical beat.

Time-form printing can play a role both in creating sound, and in responding to it. It is involved in the transform of rhythmic sound to rhythmic movement and its inverse. If not expressed as movement, the form can still be experienced in an internalized manner.

The Beginning of a Rhythmic Pattern

Where is a beginning to each repeated preprogrammed pattern in time-form printing and what is its significance? Let us consider where in the cycle the repeated initiation or "trigger" takes place as follows: If one executes a circular repetitive movement with the hand and forearm (at a rate say between 1 and 2 repetitions per second, the hand moving in a vertical plane) one mentally experiences a place of initiation (or trigger) at a specific place on that circle. Depending on where the point of initiation is along the circle, the pattern feels differently. A right-handed person performing clockwise circles will tend to place the "trigger" somewhere along the downward path of the circle. He may shift his attention however, and deliberately place it on the upper portion of the circle (Fig. 4). The motion will then feel differently, having an "upward swing" rather than a "downward swing." In either case the circular movement, beginning from the point of initiation and terminating with it, is programmed and experienced as an entity. At the location of the trigger beginning the pattern a (small) degree of effort is experienced. Other portions within the pattern are not experienced in the same way (in fact the portion of the movement opposite the trigger side may tend to be experienced as a rebound).

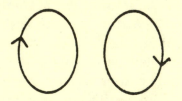

Figure 4. Initiation (or trigger) points when executing a circular, repetitive movement with the hand and forearm.

Time-form printing and its trigger point also relate to how a number of sounds in a sequence are mentally grouped together.

Stability of Tapping with Mentally Imagined Music

How does thinking music affect the stability of a rhythmic pattern, of time-form printing?

Recent experiments were carried out with tapping series of several thousand taps under a number of conditions (Clynes and Walker, 1982). Between series the subject generally continued to tap for 50–100 taps that were not measured.

Results showed that tapping stability by a musician between consecutive runs of 1000 taps when imagining Mozart's C major piano concerto K467 (first 16 bars) was .5110 sec ± .0026 during 4000 taps, and .5109 sec ± .0007 the following day with 3000 taps (same subject). (No temporal cues were given in either experiment. Excerpts from a recording of the concerto—Arthur Schnabel with the London Philharmonic Orchestra—had been played in a different test three times, weeks before the test.)

Results typically show an improvement by a factor of 5 in medium term stability (30 minutes) when a musical phrase is repeatedly thought by a musician as compared with repeating a verbally imagined phrase such as "Saturday, Sunday," and a further factor of 3 when compared with tapping without a particular thought. Results further show that mean short term "errors" for the music image series were 10 times larger than the longer term drift—the "errors" between successive 1000 series. Short term errors (beat to beat) were of similar magnitude in all series. They appear largely like noise introduced inside the control loop.

Results are summarized in Table 1. Increased stability with increasing number of taps is shown by this table. Individual taps typically show errors of several centiseconds, but larger tap groups show an increasing stability. Thus it seems that the idea or concept of the tempo of the music is more stable than the ability to execute taps in accordance with it. Errors of individual taps tend to compensate each other, showing presence of a higher hierarchical control. Improvement of errors with larger groups is only 3 dB less than the theoretical signal/noise improvement ratio for a perfectly stable signal in the presence of noise equivalent to the tap to tap errors.

Comparison of the Tempo of Imagined and Performed Rhythm

We have studied the durations of thinking a musical rhythm, as well as in actual performance—thinking the music at the rate at which we would

Table 1

Increased stability with increasing number of taps is shown by this table. Although individual taps typically shows errors of several centiseconds, larger tap groups shows an increasing stability. Thus it seems that the idea of the tempo of the music is more stable than the ability to execute taps in accordance with it. Errors of individual taps tend to compensate each other showing presence of a higher hierarchical control. Improvement of errors with larger groups is only 3 dB less than the theoretical signal/noise improvement ratio for a perfectly stable signal in the presence of noise equivalent to the tap to tap errors.

Stability of Tapping White Thinking Mozart Piano Concerto K 467 (First 16 Bars) Repeatedly

		June 25	June 26
Number of Taps		4000	3000
		Means (seconds)	
Entire Run		.5112	.5092
First 1000		.5117	.5086
Second 1000		.5109	.5092
Third 1000		.5085	.5099
Fourth 1000		.5137	

Stability Analysis of Run of 4000 Taps						
			Per Groups of			
	1	10	100	200	500	1000
mean error	.0128	.00529	.00338	.00283	.00172	.00150
standard dev.	.01936	.00610	.00416	.00378	.00285	.00216

Examples of Consecutive Individual Values			*Consecutive Means*		
.5010	.5174	.5154		.5122	.5117
.5313	.5189	.5117		.5113	.5109
.5155	.5181	.5122		.5099	.5085
.5002	.5227	.5106		.5119	.5137
.4757	.5234	.5110		.5056	
.4990	.5168	.5131		.5114	
.4853	.5133	.5096		.5113	
.5189	.5098	.5127		.5160	
.4992	.5110	.5126			
.5077	.5071	.5080			
...	...	...			
...	...	...			

Slope of line of best fit for 4000 taps: less than   −0.1 microsec/tap
                                                  −0.2 microsec/sec

perform it in real time compared with that of an actual performance by the same person, on the same occasion. (In imaging on a real time scale, subliminal motor activity of a glottal, tongue or palatal nature is almost unavoidable.) Experiments in which pieces or portions of pieces of music less than 1 minute long are executed (1) mentally only; (2) conducting; (3) playing (particular pieces are executed five times for each condition by each of 8 musician subjects, with a total of 240 trials) show the following: (a) mean standard deviation for pieces performed by a given musician is 1.92% for playing, 3.48% for thinking; (b) a consistently slower mental execution (mean 8.9%; p < .0001), when thinking, only (Clynes and Walker, 1982).

MUSIC AS TIME'S MEASURE

Time and Psychobiologic Clocks

In this section we are concerned with temporal stabilities illustrated in performances of large works involving four individuals working together musically over many years, the Sydney String Quartet. We shall show how musical concepts shared by several individuals can interact with psychobiologic clocks that may be involved in thinking and producing music. Temporal stabilities are revealed in this study—as also have been reported with single musical performers (Clynes and Walker, 1982), greater by an order of magnitude or more than those typically observed with nonmusical time intervals (Eisler 1976).

The representation of time in the central nervous system is one of the important unsolved problems in neuroscience. The problem has two main aspects:

(1) The experience of time.
(2) The temporal organization of behaviour and of central nervous system functions.

Relatively little work has been reported in the literature on the perception of time on the scale of minutes and hours. Our work with musicians involves time stabilities encompassing that range as well as shorter time spans concerned with musical rhythms.

Sensing of time and music are intimately interwoven. In the functioning of our brain we may even consider music as a measure of time: musical thought and musical memory are an indication of mental time rate and direction. (Physical law does not prescribe the direction of time, but conscious memory does; rational thought would not be possible without the inherent knowledge of which of two events was "later"—shared indeed with animals.) Clearly, music engages and programs a psycho-biologic clock, or clocks, which function subconsciously but give conscious readouts, and what in computer function are called "interrupts." These "interrupt" signals can be considered to guide the realisation of the proportions of musical rhythm and duration. Much remains to be known about the mechanisms of the psychobiologic clock or clocks involved (Church, 1984; Kristofferson, 1984; Gibson, 1984).

The resolution of the conventional metronome is 5% between successive steps. Most composers have limited themselves to this resolution—with some notable exceptions such as Bartok who decreased the step by a factor of two or three. However it was found that actual stabilities and resolutions of performances by Toscanini proved to be an order of magnitude greater than his own metronome indications for these performances, which he himself marked on his scores (Clynes, 1969). Moreover, the total time of performances as much as twelve years apart showed an extraordinary stability greater even than that of individual sub-units. Such studies, not previously practicable, had become possible through modern tape-recording methods.

Later it became clear (Clynes and Walker, 1982) that this extraordinary stability was not the particular province of the great and unique musical mind of Toscanini, as was first thought, but that other performers can unconsciously exhibit the same remarkable temporal stability with respect to the overall length of the piece. Thus a thoroughly known musical piece of duration of the order of one thousand seconds appears to exist in the mind of a musician as an entity of precise temporal size although he is not aware of this. Changes in duration of sub-sections from one performance to another often tend to be compensated by changes in other subsections so as to maintain the same overall duration.

We have seen in an earlier section that for shorter time periods it is found that the precision and stability of musical thought exceeds the possible precision of execution. Short term deviations from this thought precision seem to be like random noise which tends to cancel out over longer periods, as the musical rhythm or beat is repeated.

In these previous studies the temporal stability observed was that of a single musical mind, as conductor or as performer.

Timing Stability in Group Performance

In the following we shall describe findings of similar stability in the performance of a string quartet—four individual musical minds who work together over a number of years. Performance in different cities and concert halls of the Sydney String Quartet, an internationally recognized quartet of high standard,[5] were analysed covering a period from 1975–1979 and comprising the following works:

6 performances of Haydn Quartet Op 76, No. 5
7 performances of Beethoven Op 130
12 performances of the Ravel Quartet
11 performances of Janacek Quartet No. 2, and
3 performances of the Bartok No. 6 Quartet

In a quartet performance individual parts predominate at various portions of the music. In general each performer has some responsibility for setting the tempo at various places in the course of the music. (In general the voice with the most notes per time unit tends to lead the tempo.)

Significantly and surprisingly, **the stability observed with four performers was as great as that of single performers previously studied,** including Toscanini. This appears to show that the overall time concept of a piece can exist in the context of social music making, (ensemble playing) as a **collective** mental concept.

Methods

All the performances were public performances at various concert halls, seating from 500–3,000 people, held at various seasons in different cities. They were either evening or afternoon performances. All performances had been recorded on the same Nakamishi 500 tape-recorder. Each recorded performance was timed three times with a digital timing clock and mean times taken. Each day the playing tape-recorder (a Nakamishi 680) was time calibrated both before and after measurement. Calibrations were done by timing, three times, a ten minute tape having ten timing clicks spaced one minute apart. All tapes were also checked against tuning—the tuning process of the quartet had also been recorded. (The latter, however, can be taken only as a crude timing guide.) Timing stability of the equipment proved to have a standard deviation of $\pm$ 0.06 sec in 10 minutes or $\pm$ 0.01%.

All subsections were timed to end at the beginning of the last tone of the music. This was in order to avoid distortions in timing due to the difficult timing determination of the end of a decaying tone. Each piece was timed cumulatively. All timing was done by playing on a Nakamishi 680 tape-recorder, a machine of greater precision than the Nakamishi 500. Standard deviation between repeated timings of the same performance was 0.01% or 0.1 sec per 16 minutes.

The stability of the Nakamishi 500 during the years of recording is not known. At the time of this study it was $\pm$ 0.08 sec std. in 10 minutes, or + 0.13%, compared with 0.01% of the Nakamishi 680. We can be reasonably assured, however, that it did not get better with age.

The stability of the performance times might possibly have been even somewhat greater than was observed, since, of course, all sources of error would tend to decrease the measured stability.

Results

Performances of Haydn Op. 276, No. 5

Table 2 and Figure 5 show the performance times of the four movements of this quartet, at the dates shown. The greatest variability is shown in the slow Largo movement; a finding that is typical—the tempo stability of movements with a moderate or fast beat seems to be greatest and that of slow, lyrical pieces least.

It can be seen that the four stablest performances of the 6 performances of the Minuet have only a .4 second standard deviation in more than 3 minutes, or 0.2%. Because of this high stability these four performances were chosen to investigate the detailed course of the subsections in relation to the overall stability.

The subsections here are clearly demarcated as the halves of the Minuet and Trio respectively, and are repeated except in the reprise of the Minuet. Figure 6 and Table 3 show the stability of subsections of the Minuet. It is seen that the subsections are also stable, but the stability is less than that of the overall time duration. Where portions of the performance are slightly faster, as in the performance of 20/9/77, a compensation occurs in a later section (in this instance the Trio). The total duration of the Minuet is in all four performances practically identical. The proportions of the larger sections are generally preserved, except

Table 2

Four performances showing especially high stability in the minuet. Note also that performances group themselves into two pairs (1, 3 and 2, 4) in regard to total playing time.

HAYDN—Op. 76, No. 5
Times for 4 Performances

	20/9/77	6/10/77	24/11/77	28/10/78	St. Dev. %	
Allegretto	4:55.6	4:59.8	4:51.8	4:52.7	1.22	Allegretto
Largo	7:44.0	8:02.2	7:50.4	8:03.2	1.96	Largo
Menuetto	3:14.0	3:13.6	3:13.6	3:14.4	0.20	Menuetto
Finale	3:33.2	3:27.0	3:31.1	3:30.7	1.38	Finale
Total playing time	19:26.8	19:42.6	19:26.9	19:41.0	.737	Total playing time

for a slight trade off between the duration of the trio and the first playing of the minuet.

The first movement and finale of the Quartet, which have a relatively fast beat, have next higher degree of stability and the slow movement is

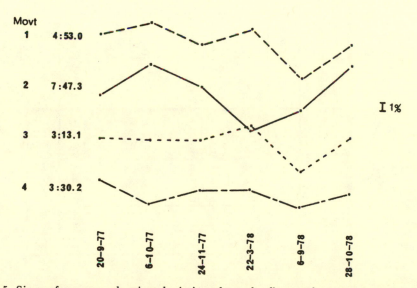

Figure 5. Six performances showing deviations from the first performance on a percentage scale. Times for the first performance (20-9-77) for each movement are stated on the left. The horizontal axis shows the sequence of performances, and is not a linear time axis.

Table 3

An analysis of four performances showing subsections and repeats as well as cumulative times. In addition to great overall stability, consistent proportions are observed within the subsections. Compensation is also evident so that when the first playing of the minuet is somewhat faster the trio tends to be correspondingly slower.

24/1/77			20/9/77			6/10/77			28/10/78		
0:09.5			0:09.6			0:09.9			0:09.4		
0:09.9	0:19.4		0:09.7	0:19.3		0:09.9	0:19.8		0:09.9	0:19.3	
0:28.5			0:28.4			0:28.6			0:28.3		
0:29.3	0:57.8	1:17.2	0:29.1	0:57.5	1:16.8	0:29.7	0:58.3	1:18.1	0:29.2	0:57.5	1:16.8
0:14.1			0:14.3			0:13.8			0:14.3		
0:14.0	0:28.1		0:14.3	0:28.6		0:14.0	0:27.8		0:14.5	0:28.8	
0:24.5			0:24.9			0:24.5			0:24.7		
0:25.4	0:49.9	1:18.0	0:25.6	0:50.5	1:19.1	0:24.8	0:49.3	1:17.1	0:25.4	0:50.1	1:18.9
0:10.0			0:09.9			0:10.0			0:09.8		
0:28.4	0:38.4	0:38.4	0:28.6	0:38.5	0:38.5	0:28.4	0:38.4	0:38.4	0:28.5	0:38.3	0:38.3
		3:13.6			3:14.4			3:13.6			3:14.0

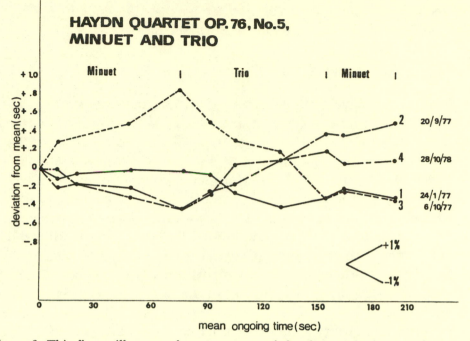

Figure 6. This figure illustrates the convergence of the time tracks for 4 performances illustrating the tendency to conserve the total performance time in spite of small fluctuations of the timing subsections. The vertical axis shows the cumulative deviation from the mean of the four performances at any point of the performance. The slope of a line segment thus indicates how much faster or slower than the mean rate that particular section was played. 1% faster and slower slopes are given as calibration marks at the right bottom portion of the figure. The figure shows that most segments were played at tempos well within one percent deviation from the mean tempo for that segment, and that the maximum deviation from the cumulative mean of any performance was less than 0.9 seconds (0.4% of the total time) and was mostly much less than that.

least stable. ($F_{3,3}$ test comparing these movements to the slow movement shows p < .01). Note that the standard deviation of the whole work in seconds is actually less than that of the slow movement alone—a trend also illustrating compensation.

For the first movement (Allegretto) we note that two performances cluster around 4 minutes and 58 seconds and the other two around 4 minutes and 53 seconds. In the Largo also two performances cluster around 8 mins., 3 seconds while two others are around 7 mins., 47 secs. The total playing time for the four movements of the two performances with the slower Largo was 19 mins., 41.8 secs. ± 0.8 secs., while the two performances with the faster largo show a playing time of 19 mins., 26.8 secs. ± 0.1 secs. The difference between the two sets of total times of 15 ±

0.9 seconds is essentially accounted for by the difference in the Largo (15.5 ± 3.7 seconds) in these four performances.

Beethoven Ops. 130, With and Without the Grosse Fuge

Seven performances of Beethoven's Ops, 130 are presented in Table 4, Figs. 7–9. This quartet consists of six movements. The last four performances substituted the Grosse Fuge (Op. 133) in place of the Allegro movement as a finale (6th movt.). All the other five movements show a considerable slowing in every performance where the Grosse Fuge was played as the last movement. (The test for equality of means for each movement without the Grosse Fuge vs. with the Grosse Fuge shows this to be significant at the p < .01 level.) The lowest degree of stability occurs in the fifth movement (Cavatina), a very slow movement. But even for this movement every single performance was slower when the Grosse Fuge was played than any one of the three performances with the shorter finale.

Remarkable stability is shown by the first movement in the three performances with the Allegro finale. This movement is quite complex in structure. The movement is composed of both slow (Adagio) and fast (Allegro) sections. Grouping the Adagio sections together we may note also here that compensation occurs so that the performances where the Adagio sections are slightly slower the Allegro sections are correspondingly slightly faster, resulting in an overall duration of 9 mins., 11.6 secs. ± .7 secs.

The time courses of these Beethoven performances are graphed in figures 7 and 8. High degrees of stability are also shown by the second and third movements. The total times of the three performances are also consistent. The first two performances differ by only 1 second in 34 minutes. The third performance is longer largely as a result of an extended time for the Cavatina. Between the first two performances one can note a compensation: movements 1–3 taken together correspond closely but between themselves show some degree of divergence. Further light on the nature of such divergences is shown by the fact that the timing for the second, fourth and sixth movements of the second performance are then almost identically preserved in the third performance; the second and third performances differ mainly in the slower performance of the Cavatina in the third performance. Note that the standard deviation in seconds of the total performance time (7.3 secs.) is much less

Table 4

Three performances of Opus 130 (left) and four performances of Opus 130 with the Grosse Fuge as finale (Opus 133) in lieu of the finale of Opus 130. Note that all movements are slower in the performance that includes the Grosse Fuge. Standard Deviations are less for the entire performances than may be expected from the standard deviations of individual movements. Note the high degree of stability of the first and third movements in the performances without the Grosse Fuge and also of the Grosse Fuge itself.

	5/8/76	6/8/76	13/8/76	Means	St. Dev. %	12/9/77	22/9/77	19/5/78	24/5/78	Means	St. Dev. %
First Movement	9:12.2	9:11.9	9:10.9	9:11.67	.12	9:41.4	9:35.8	9:39.4	9:52.6	9:42.3	1.24
Second Movement (Presto)	1:52.4	1:50.9	1:50.8	1:51.37	.81	1:56.6	1:56.9	1:56.9	2:00.3	1:57.67	1.49
	11:04.6	11:02.8	11:01.7			11:38.0	11:32.7	11:36.3	11:52.9		
Third Movement (Andante)	6:38.4	6:39.7	6:37.1	6:38.4	.33	6:48.5	6:45.2	7:00.0	7:19.1	6:58.2	3.66
	17:43.0	17:42.5	17:38.8			18:26.5	18:17.9	18:36.3	19:12.0		
Fourth Movement (Alla danza tedesca)	3:13.4	3:06.6	3:07.5	3:09.17	1.95	3:21.5	3:20.9	3:24.6	3:27.2	3:23.55	1.43
	20:56.4	20:49.1	20:46.3			21:48.0	21:38.8	22:00.9	22:39.2		
Fifth Movement (Cavatina)	5:35.4	5:52.8	6:07.3	5:51.83	4.54	6:20.3	6:11.6	7:09.3	7:04.7	6:41.47	7.41
	26:31.8	26:41.9	26:53.6			28:08.3	27:50.4	29:10.2	29:43.9		
Sixth Movement (Grosse Fugue)	7:57.3	7:48.2	7:48.6	7:51.37	1.09	16:05.9	16:17.2	16:12.9	16:29.6	16:16.15	.97
	34:29.1	34:30.1	34:42.2	34:33:76	0.35	44:14.2	44:07.6	45:23.1	46:12.5	44:59.35	2.20

Cumulative times are given below and to the left of the timings of each movement (without pauses between movements as they often included tuning).

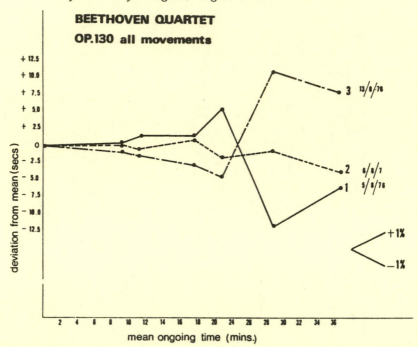

Figure 7. Cumulative timing of the 3 entire performances, (each of 6 movements) showing tendency to converge, maintaining total performance time. Cumulative deviation from mean does not exceed 10 seconds in 36 minutes (0.5%) anywhere, and is mostly less. Largest deviations occur in the fifth movement (Cavatina), a slow movement. Calibration as in Figure 2.

than the standard deviation of the Cavatina (16.0 secs.) and the standard deviation of the movements taken together considered independently (17.3 secs.), indicating compensation, $p < .005$.

All performances are generally slower when the Grosse Fuge is introduced. Moreover, in the last four performances we can also note a decrease in stability of the other movements. (An $F_{3,2}$ test for equality of variances shows this to be significant at the $p < .05$ level.) The string quartet had been used to perform the piece without the Grosse Fuge. Introducing this had a somewhat destabilizing effect, as well as increasing the duration of all other five movements. The stability remains high, however, by conventional standards (standard deviation 0.4 of a step of the metronome).

Two performances of the Grosse Fuge itself are analysed in detail in Table 5. Noteworthy is the exquisite balance between the various sections of the fugue, a balance brought about entirely subconsciously, as it would have been beyond human capacity to select the tempo deliberately in order to bring it about.

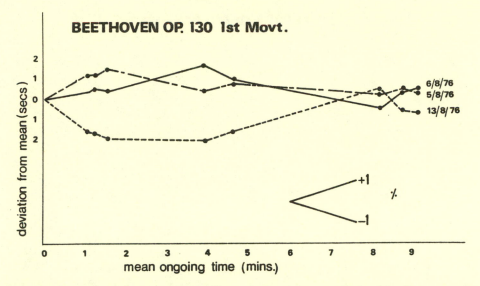

Figure 8. The same performances as in Figure 7, showing an analysis of the first movement only and its subsections. This illustrates a similar convergence and conservation of total time as does the entire performance. The cumulative deviation from the mean is less than one second in 9 minutes (0.2%) at the end of the first movement, and maximally 2 seconds (0.4% of total time). Calibration as in Figure 2.

Thus the main allegro part of the fugue, bars 30 to 158, has its transformed counterpart in bars 233 to 492. The first section is in quadruple time, but the later one is in 6/8. The first section has 128 bars (512 beats) while the later has 260 bars (520 beats). Yet the performers timed the sections at 237.8 and 237.9 secs. respectively in one performance and at 239.2 secs. and 235.4 secs. in another.[6] This corresponds to a metronome mark of 129.2 and 131.1 for the beat of quarter notes and of dotted quarter notes respectively for the first performance. For the other performance the corresponding metronome marks are 128.5 and 132.5. Together the two sections accounted for 475.7 secs. in one performance and 474.6 secs. in the other (mean metronome mark 130.1 and 130.5 beats per minute respectively). Such a remarkable outcome in proportion is a significant clue to the subconscious processes involved.

Furthermore, the cumulative performance time shows 293.4 vs. 292.6 secs. to the end of section one, 705.1 vs. 707.6 secs. to the end of the transformed section. The total performance time was 965.7 vs. 977.2 secs., but much of that difference is attributable to only two connecting passages or sections played at a considerably different tempo, viz. bars 494 to 533, 64.5 secs. vs. 70.6 secs.—probably a changed interpretation—and bars 159 to 233, 119.3 secs. vs. 123.3 secs. respectively.

BEETHOVEN QUARTET OP.130

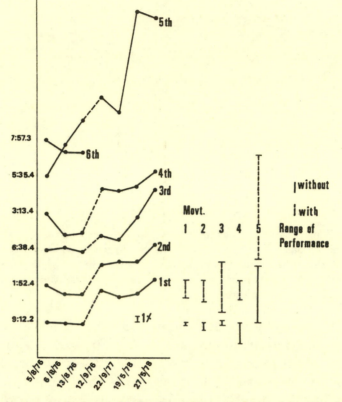

Figure 9. 7 performances, the last 4 with the Grosse Fugue in place of the Allegro Vivace finale of Opus 130. Each movement is plotted at the same vertical percentage scale. Performance times of the first performance of each movement are stated on the left of the figure. On the right side of the figure, the range of performance time is shown as a bounded vertical line in percentage deviation from the first performance for each movement with (solid) and without (broken line) the fugue. There is no overlap in the two ranges for any movement. Performances with the Grosse fuge of movements 1–5 are all considerably slower. (Dotted lines on left side of figure connect the first 3 performances to the last 4 which include the Grosse Fuge.)

We see this subconscious sense of temporal proportion exemplified here, in addition to the remarkable stability of the musical ideas and concepts. The more significant, then, that these proportions and stabilities are subject to influence and show flexibility in relation to the larger musical context within which they are placed. That the substitution of the much longer and weightier Grosse Fuge should cause all other movements to increase in temporal dimensions shows a surprising depen-

Table 5

Bracketed timings show total time for the statement of the fugue (128 bars long) and its later transformation to 6/ time (260 bars long).

BEETHOVEN GROSSE FUGUE Opus 133

Analysis of 2 Performances - 22/9/77 and 12/9/77

(Brisbane)   (Towoomba)

Section Bar Nos.	Time Sec	Cumulative Time	Time Sec	Cumulative Time
17	19.6	19.6	20.3	20.3
30	33.8	53.4	35.3	55.6
58	49.3	102.7	49.5	105.1
79	38.3	141.0	38.3	143.4
109	56.4	197.4	56.0	199.4
139	57.2	254.6	56.7	256.1
158	38.0	292.6	37.3	293.4
		239.2		237.8
209	123.3	415.9	119.3	412.7
233	56.3	472.2	54.5	467.2
272	33.9	506.1	34.4	501.6
324	45.8	551.9	46.3	547.9
358	29.5	581.4	30.0	577.9
404	41.1	622.5	41.4	619.3
453	46.5	669.0	46.8	666.1
477	22.0	691.0	22.3	688.4
493	16.6	707.6	16.7	705.1
		235.4		237.9
533	70.6	778.2	64.5	769.6
565	27.0	805.2	27.2	796.8
609	38.6	843.8	38.3	835.1
663	64.8	908.6	63.2	898.3
701	35.7	944.3	34.6	932.9
741	32.9	977.2	33.0	965.9

dence of otherwise stable concepts on the larger temporal frame within which they are placed musically.

Ravel Quartet

Twelve performances were recorded between June 1975 and June 1978, (Table 6, Fig. 10). These fall into two groups (the first group of five was recorded on a different tape recorder no longer available and thus cannot be directly compared with the last group of five). The first five from June 1975 to June 1977 appear to start from stable versions and gradually tend to become faster in the first and third movements. The second and fourth movements are stable throughout the first four performances and become faster in the fifth. This is reflected by a gradual decrease of the total time, from performances two to five.

After the fifth performance, a rethinking of the interpretation took place and performances No. 6–12, between August 1977 and June 1978, show a considerably slower tempo for all of the movements except for the fourth.

In the case of the Ravel Quartet there does not appear to be an overall length of the piece fixed in the mind of the musician, in spite of remarkable stabilities of certain of the movements.

An interesting observation is a tendency for the timings to fall into distinct groups rather than random values. If we look at the last four performances, for example, the times of the second movement are almost identical in performances 1–3 and also in performances 2–4. The first and third movements have a similar pattern so that performances 1–3 and performances 2–4 appear to group together. This is also reflected in the total time so that performances 1–3 and performances 2–4 appear to group together.

This tendency of timings to fall into discrete values or subgroups which here would seem accidental is further explored in the analysis of thirteen performances of the Janacek Quartet No. 2, where this pattern can be observed with systematic regularity.

Janacek Quartet No. 2: Balanced and Quantized Tempo Changes

Eleven performances were recorded between September 1977 and May 1978 (Fig. 11). We can consider the first four performances as learning stages through which the piece gradually settled to a highly stable concept. The performances tend to become slower and then faster before

Table 6

Groups of 5 and 7 performances. The latter group was recorded on a different tape recorder and is not directly comparable. Comparisons can be made within each group (separated by a vertical line).

RAVEL STRING QUARTET - TIMINGS

	9/6/75	30/4/76	25/9/76	7/2/77	9/6/77	St. Dev. % Perf.1-4	St. Dev. % Perf.1-5
1st Movt.	7:41.5	7:42.7	7:38.3	7:32.8	7:19.1	.96	2.11
2nd Movt.	6:01.3	6:05.0	6:05.7	6:02.1	5:39.7	.59	3.01
3rd Movt.	8:08.1	8:08.7	8:01.7	7:49.6	7:35.8	1.84	2.20
4th Movt.	4:42.2	4:39.8	4:39.9	4:45.4	4:25.4	.99	2.76
TOTAL	26:33.1	26:36.2	26:26.6	26:09.9	25:00.0	.74	2.55

	8/9/77	15/9/77	13/5/78	18/5/78	25/5/78	23/5/78	29/6/78	St. Dev. % Perf.6-12
1st Movt.	7:53.3	8:11.4	8:06.8	8:09.7	7:52.1	8:14.6	7:56.4	1.92
2nd Movt.	6:16.7	6:25.5	6:17.6	6:32.1	6:19.3	6:32.9	6:19.3	1.79
3rd Movt.	8:16.5	8:27.4	8:12.0	8:19.0	8:04.6	8:20.9	7:55.9	2.15
4th Movt.	4:54.3	5:01.8	4:44.6	4:49.2	4:50.7	4:50.3	4:50.4	1.82
TOTAL	27:20.8	28:06.1	27:21.0	27:50.0	27:06.7	27:58.7	27:02.0	1.56

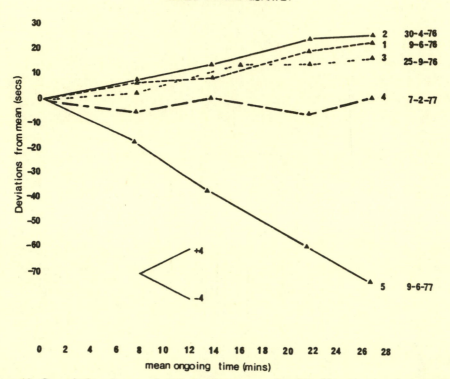

Figure 10. Cumulative time tracks of all movements showing diverging tendency and no overall compensation and conservation of total time for these initial five performances, distinctly different behaviour patterns than for the Beethoven and Haydn quartets.

settling into a range maintained throughout the last seven performances. The stability here is of a very high order. Again, it is greatest in the faster movements. In performances 5–8 the first movement varies only between 6 mins., 9.5 secs. and 6 mins., 11.1 secs., with a mean of 6 mins., 10.1 secs. and standard deviation of 0.7 secs. The fourth movement varies between performances 7–10 only in the range from 7 mins., 42.1 secs. to 7 mins., 43.6 secs. (mean 7 mins., 43.0 secs.; standard deviation 1.1 secs.). System-atic changes in the seven performances are illustrated in Tables 7 and 8. If we begin with performance one of this series of seven performances and tabulate the changes from the first performance we find that the changes appear to be organised into distinct groups. We can consider performances of the first movement to fall into three groups: A, B and C, where a change from group A to B or to C is a major change, while deviations within each group are quite small in comparison. We can tabulate the changes accordingly to whether they increase (S) or decrease

(F) the duration. Table 8 shows that after seven performances the result of the changes is to leave the second, third and fourth movements essentially unchanged while the first movement has a distinct change of 1.8%. Timing deviations are plotted in Figure 12 and show the tendency for the deviations to be of discrete rather than random nature. In fact the mean fluctuation within groups is twelve times less than between groups.

In order to test further whether the distribution of timings has statistically significant gaps—that is regions of zero probability—we used the data of the seven performances of the four movements. Taking the first performance as reference point and considering the percentage timing difference between this and subsequent performances yields $6 \times 4 = 24$ observations which were pooled.

A null hypothesis of a distribution having no "gaps" was required, and the most reasonable choice seemed to be the normal distribution with mean and variance estimated from the data. The observations were grouped into cells of size 0.5% for the absolute value. A value of 16.3 was obtained for chi-square, compared with the 1% value of 15.1, and 0.5% value of 16.7 indicating with a $p < .01$, that the gaps are not due to chance.

Thus the quantized nature of the deviations seems to indicate that preferential values of timings exist. It may be that these correspond to quantized differences in the tempo concept of the music. This seems more likely than purely physiologic reasons for the quantized behaviour since performances were carried out in greatly varying environmental circumstances: halls, temperature and humidity.

Metronome Marks of the Mind?

Having found evidence of quantumization in the Janacek performances, we could test this now predictively on previous results. We may now examine the data of previously presented performances of the twenty-four Beethoven, Haydn and Ravel performances (84 movements), to see if studying the percentage deviation from the first performance of each series for all 84 movements reveals a like quantization.

A surprising result was obtained: Fig. 13 displays the autocorrelation function of the histograms of the timing deviations of the 84 movements of these works. The figure shows a distinctly preferred timing quantum of $0.48 \pm .02$. This would seem to indicate a preferred quantum step in the tempo of musical thought—a metronome mark of the mind (one tenth the size of the conventional metronome mark), applicable in a time

Table 7

Timings of 11 performances. The first four may be considered as learning phases. The last 7 performances show as great a stability as may be found in the Haydn and Beethoven performances. For each
performance the first line is the timing for each individual movement and the second line represents
the cumulative time from the beginning of the performance without pauses between movements.
The specific patterns of stability and change are analysed schematically in Table 8.

JANACEK STRING QUARTET No. 2

Perform. Date	1st Movt	2nd Movt	3rd Movt	4th Movt
2/9/77	5:57.6	5:46.8	5:48.1	8:02.3
		11:44.4	17:32.5	25:34.8
8/9/77	6:14.3	6:06.7	5:45.6	8:15.2
		12:21.0	18:06.6	26:21.8
15/9/77	6:27.3	6:08.9	6:06.4	8:34.8
		12:36.2	18:42.6	27:17.4
20/9/77	6:15.8	5:56.1	5:47.6	8:11.5
		12:11.9	17:59.5	26:11.0
6/10/77	6:09.5	6:02.8	5:40.3	7:57.9
		12:12.3	17:52.6	25:50.5
24/11/77	6:09.6	6:01.7	5:49.3	7:49.4
		12:11.5	18:00.8	25:50.2
22/3/78	6:11.1	6:02.2	5:41.5	7:43.0
		12:13.3	17:54.8	25:37.8
15/5/78	6:10.1	5:56.7	5:29.8	7:42.1
		12:06.8	17:36.6	25:18.7
17/5/78	6:02.6	5:52.9	5:27.1	7:43.3
		11:55.5	17:22.6	25:05.9
19/5/78	6:10.2	5:54.7	5:29.5	7:43.6
		12:04.9	17:34.4	25:18.0
27/5/78	6:16.0	6:01.5	5:38.8	7:56.9
		12:17.5	17:56.9	25:53.2

St. Dev. %   1.06   1.13   2.40   1.46
Last 7 Performances   ENTIRE   1.25

Table 8

This table schematically illustrates the progression of changes throughout the 7 performances in each movement. "A" represents the initial version, "B" and "C" discretely different subsequent versions. f and s indicate whether the change is to a faster or slower version, respectively. Note that the 7th performance is identical to the first except for a distinctly slower first movement. Two distinct changes occur simultaneously as between performance 1 and 2. They may mutually compensate or not as between performances 2 and 3, and 3 and 4. However, with regard to movements 2, 3 and 4 the cumulative effect of the changes of the 7 performances is to revert to the timings of the first performance. All versions belonging to Group A have less than 1.6 second deviation from one another.

JANACEK   STRING   QUARTET   No.   2

7   Performances

	1st	2nd	3rd	4th	Movements
1	A	A	A	A	comp.
		s		f	A + A = B + B
2	A	A	B	B	
			f	f	
3	A	A	A	C	2 changes
		f	f		no. comp.
4	A	B	C	C	2 changes
	f				no. comp.
5	B	B	C	C	1 change
	s				
6	A	B	C	C	1 change
	s	s	s	s	
7	C	A	A	A	4 changes (back to essentially (1))

Performances

range of 3–8 minutes. One is not consciously aware of such a step.

A quantized rate in the main clock governing the possibility of choosing a tempo would manifest itself in a given percentage quantumization of timing duration appearing in various pieces in a given duration range.

The resolution of such a biologic clock rate may indeed be expected to

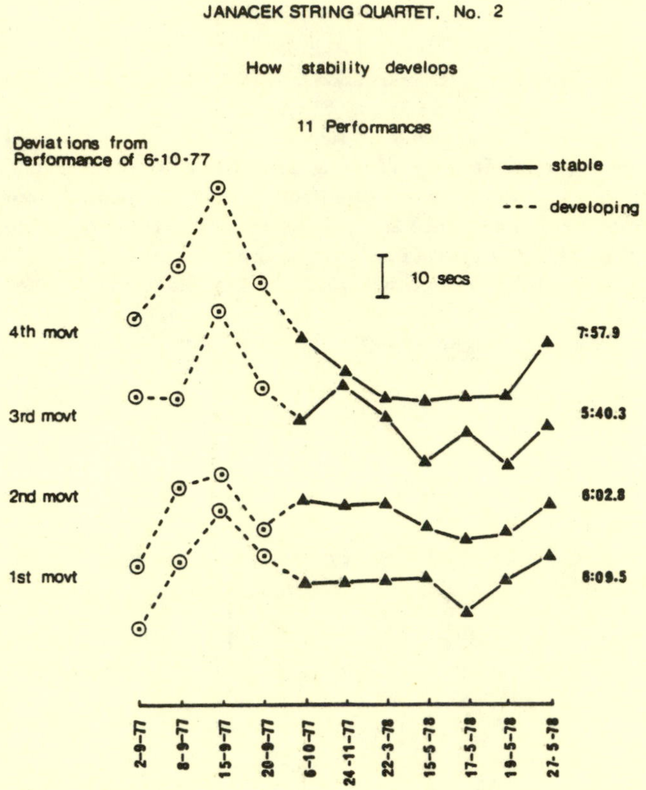

JANACEK STRING QUARTET, No. 2

How stability develops

11 Performances

Deviations from
Performance of 6-10-77

——— stable

--- developing

10 secs

4th movt   7:57.9

3rd movt   5:40.3

2nd movt   6:02.8

1st movt   6:09.5

2-9-77 8-9-77 15-9-77 20-9-77 6-10-77 24-11-77 22-3-78 15-5-78 17-5-78 19-5-78 27-5-78

Figure 11. Of the 11 performances, the first four may be considered as training phases towards the stability achieved in the last 7 performances. Note also the compensation shown in the first and third movements for the performance of 17/5/78 in comparison with the previous and following performance. These results indicate that such remarkable stability can exist also in performances of modern works.

be discrete rather than continuous. Whatever the actual construction of the clock, both molecular process considerations and neural firing events dictate the likelihood of a discrete rate resolution involved in voluntary tempo choice on any one occasion. In this respect it may be compared to the function of the metronome's discrete marks. Moreover, we have also observed longer term stability of the rate, i.e., clock. The question becomes then, what are the sizes of the "metronome steps" of the clock allowing tempo to be thought. Of course such quantumization may be expected to be linear over a restricted range only.

To determine the degree of confidence of these observations from only 84 data points, which cannot be estimated from the autocorrelation function (Vroon, 1974) a quantum model was made on a computer and fitted to the data. This model represented each timing deviation (d) from the

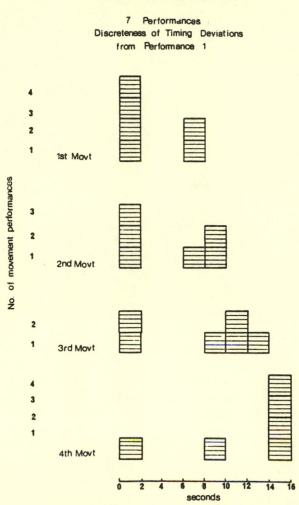

7   Performances
Discreteness of Timing Deviations
from Performance 1

Figure 12. Each shaded block represents one timing data point in this histogram with 2 second bins. Note the absence of data points in the third and fourth bin and discrete patterning.

first performance of each series as the nearest integral number of quanta(q), plus a remainder(r) (which could be either +ve or −ve); d = nq + r.

To estimate the confidence level of this observation, a test model was constructed in which the distribution was tested by the Monte Carlo method i.e., iteration using simulated data. In the simulated data, as hypothesized in the real data, a data point consisted of an integral number of quanta plus an amount of noise. Using an appropriate distribution of noise, iterations of 1000 runs were repeated for various amounts of noise.

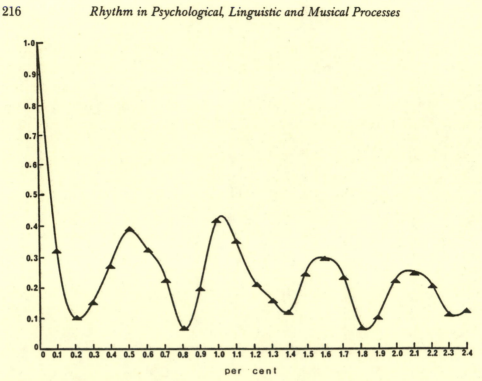

Figure 13. Autocorrelation function of the histogram of the timing deviations from the first performance, in percent for each movement of the Haydn, Beethoven and Ravel quartets given in this paper. The bin size is 0.1%. Note the prevalence of a maintained periodicity of close to 0.5% wave length. These data do not include the Janacek performances in which discontinuous timing behaviour was originally observed (see Figure 12).

The results, when compared to that observed with the actual data, gave a significance of $p < .01$ to the observation that there was a quantum in the range of $.48 \pm .02$. This accorded well with the visual interpretation of the autocorrelation function of the histogram of timing deviations (Fig. 13). Nevertheless this finding should be treated with caution pending further confirmation. Such apparent quantumization would be expected to be found in single performers though we found it here in the performances of a group.

Discussion

How does our mind unconsciously calculate what music is and should be? The findings as reported here pertain to the stability of such unconscious calculations: the forming of small scale and large scale musical images.

Trying to look for an understanding of how such stability in musical thinking and performance of four different individuals can occur, we need to reflect that performances of a particular movement represent an "agreed" version—agreed to by four individuals, and that the performance of the whole work represents an agreed concept of the work. The concept of each movement gradually achieves a more and more defined form in the minds of the players.

This very clear and definite form is then reproduced whenever a performance takes place except when there is a deliberate change in interpretation, or a major accident (the latter appears to be quite rare in the performances analysed here).

Ordinary environmental influences such as different halls, temperatures, humidity, food eaten and time of the day seem to have no detectable effect on stability. On the other hand the substitution of a different finale in Beethoven's Ops 130 has a very strong effect on the timing of the other five movements. The new finale is much longer and weightier than the one it replaces, and all other five movements are appreciably slowed as a result. Whether such influences would work in a similar direction in other cases remains to be explored. This behaviour also further strengthens our findings that the total duration of a piece exists in the mind of the musician as a stable entity, although he is not consciously aware of this.

It is remarkable that such mutually agreed concepts can remain stable in four different individuals over a long period of time. As in a group of dancers a harmoniously planned execution of a multitude of organized movements produces a total performance, so the movements of musicians both in detail and in their totality are governed by overriding concepts. That these concepts can be so precise and have such definite form appears to be the important aspect of these findings. Stabilities in concept or idea and execution could be noted before in the execution of single patterns of movements such as throwing a dart, or a ball, to hit a target. The results with large musical works are, it is believed, the first time such stable mind—body interactions have been shown over such long time spans and such complex motions.

Of course the stabilities observed in our studies are far greater—by more than an order of magnitude even—than those observed in the estimation and production of time intervals in which music plays **no** role (see Eisner, 1975 for a review of the data on such experiments). Such intervals may be said to be musically empty (but note: a rest in a musical context is not an empty interval). It appears that musical significance gives time the precise measure that these performances show—greatly beyond that of musically empty intervals. And only when that musical significance has stabilized in the mind is the corresponding temporal stability observable.

To be able to image and space-out musical tones in a time frame implies the existence of a psychobiologic clock. A signal must be given when it is time to do the next thing (Kristofferson, 1984; Gibbon, 1984; Church, 1984; Wing, 1984). That signal is clearly preprogrammed— something like setting an alarm clock on a miniature scale. Neither an alarm nor a computer interrupt can operate without a clock and somebody has to set the alarm or set the number of ticks to be counted for the next event. These appear to be minimum requirements for a psychobiologic clock whose unconscious function would help to translate a musical concept into a moving performance.[7]

Even more mysterious is the way in which the music concept is converted to the right alarm setting. Our studies of the inner pulse and essentic form offer some guidance to this question. These studies, aspects of which were described in this chapter, have isolated forms in time as precise entities associated with the expression of specific qualities and emotions (Clynes, 1973, 1977, 1980, 1983). Time form printing by the central nervous system (Clynes, 1977; Clynes and Walker, 1982) described earlier requires that only one decision be made for the initial form of the inner pulse of the music—subsequent repetitions are "printed" out without substantial conscious attention. Thus the initial precision of thought in forming the musical pulse carries through subsequent repetitions. What we see in these data then is that both the thought and its repetition are highly precise for these musicians in this musical context. This does not mean that the pulse is not modulated by the musical requirements, but that it is reliably modulated according to the musical influences from one performance to another.

Findings of a high degree of timing stability and precision presented here and in our earlier reports, of interest in themselves, are significant towards further experimental work on the nature of these clocks. One may now investigate ways in which disturbing influences can be introduced biochemically, physiologically, and psychologically—as Hoagland (1933) first suggested—and search for the biological mechanism of these clocks from a base line of stability and precision considerably greater than was previously held to be the case. Better understanding of their function could shed light not only on musical thinking but also on thinking, and on our ability to experience time.

Conclusions

(1) Performances by an acclaimed string quartet of the same works over a number of years show a remarkable temporal stability. Stability is greatest in moderate and fast pieces (s.d. of the order of 0.4%).

(2) The temporal stability reported here for a Quartet is as great as that observed and previously reported for performances of individual performers, including those of Toscanini.

(3) Total duration of a work appears to be a stable entity; small deviations of durations of parts or of movements often tend to compensate another, maintaining overall stability.

(4) When the overall size of the work is changed, e.g., by replacing the finale of Op 130 with its original finale, the Grosse Fuge, Op 133, the durations of the other unchanged constituent parts can be substantially altered.

(5) Stability appears to grow over an initial period of the order of a year; after this period stability may maintain itself.

(6) The stability is more than an order of magnitude greater than the best results described in the research literature with time intervals without music.

(7) This stability appears to exist in spite of environmental changes, such as different halls, temperature, humidity or time of day encountered in the working life of concertizing musicians.

(8) Statistical analysis of the highly stable performances of Janacek's second quartet indicates that very small changes in durations of such stable performances appear to occur in preferred or quantised magnitudes.

(9) When the previous data of this paper were examined for similar quantization, 0.5% appeared as a preferred quantum of tempo deviation for the 84 performances considered together. This was indicated by the autocorrelation function of the histogram of percentage total time deviation.

(10) The existence of such stability is significant in terms of the problem of mind-body interaction. Musical concepts appear to precisely engage central nervous temporal processes—as their embodiments.

(11) This stability creates opportunities for study of the effects of drugs or other environmental factors on the temporal integrating function of the psychobiologic clocks and central nervous processes involved.

CONCLUDING REMARKS

Finally let us return to the beginning of this chapter, to its title, When Time is Music.

Two new properties of time emerge in evolution (as we have seen) where there is consciousness—the finite duration of the present moment, and the rate of passage of time. These are fundamental to rhythm, and indeed music. Time is music only when there is time consciousness. Not in the inorganic world; there, without ordered memory, time is a dimension, a process. Yet one could speculate that perhaps for God, too, time would not be music—God is not likely to be driven by musical rhythm, like we can be. He is not likely to use mental automatism for anticipation like we do in the pulse. Newness of the moment and knowledge of all time would be integrated in Him in a way humans cannot conceive. We can only conceive of music—our wondrous gift horse—and make the best of it.

In this chapter we have seen how our own clocks may be involved, through music, in the bridge between concepts and the physical world; and also how, biologically, meaning has coopted time to create expressive forms through which we communicate and share the evolving story of our feelings.

ACKNOWLEDGMENT

The author gratefully acknowledges the careful and painstaking work of repeated timings carried out by Janice Walker. Special thanks are due to the members of the Sydney String Quartet for providing the many tapes of their performances. The help of Nigel Nettheim in the statistical evaluation of the data is also gratefully acknowledged. Thanks are also due to Jane McGlone and Dorothy Capalletto in tabulating the data and preparing the manuscript.

REFERENCES

Allan, L. G. Contingent aftereffects in duration judgements. In J. Gibbon and L. Allan (Eds.), *Timing and time perception.* New York: New York Academy of Sciences, 1984, *423,* 116–130.

Allan, L. G. Magnitude estimation of temporal intervals. *Perception & Psychophysics,* 1979, *26,* 340–354.

Allan, L. G. The perception of time. *Perception & Psychophysics,* 1979, *26,* 340–354.

Bargiello, T. A., & Young, M. Y. Molecular genetics of a biological clock in Drosophila. *Proceedings of the National Academy of Science,* 1984, *81,* 2142–2146.

Becking, G. *Der Musikalische Rhythmus als Erkenntnisquelle,* Ausburg: B. Filsner, 1928.

Bernstein, L. The unanswered question: *Six talks at Harvard.* Cambridge, MA: Harvard University Press, 1976.

Church, R. M. Properties of the internal clock. In J. Gibbon and L. Allan (Eds.), *Timing and time perception.* New York: New York Academy of Sciences, 1984.

Clynes, M. Music as time's measure, *Journal of Music Perception,* in press.

Clynes, M., Jurisevic, S., Rynn, M. In preparation.

Clynes, M. Secrets of life in music, in *Analytica;* Studies in the description and analysis of music, in honour of Ingmar Bengtsson. Stockholm: Publication issued by the Royal Swedish Academy of Music, 1985, *47,* 3–15.

Clynes, M. Music beyond the score, presented at Symposium on Music, Reason and Emotion held in Ghent, Belgium, 1983.

Clynes, M. Expressive microstructure in music, linked to living qualities. In J. Sundberg (Ed.), *Studies of Music Performance.* Stockholm: Publication of Royal Swedish Academy of Music, 1983, *39,* 76–181.

Clynes, M., & Nettheim, N. The living quality of music: Neurobiologic basis of communicating feeling. In M. Clynes (Ed.), *Music, mind and brain: The neuropsychology of music.* New York: Plenum Press, 1982.

Clynes, M., & Walker, J. Neurobiologic functions of rhythm, time and pulse in music. In M. Clynes (Ed.), *Music, mind and brain: The neuropsychology of music.* New York: Plenum Press, 1982.

Clynes, M. The communication of emotion: Theory of sentics in emotion. In R. Plutchik and H. Kellerman (Eds.), *Theory, research and experience.* New York: Academic Press, 1980.

Clynes, M. *Sentics: The touch of emotions.* New York: Doubleday Anchor, 1977(a).

Clynes, M. Space-time form printing by the human central nervous system. Presented at the Society for Neuroscience, Los Angeles, 1977b.

Clynes, M. Communication and generation of emotion through essentic form. In L. Levi (Ed.), *Their parameters and measurement.* New York: Raven Press, 1975.

Clynes, M. Sentics: Biocybernetics of emotion communication. *Annals of the N.Y. Academy of Science,* 1973, *220,* 55–131.

Clynes, M. Towards a theory of man, precision of essentic form in living communication. In K. N. Leibovic and J. C. Eccles (Eds.), *Information processing in the nervous system.* New York: Springer-Verlag, 1969.

Cooke, D. *The language of music.* London: Oxford University Press, 1959.

Cooper, G. W., & Meyer, L. B. *The rhythmic structure of music.* Chicago: University of Chicago Press, 1960.

Deutsch, D. *The psychology of music.* New York: Academic Press, 1982.

Eisler, H. Applicability of the parallel-clock model to duration discrimination. *Perception & Psychophysics,* 1981, *29,* 225–233.

Eisler, H. Experiments on subjective duration 1868–1975: A collection of power function exponents. *Psychological Bulletin,* 1976, 83, 1154–1171.

Gabrielsson, A., Bengtsson, I., & Gabrielsson, B. Performance of musical rhythm in 3/4 and 6/8 meter. *Scandinavian Journal of Psychology,* 1983, *24,* 193–213.

Gibbon, J., Church, M., & Meck, W. H. Scalar timing in memory. In J. Gibbon, and

L. Allan (Eds.), *Timing and time perception*. New York: New York Academy of Sciences, 1984.

Hoagland, H. E. The psychological control of judgement of duration: Evidence for a chemical clock. *Journal of General Psychology*, 1933, *9*, 267–287.

Hopkins, G. W. Ultrastable stimulus-response latencies: Towards a model of response-stimulus synchronization. In J. Gibbon and L. Allan (Eds.), *Timing and time perception*. New York: New York Academy of Sciences, 1984.

Hopkins, G. W., & Kristofferson, A. B. Ultrastable stimulus-response latencies: Acquisition and stimulus control. *Perception & Psychophysics*, 1980, 241–250.

Hornstein, A. D., & Rotter, G. S. Research methodology in temporal perception. *Journal of Experimental Psychology*, 1969, *79*, 561–564.

Imberty, M. Entendre la Musique. *Semantique Psychologique De La Musique*. Paris: Dunod, 1979.

Klages, L. *Grundlegung der Wissenschaft vom Ausdruck*. Bonn: Barth, 1950.

Konopka, R. J., & Benzer, S. Clock mutants of Drosophila Melanogaster. *Proceedings of the National Academy of Science, USA*, 1971, *68*, 2112–2116.

Kristofferson, A. B. Quantal and deterministic timing in human duration, discrimination. In J. G. Gibbon and L. Allan (Eds.), *Timing and time perception*. New York: New York Academy of Sciences, 1984.

Kristofferson, A. B. A quantal step function in duration discrimination. *Perception and Psychophysics*, 1980, *27*, 300–306.

Kyriacou, C. P., & J. C. Hall. Circadian rhythm mutations in Drosophila melanogaster affect short-term fluctuations in the male's courtship song. *Proceedings of the National Academy of Sciences, USA*, 1980, *77*, 6724–6733.

Langer, S. K. *Feeling and form: A theory of art developed from philosophy in a new key*. London: Routledge & Kegan Paul, 1953.

Lashley, K. S. The problem of serial order in behaviour. In L. Jeffress (Ed.), *Cerebral mechanisms in behaviour*. New York: Wiley, 1951.

Latour, P. L. Evidence of internal clocks in the human operator. *Acta Psychologica*, 1967, *27*, 341–348.

Mach, E. *Die Analyse der Empfindungen und das Verhaltnis des Physischen zum Psychischen*. Jena: G. Fischer, 1885.

Mach, E. Untersuchungen uber den Zeitsinn des Ohres. *Sitzungsberichte der mathem. —naturwiss. Klasse d. Kaiserl. Akademie d. Wissenschaften*, 1865, *51*, 11. Abt. Heft 1–5, 133–150.

Martin, J. G. Rhythmic (hierarchical) versus serial structure in speech and other behaviour. *Psychological Review*, 1972, *79*, 487–509.

Meyer, L. B. Explaining music: *Essays and explanations*. Berkeley: University of California Press, 1973.

Michon, J. A., & Jackson, J. L. Attentional effort and cognitive strategies in the processing of temporal information. In J. Gibbon and L. Allan (Eds.), *Timing and time perception*. New York: New York Academy of Sciences, 1984.

Minsky, M. Music, mind and meaning in music. In M. Clynes (Ed.), *Music, mind and brain: The neuropsychology of music*. New York: Plenum Press, 1982.

Polzella, D. J., Dapolito, F., & Hinsman, M. C. Cerebral asymmetry in time perception. *Perception & Psychophysics*, 1977, *21*, 187–192.

Poppel, E. Time perception. In R. Held, W. Leibowitz and H. L. Teuber (Eds.), *Handbook of sensory physiology (VIII): Perception*. Heidelberg, Germany: Springer, 1978.

Pribram, K. H. Brain mechanism in music: Prolegomena for a theory of the meaning of music. In M. Clynes (Ed.), *Music, mind and brain: The neuropsychology of music*. New York: Plenum Press, 1982.

Schenker, H. *Der Freie Satz*. Vienna: Universal Edition, 1953.

Sessions, R. *Questions about music*. Cambridge, MA: Harvard University Press, 1970.

Shaffer, H. Timing in musical performances. In J. Gibbon and L. Allan (Eds.), *Timing and time perception*. New York: New York Academy of Sciences, 1984.

Sorantine, E. *The problem of musical expression*. Nashville, TN: Marshall & Bruce Company, 1932.

Stelmach, G. E., Mullins, P. A., & Teulings, H. Motor programming and temporal patterns in handwriting. In J. Gibbon and L. Allan (Eds.), *Timing and time perception*. New York: New York Academy of Sciences, 1984.

Sternberg, S., Knoll, R. L., & Zukofsky, P. Timing by skilled musicians. In D. Deutsch (Ed.), *The psychology of music*. New York: Academic Press, 1982.

Sundberg, J., Fryden, L., & Askenfelt, A. *What tells you the player is musical?: An analysis-by-synthesis study of music performance*. Stockholm: Publication of Royal Swedish Academy of Music, 1983.

Sundberg, J. On the anatomy of the retard: A study of timing in music. *Journal of Musical Theory*, 1980, *24*(2), 205–243.

Treisman, M. Temporal rhythms and cerebral rhythms. In J. Gibbon and L. Allan, (Eds.), *Timing and time perception*. New York: New York Academy of Sciences, 1984.

Vroon, P. A. Is there a time quantum in duration experience? *American Journal of Psychology*, 1974, *87*, 237–245.

Wing, A. M., Keele, S., & Margolin, D. I. Motor disorder and the timing of repetitive movements. In J. Gibbon and L. Allan (Eds.), *Timing and time perception*. New York: New York Academy of Sciences, 1984.

NOTES

1. Most of this chapter is based on two publications, Music Beyond the Score published in Communication and Cognition, 1985 and Music as Time's Measure, in Music Perception, 1986, with grateful acknowledgment. Material from Clynes and Walker, in Music, Mind and Brain, the Neuropsychology of Music, 1982, ed. Clynes, is also included.

2. "It is the quality and character of the musical gesture that constitutes the essence of the music, the essential goal of the performer's endeavours . . . We experience music as movement and gesture . . . One must emphasize that a real gesture is in its very nature organic. It takes precise and characteristic shape by virtue of its

own energy, its own inherent laws, its goals, its own curve and direction. There is nothing whatever fortuitous about it." Roger Sessions (1970)

3. In particular, Western Classical Music of the period 1750–1900

4. Just as hunger includes knowledge of what to eat and how much—an extraordinary invention of nature, combining feeling and knowledge in one psychic entity—so also emotions have their own fields of knowledge, and enjoining attitudes.

5. Members and Ages in 1979:

Harry Curby 1st	Violin	(46)
Doral Tincu 2nd	Violin	(43)
Alex Todicescu	Violin	(40)
Nathan Waks	Cello	(28)

6. We show the analysis of the first two performances of the Fuge here in detail. Corresponding values for the third and fourth performance are 241.1 and 236.1 secs, and 243.8 and 243.0 secs respectively, displaying similar behaviour.

7. Oscillating circuits controlled for their frequency of oscillation (like a metronome is set by a slider) could reproduce the fine structure of the musical pulse only with elaborate non-linear programming, and would not have the flexibility in stop and start and changes that the real musical pulse has.

Chapter 9

RHYTHMIC ENTRAINMENT AS A MECHANISM FOR LEARNING IN MUSIC THERAPY

Mark S. Rider, Charles T. Eagle, Jr.

Mathew is seated on the floor directly in front of me, engaged in self-stimulatory behaviors—rocking, wringing his hands—and totally unaware of my presence.

"Math-ew," I sing on an ascending fourth...No response by Mathew, so I repeat the prompt (cue) in an attempt to obtain some communicative response from this autistic boy. After repeated unsuccessful attempts to obtain any vocalizations, I physically prompt him to strike the drum twice (to the two syllables of his name) as I accompany with his name: "Math-ew." Again, nothing. Suddenly, after several physical prompts on the drum, Mathew cries out, "Ah-ah-ah-ah" in an ascending arpeggiated style. Immediately, I imitate him—"Ah-ah-ah-ah," in the same rhythm and key. For the first time in the session, Mathew makes eye contact, laughs, and reaches out to hug me and I reciprocate. I try imitating the four-note sequence several times and finally he answers, "Ah-ah-ah-ah." After hugging Mathew again and praising him, I return to the two-beat cadence of his name, still prompting with his hand on the drum. On the third trial, he responds by saying, "Math-ew." This was his first music lesson. (Rider, 1982a)

The above excerpt demonstrates a brief moment of successful contact with a child who experiences few such moments of awareness that we would call "normal." But what was the mechanism operating in the above interaction? Was it the music environment? Was it the reinforcing and supporting atmosphere, the hugging and praising by the music therapist? Was it related simply to the multi-sensory learning system of the boy's auditory/visual/tactile modes?

Findings from experimentally controlled and descriptive research tell us that all three factors—music, reinforcement, and multi-sensory environments—are capable of enhancing learning. Thus, it has been shown that: (1) Music provides motivation and structure for the learning environment; (2) Reinforcement and support have been effective in increasing classroom discipline and client responsibility; (3) Sensory integration appears to be paramount for maximum learning and retention. However, closer observation of the interaction with Mathew reveals that the major breakthrough in the session did not occur until the therapist imitated the four-syllable outburst by Mathew in the same rhythm and key. His affect changed significantly at this juncture, and, for the moment, the interaction became more intimate; Mathew, in turn, was more responsive. Therefore, imitating, or matching, the behavior of the client through the auditory sense emerges as a possible causative component in learning.

Entraining as a Model for Music Therapy

Behavior Matching

The preceding case history demonstrates a phenomenon which can be found in much of the research in music psychology/therapy. This matching of behavior for the purpose of changing one's perception of time or mood has been dubbed the "iso-principle" by Ira Altshuler (1948). He found that depression or agitation could be relieved by presenting music which matched the initial mood of the patient and then gradually changing the music in the affective direction desired. For example if a patient entered the therapy session in a depressed mental state, Altshuler would initially present "depressing" music (relatively slow, primarily minor key). By careful observation he would determine when the mood of the patient matched the mood of the music, and, at that point, introduce slightly more "manic" music (relatively fast, primarily major key). Gradually, Altshuler matched the patient's behavior with more and more manic music, thereby moving the patient from a depressed mental state to a more manic or balanced state.[1] Altshuler also used other elements in music, such as tempo, melody, and harmony, to entrain patients (Collins, 1983).

The iso-principle is closely related to the concept we call "entrainment." The principle seems to be associated with and perhaps explained by a phenomenon in physics which causes "phase-locking" between any two or more objects having similar oscillatory or rhythmic behavior. This occurrence was reported as early as 1665 by Christian Huygens who was studying the phase-locking of two pendula (Leonard, 1978). Set in motion with unsynchronized but close periods, two adjacent, connected pendula gradually become synchronized. Usually the slightly faster oscillator will force the slightly slower one to move at the pace of the former (Bentov, 1977). This is similar to, if not the same as, the sets of oscillators found in humans, many of which function on a circadian, or daily cycle. Hormonal and electrolytic levels, body temperature, skin resistance, and sensory awareness, to name only a few of these human oscillators, all operate, many independently, on an approximate 24-hour period. Moreover, light intensity, electromagnetic field, and social phenomena can entrain the circadian oscillators of living systems to non-circadian rhythms if the entrainers, or "zeitgebers," have a similar rhythm. Whereas circadian entrainment in humans occurs in a range from 23–28 hours with a median of 25 hours (Luce, 1971), certain nonhuman species have a wider range of 18–30 hours with a median of 23.5 hours (Cloudsley-Thompson, 1961).

The mechanics explaining rhythmic entrainment are based on physical laws which tend to minimize the total energy output of a system. Nature "finds it more economical in terms of energy to have periodic events that are close enough in frequency to occur in phase or in step with each other" (Bentov, 1977, p. 21). Congruent with this theory are findings from brain research which reveal that the neural system attempts to process information based on minimum input (Roederer, 1974). This may be the basis of music processing. Music which is familiar to us and is similar to our present mood may minimize the energy of the total organismic system. If we are depressed and listen to a joyous piece of music, a maximum amount of energy is expended. This may relate to Clynes' findings that the "essentic forms" of two different emotions cannot be produced simultaneously (Clynes, 1978; Clynes & Nettheim, 1982).

Research also has suggested that emotional arousal causes an increase in subcortical information processing, thereby reducing the amount of cortical processing that can occur. This may be the reason why people who are angered prefer structurally simpler music than when they are not aroused (Konecni, 1982). Perhaps music which is unfamiliar to us or differs from our present mood causes excessive mental activity; a form of cognitive dissonance may be the result.

Rider (1982b) found that extroverted people more often like vocal music, while introverted people generally prefer instrumental music. This finding comes from data provided through use of a revised version of the **Music Preference Test of Personality** (Anderson & Cattell, 1953) and indicates that we tend to prefer music which matches certain of our personality characteristics. On a larger scale, music tends to match the social personality of a culture. For example, Lomax (1968) found that sexually restrictive cultures were permeated with songs which were nasal and narrow in vocal width, whereas the opposite held true in more open cultures. Also, musical counterpoint (use of more than one dominant musical line) was preferred to homophony (all musical parts being dependent on one melodic phrase) in cultures where the women had a role more equal to men.

Learning

Learning is related to internal circadian rhythms. For example, the memory process appears to be related to body temperature and activity. Neurotransmitters show circadian periodicity, some varying with sleep cycles and others with light intensity. Sensory acuity as well as mental and physical dexterity also exhibit periodic activity (Luce, 1971). However, learning **per se** seems to have a unique non-circadian rhythm which is related to the skill or concept to be learned. Precision teaching specialists, having identified four levels in the learning of any concept—acquisition, proficiency, generalization, and adaptation (Haring, Lovitt, Eaton & Hanson, 1978)—have shown that dysfunctions arise when teaching is not "in-synch" with the "rhythm" of these four levels. For instance, the teacher who neglects the last two levels (generalization and adaptation) and moves on to an advanced concept may be said to be 180 degrees out-of-phase with the student.

Piaget (1952) also posited a cyclic characteristic to learning. In his theory the child is constantly moving, like a pendulum, between "assimilation" and "accomodation." In assimilation, the child is in free play where s/he is organizing, changing, and interpreting the external world with her/his present cognitive structures. In accomodation, the child is imitating or changing the cognitive structures to make sense of the external world. According to this theory, then, the child is more accessible to externally controlled learning (imitating) at certain times and to internally controlled learning (improvising) at others. Furthermore, people seem to continually oscillate between these two types of learning throughout life-long cognitive development.

An extensive search of the effects of music upon learning in children, including those with developmental disabilities, reveals three distinguishable categories into which teaching, or treatment, methods may be grouped. In **primary entrainment**, the music, or some attribute of it, is matched directly to the physical or cognitive behavior of the client. Once synchronized, modulation of the music causes change in those personal behaviors. In **secondary entrainment**, the music is synchronized with the material, skill, or concept to be learned. Many of the mnemonic uses of music utilize this process. Finally, in **tertiary entrainment**, the music is matched to the child's functioning or preference level to cause a change in an unrelated behavior. As will be explained later, facilitating development through contingent reinforcement makes use of this process.

In music therapy procedures, some or all of these three processes are involved. No music therapy technique can be used effectively without making use of at least one of these three levels of entrainment. In the following discussion, clinical methods in music therapy will be organized accordingly.

Learning Through Primary Entrainment

Primary entrainment is the process by which music is synchronized to a psychophysiological behavior to cause a change in that behavior. Clinically, the musical stimulus is matched directly with the client's behavior for the purpose of the client effecting control of that behavior. Although primary entrainment through music has been observed in the treatment of a variety of handicapping conditions, examples of the process are given here only for persons who have cerebral palsy or who exhibit autistic behaviors. In the latter part of the present section, primary entrainment as used in relaxation-enhanced learning will be discussed. Throughout the section, reference can be made to Table 1, which presents a listing of musical elements that are primary entrainers of some target behaviors in several different client groups.

Physical Control of Children with Cerebral Palsy[2]

Several examples of primary entrainment through music therapy exist in the literature on cerebral palsy. Palmer (1952) developed a technique

Table 1
Primary Entrainment of Diagnostic Groups Through Elements of Music

Diagnostic Groups of Clients	Target Behaviors	Elements of Music Matched to Target Behaviors
Athetoid cerebral palsy	Reduction in tremors	Tempo
Athetoid and spastic cerebral palsy	Increase in physical control	Sedativeness/stimulativeness
Autistic and severely/ profoundly retarded	Reduction of perserverative behavior	Tempo, pitch, rhythm
All	Development of cognitive concepts	Loudness, timbre, imagery, tempo, duration
All	Increase in relaxation (decrease in brain-wave frequency and muscle tonus)	Rhythm, sedativeness

with children disabled by athetoid cerebral palsy in which different types of auditory stimuli were matched with the rate and amplitude of unpredictable athetoid movements. Once the matching occurred, the amplitude of the tremor increased and the tremor itself became much more regular. Termination of the auditory stimuli resulted in temporary remission of the tremor and in general relaxation. Through these procedures, relaxation periods were extended for longer periods of time so that learning under normal conditions could be experienced.

In research on the effects of background music on the muscular control of children with cerebral palsy, an interaction has been found between the variables of musical tempo and cerebral palsy types. Of the two main types, spastic children generally have far greater hypertonicity than athetoid children while the latter group is characterized by slower, writhing movements. From our model of primary entrainment, we hypothesize that children showing more hypertonicity (spastic) will entrain better to stimulative (primarily, fast) music; conversely, athetoid children should entrain better to sedative (slow) music. In other words, tempo is matched to muscular activity.

The primary entrainment hypothesis was substantiated in at least three separate studies in which cerebral palsied children were evaluated on tasks of physical dexterity (Schneider, 1956), bicycle riding (Lathom,

1961), and reproduction of rhythm (Sato, 1962) under conditions of sedative and stimulative music. Resulting data from all three studies indicated that spastic children evidenced better performance under stimulative music, and the athetoids better performance with sedative music. On the physical dexterity tasks, both quantity and quality of performance improved, as predicted, for each group under the respective facilitative music condition. Interestingly, no modulation of the music was required beyond matching the tempo with the diagnostic type of cerebral palsy.

Communicative Responses of Children with Autistic Behavior[3]

Nordorf and Robbins (1971, 1972, 1977) have done some of the pioneering work using primary entrainment procedures to reduce autistic behaviors. Their method involves the autistic child participating in music ensembles with two therapists. The emphasis in the Nordoff and Robbins approach is on musical improvisation with the child. In the musical environment, the autistic child will exhibit his sterotyped, often compulsive, behavior in a "musical" way. Nordoff and Robbins (1977) investigated these musical characteristics and determined that the dimensions of loudness and/or tempo were the most identifying features. The client's playing on a drum, piano, or other instrument usually was loud and fast (ordinarily, greater than 200 beats per minute). Sometimes, the playing was very soft and slow, listless and inhibitive, even fearful. Nevertheless, the important feature of the playing, whether loud or soft, fast or slow, was that the patterns (a) kept repeating and (b) were unchanging, particularly to persistent external prompting.

Nordoff and Robbins found that the best method for reducing the stereotyped behavior of autistic and severely handicapped children was to match loudness, tempo, and possibly pitch levels of the (drum) beating or vocalizing. Through progressive musical imitation of the child's behaviors, the therapists entrained a child and gradually directed the child toward less compulsive and more appropriate behavior. We analyzed children's behaviors heard on an audio tape (Nordoff & Robbins, 1977), and shown in a film (Parry, 1976) of therapy sessions by Nordoff and Robbins. We found that, initially, the children exhibited withdrawal in their "non-musical" playing until the point in time when they became aware they were being mirrored in the therapist's music. Then, there was almost universally a laugh, a smile, or some observed affective change which seemed to indicate the children were willing to enter into a more therapeutic relationship. The role of "lead improvisor" changed back and forth from therapist to child, with the child adding new rhythmical, melodic, and dynamic patterns to his musical repertoire. It also was apparent that, during this process, vocalizations often came into being, which led to appropriate verbalization of words.

This approach has also been found to be successful with severely and profoundly mentally retarded children. Saperston (1973) assigned musical patterns on the piano to each of several types of stereotyped movements exhibited by a profoundly retarded child so that the child could control the music by changing his behavioral response to the music. Over a period of 1½ years, the child significantly increased basic communication skills, such as awareness, attention span, eye contact, and vocalizations, and showed positive affective changes toward increased laughter and socialization.

Background music, when synchronized in some way with stereotyped behaviors of severely and profoundly handicapped children, has a considerable effect upon these behaviors. Reardon and Bell (1970) and Smeets (1972) found that stimulative background music had a more quieting effect upon the activity level of mentally retarded persons than sedative music. Stevens (1971), however, showed that the rate of stereotyped behavior may be an important factor. She found that retarded adolescents who body-rocked at different speeds responded differently to varying tempi of music. Generally, (a) fast rockers tended to slow down when the music's tempo was **slightly below** that of their rocking tempo. (b) Slow rockers slowed down even further when the tempo of the music was **slightly faster** than their rocking tempo. (c) Music that **matched** the tempo of the rocking had a stimulative effect on the rocking of both groups. This last finding parallels that of Palmer (1952) who found that matching the music with the tremor in a person with cerebral palsy resulted in regularity of the tremor along with an increase in its amplitude; however, a subsequent reduction in musical tempo produced relaxation of the tremor. Perhaps if Stevens (1971) had reduced the tempo of the music after first matching it to the rocking of her clients, the rocking rates would have decreased. It also seems that perseverative rocking behaviors of children are entrained best to musical tempi which are near, but not precisely the same as, the rocking state.

Cognitive Processes

Reducing self-stimulatory behaviors through primary entrainment appears essentially cognitive. Piaget called these behaviors the "primary circular reaction" stage of sensori-motor intelligence (Rider, 1982c). Furthermore, each of the different stages of cognitive development has been found to be correlated with different levels of musical perception (Rider, 1977, 1981). As determined through the **Musical-Perception Assessment of Cognitive Development (M–PACD)** (Rider, 1982c), perceptions of the rhythmic components of tempo and duration were found to be the musical attributes most closely related to cognitive developmental level. The stages of cognitive development, corresponding approximate age levels, and musical-perceptual behavioral characteristics of each stage are shown in Table 2. As can be seen in this Table, a child of 18 months to three years of age may develop his symbolic functions when he plays a musical instrument both loudly and softly. A child **not near** this stage would be difficult to entrain in loudness discrimination. Such is the case when a toddler gladly imitates the father in shaking a rattle but shows no ability in playing it softly or loudly. Since musical participation demands many of the cognitive abilities of dynamic and tempo control, imagery, seriation, and meter conception (conservation of tempo and duration) as well as some abilities which are relatively non-cognitive (e.g., pitch control), it follows that music activities which are age-appropriate may facilitate intellectual development. Confirmedly, a number of researchers have demonstrated cognitive gains through musical participation, e.g., Rosene (1976), Wagley (1978), and Wingert (1972).

Relaxation Techniques

There is increasing evidence that relaxation is a prerequisite to successful learning activities. When threat, fear, anxiety, and other strongly arousing emotions confront the learner, "downshifting" may occur in which older subcortical parts of the brain predominate, reducing the efficiency of the neo-cortical function (Hart, 1975). It seems that music commonly makes learning—sometimes a threatening activity—less anxiety-provoking. This is seen dramatically in a learning technique developed in Bulgaria, which makes extensive use of music and relaxation. "Suggestology," or the Lozanov method (named after its creator), uses relaxation and other procedures as a prerequisite to learning. Research in

Table 2
Developmental Stages and Corresponding Age Levels and Musical Behaviors*

Stages of Cognitive Development	Approximate Age Levels	Musicial Behaviors
Sensori-motor	0–1½ years	Ability to create sounds through vocalization and playing of simple music instruments
Symbolic	1½–3 years	Ability to demonstrate (in order) simple discrimination of loudness, timbre, tempo, and finally, duration.
Pre-operational	3–6 years	Ability to demonstrate gradual changes in tempo and duration
Concrete operational	6–11 years	Ability to simultaneously attend to more than one musical concept, such as melody and beat

*Taken from Rider (1982c).

Suggestology indicates that learning can be accelerated dramatically (Ostander & Schroeder, 1979). (See the following major section on secondary entrainment for a more complete discussion of Suggestology.)

Researchers have corroborated the need for relaxation preceding learning. In a study of highly and minimally creative college students, sedative music played prior to taking a maze test produced significantly higher scores in both groups than stimulative music (Borling, 1981). Sedative music also induced more alpha frequency brain-wave (EEG) production than stimulative music, but only in highly creative individuals. The use of music to entrain alpha production is well-documented, and many auditory stimuli of a rhythmic nature have been shown to stimulate alpha brain waves (Johnston, 1973, Oswald, 1959). Musicians have consistently outproduced alpha levels of non-musicians when listening to music (Wagner, 1975a, 1975b; Wagner & Menzel, 1977). This relative dominance of alpha waves, which generally indicates relaxed states, suggests a positive relationship between musicality and the ability to relax.

Rhythmic physiological responses, such as those recorded as galvanic skin response (GSR), and through electromyography (EMG), and electro-encephalography (EEG), as well as various circadian rhythms probably act in concert. For example, the EEG "alpha state" (relaxation) is usually acompanied by reduced GSR and EMG activity. Rather than entrain any

one physiological function, music may affect many physiological operations and also affect cooperation among these and circadian rhythms.

Learning Through Secondary Entrainment

In secondary entrainment, music is synchronized with the skill, concept, or material to be learned. This process is slightly more indirect than in primary entrainment in which some aspect of the music is matched directly to the client's behavior to cause a change in, or a more effective control of, that behavior.

Some psychophysiological responses may be affected by music even if one is auditorially unaware of that music; however, if the client is **overly** aware of the music, that is, if the amount of energy needed by a client to entrain to a certain piece of music is too great, little else can be attended to. Therefore, if non-musical information is going to be learned through music, the music should be compatible in one or several ways with that information, thereby reducing the total energy expenditure. Throughout the present section, reference can be made to Table 3, which presents music-matching procedures that are secondary entrainers in the learning process believed to provide this compatibility.

Table 3
Secondary Entrainment in Learning Processes Through Music-matching Procedures

Learning Process	*Music-matching Procedures*
Cueing	Music elements matched to target recall words
Chunking	Rhythms matched to series of words or digits to be recalled
Multi-sensory synchronization	Music elements matched to information in other modes (e.g., visual and tactile)
Pacing	Sedative music matched to slow breathing rhythm and pacing of target verbal information

Cueing

Cueing refers here to providing a sensory prompt for learning material. Background music generally has been found to have a negative effect upon academic behaviors (such as reading and arithmetic) of the "normal" population (Fogelson, 1973; Purvis, 1971; Zimmer & Brachulis-Raymond, 1978). However, there is evidence that students who regularly study with background music are not as negatively affected as those who do not study with music (Etaugh & Michaels, 1975). Furthermore, reading comprehension has been shown to be significantly higher under conditions of familiar music than with unfamiliar music (Hilliard & Tolin, 1979). One explanation for this finding is that the energy in learning the information content was minimized under musical conditions familiar to the subject. The accomplishment of this energy minimalization possibly occurs through synchronization and enhancement of the neural coding of sensory stimuli.

Certain handicapped populations seem to benefit more from learning environments with background music than non-handicapped populations. Spudic and Sumervill (1978) found no detrimental effects of music on arithmetic performance of retarded persons. Stainback, Stainback and Hallahan (1973) and Sternlicht, Deutsch, and Siegel (1967) concluded that sedative, or calm, classical music aided retarded persons in learning complex tasks. One of two explanations seems plausible: Either the music (a) contained low-information content (i.e., not distracting) or the music (b) entrained the subjects into a relaxation stage of the learning cycle. Because sedative music aided learning, the second explanation seems more likely. However, Scott (1970) indicated that popular music of a more stimulative nature (Beatles) significantly increased arithmetic performance over no-music conditions in hyperactive boys. Thus, it is quite possible that tempo plays an important, if not the most important, role in such musical entrainment. "Personal tempo" may influence learning because normal **and** retarded persons relax to sedative music while hyperactive children relax to stimulative music (as they apparently do to chemical stimulants). This matching of musical tempo to personal tempo, and vice versa, is, however, perhaps more demonstrative of the process on primary entrainment. (See the preceding major section of primary entrainment.)

"Catchy" rhythms, melodies, and rhymes have been very effective in increasing recall and retention. Proper synchronization of music and material to be learned seems to result in a reduction of information input; and certain features of the musical stimuli, such as their tempi and loudness levels, may enable further reduction in processing through cueing (i.e., providing a sensory prompt for learning material).

Story content has been retained by retarded children at a significantly higher level when sung rather than spoken (Isern, 1961; Lathom, 1970). Spelling also has been improved when combined with music or poetry rather than through traditional approaches (Mickens, 1972). In these studies, procedures were used in which music was generally employed as a cue for the content to be remembered. For example, in a song teaching the concept "up-down," musical pitch was used to rise on "up" and fall on "down," thereby synchronizing with the meaning of the words. Wooderson (1978) found that cues provided by musical instruments— melodies directing attention to certain words—were significantly more effective in improving word-reading in normal first-graders than simply singing the clue words with an accompaniment. Still, the latter method was successful in teaching severely retarded children to match random shapes with nonsense syllables (Austen, 1977). The synchronization of music to subject matter may need to be more precise the higher the developmental level of the children.

Chunking

Several researchers have investigated the mnemonic effects of rhythm and melody. Although melody has been found to facilitate memory for digits (Jellison, 1976) and rhythmic patterns (Maydian, 1982), rhythm seems to be a more powerful mnemonic device. Marple (1979) and Prickett (1974) demonstrated that rhythmic presentation of serial information aided significantly in recall, enabling normal elementary school students to "chunk" the materials to be learned, that is, to organize bits of material into larger units. In a memory task of serial order of two tones positioned in the middle of a melodic-rhythmic series, Jones, Kidd, and Wetzel (1981) determined that rhythm accounted for more of the variance in recall performance than melody. Paired-associate learning also has been improved to a significantly greater degree using rhythmic over melodic mediators (Staples, 1968). Even rats have demonstrated better discriminative learning under conditions of more rhythmic rather than less rhythmic music (Bates & Horvath, 1971)!

Multi-Sensory Synchrony

Findings from two studies on paired-associate learning failed to demonstrate differential effects of melodic, spoken, or visual mediators (Myers,

1979; Shehan, 1981). However, Shehan did find a significant increase in recall with a combination of music and visual or verbal and visual presentations. In other words, a rhythmic synchronization of two or more sensory modalities produced the most efficient learning. In a related study, Dale (1974) found that recall and retention were directly proportional to the number of sensory modalities used in learning.

Music with its ability to entrain muscle responses (Sears, 1960) and tactile sensitivity (Madsen & Mears, 1965), engages the proprioceptive and tactile senses. If matched to the material to be learned, the music then helps create a synchronized multi-sensory environment. It may be for this reason that a number of researchers have demonstrated more significant gains in speech and language skills development through music therapy than with traditional speech therapy techniques (Krauss & Galloway, 1982; Seybold, 1971; Walker, 1972).

Rhythmic synchronization plays such an important role in much learning that its function cannot be overstated. The learning of motor skills, such as jumping and balancing, has been facilitated when accompanied with synchronizing rhythmic music (Beisman, 1967). Rhythmic activities and action songs in which the rhythms and actions were synchronized to speech have resulted in significant gains in body image, receptive and expressive language, and fine and gross motor skills (Galloway & Bean, 1974; Price, 1979). Speech discrimination also has been improved significantly by the use of rhythmic music (Palmer, 1980). Coordinating music hand signs (the Kodaly method) with pitch (Hurwits, Wolff, Bortnick, & Kokas, 1975) and synchronizing body-part movements in association with sequences of colored lights (Larson, 1978) are said to have enabled learning disabled children to improve sensori-motor integration. Clearly, music can help integrate the cognitive, affective and psychomotor domains.

Pacing

Suggestology is a relatively new learning strategy developed by Dr. Georgi Lozanov that makes use of secondary entrainment and has been labeled by some as enabling "supermemory" or "superlearning" (Ostrander & Schroeder, 1979). One of the features of Suggestology is the establishment of a relaxed atmosphere, created by primary entrainment through music. During the actual learning portion of suggestology, however, pacing through the use of rhythm plays a strong role.

Pacing the material to be learned in 8-second cycles was found by Lozanov to be the most beneficial. The first 4 seconds of the cycle are spent inhaling, while during the last 4 seconds the subject reads from a list while listening to a tape of the same material. In other words, synchronization of the senses is obtained while pacing the reading into a constant rhythm of 4 seconds on, 4 seconds off, etc. The complete Suggestology lesson is usually repeated a second time while the person listens to a tape recording of the material to be learned, accompanied by sedative background music. No visualization of the material occurs during this second session. In one report of Suggestology with learning disabled children, significant gains were found in math, reading, and affective relations (Schuster & Vincent, 1980).

Learning Through Tertiary Entrainment

In tertiary entrainment, the process is more indirect than in either primary or secondary entrainment. At this level, music preferred by the subject is used as a contingent reinforcer in the modification of an unrelated non-musical behavior such as academic performances in mathematics or reading. This process works well if the music and the material to be learned are so incompatible that the other two modes of entrainment are no longer feasible.

The Premack (1959) principle seems to be involved in the mechanism of this tertiary process. Listening to the music, if it is properly matched to the functioning and preference level of the client, is the "more desirable behavior" which can reinforce or make effective and efficient the "less desirable behavior" (non-musical). While non-contingent background music may be sufficient to increase performance of non-musical behaviors, music that is contingent upon rate and quality of performance has been found to be more effective (Bellamy & Sontag, 1973; Metzler, 1974; Underhill & Harris, 1974). The range of behaviors which have been increased or improved through the use of contingent music includes language discrimination (Madsen, Madsen, & Michel, 1975; Madsen & Seringer, 1976; Seybold, 1971), mathematics (Madsen, Moore, Wagner, & Yarbrough, 1975; Madsen & Forsythe, 1973; Miller, 1977), reading (Eisenstein, 1974; Gordon, 1977; Steele, 1971), and social skills (Reid, Hill, Rawers & Montegar, 1975; Steele, 1968).[4]

Music as a contingent reinforcer may prompt or entrain the individual to enter into a rhythmical sequence and pattern of non-musical behavior which is predictable and optimizes adaptation. Children who do not make maximum use of their time during work and play may not be synchronized into a schedule of optimum efficiency. This concept may be similar to the basic-rest-activity-cycle (BRAC) of the brain found by Dement and Kleitman (1957) to run continuously throughout the 24-hour day. Without intrinsic or extrinsic motivation to excel, the problem learner (particularly the low-motivation student) possibly over-extends time spent in mental rest.

Reinforcers, such as music, may provide the extrinsic motivation which ultimately regulates the BRAC. In this regard, contingent music was found to be significantly more effective in improving math scores in low ability children than in middle or high ability groups (Yarbrough, Charnoneau, Wapnick, 1977). Perhaps the higher ability children were already entrained to a maximum efficiency cycle, whereas the contingent music program helped establish this rhythm in the low ability group. It may be that learning to self-regulate the BRAC is a basic prerequisite to intrinsic motivation for cognitive pursuits. Several studies from music therapy research have demonstrated transfer of learning to other situations, indicating that a global concept—possibly entrainment to an internal synchronized cycle such as the BRAC—has been acquired, not merely the learning of the antecedent behavior (Hanser, 1974; Johnson & Phillips, 1971). Perhaps related to this, Luce (1971) notes several examples of the correlation between lack of health, or "dis-ease," and a lack of synchrony among the physiological rhythms.

A recent study by one of us (Rider, Floyd & Kirkpatrick, in press) demonstrated that shiftworking conditions led to considerable circadian dysynchronization between body temperature and adrenal corticosteroid rhythms. Furthermore, autogenics training using progressive muscle relaxation and music was found to significantly re-entrain these rhythms. The relationship between relaxation and learning discussed in the previous two sections may be such that synchronized or regulated neuro-behavioral rhythms yield optimal performance and learning potential.

Concluding Statement

The prevalence of rhythms in learning is undeniable. There are circadian rhythms for memory, sensation, and perception. There are recurring times when we are more amenable to imitative learning and other times when we need more creative experiences. Even within the learning of a single concept, a cyclic process from relaxation to complete mastery seems involved.

Music is a rhythmic phenomenon in both its horizontal and vertical structure. Most obvious is the horizontal movement of music through time, from a beginning to an ending point. This movement, of course, is best heard in melodic continuance with its enhancing melodic configurations. Utilization of tempo, duration, and perhaps dynamics lend to this perception. Less obvious is the vertical movement of music. Pitches with their inherent overtones and timbres with their overtone strengths which identify differences among musical instruments are both physical frequencies that are cyclical, or rhythmical. Therefore, melody and harmony—no matter how simple or complex—contain these horizontal and vertical features which are metrical in nature.

If, as some believe, organisms (including humans) contain sets of complex patterned vibrations, frequencies, or rhythms, it may be that the rhythms of music can entrain with the rhythms of an individual or even with the rhythms of a group of individuals. More obviously, entrainment is a phenomenon by which rhythmic events affect **and** effect each other through synchronization; entrainment occurs more easily when two (and perhaps more) cyclic events are similar in period. For example, humans can be entrained quite readily to a 24-hour cycle of light/dark or daylight/night; but when not exposed to external entrainers (such as light and magnetic fields) most exhibit a cycle slightly longer than 24 hours (Luce, 1971).

It seems that music can be used to entrain many types of behavior. (One may speculate that this is related to humans being composed of a multitude of oscillators or encased vibrations and frequencies.) In **primary entrainment**, tempo and sometimes pitch and dynamics are matched to behavioral and cognitive characteristics of clients, thereby causing a change in those characteristics. Muscular control in children with cerebral palsy, elimination of self-stimulatory behaviors in children with autistic behaviors and severely handicapping conditions, and development of cognitive functioning in all people are examples of some of the uses of music in primary entrainment. In **secondary entrainment**, music is matched with the material to be learned rather than to the client behaviors. Rhythm and tempo are effective mnemonic devices when matched with similar characteristics of verbal content. Music also aids in synchronizing the human sensory systems, thereby enhancing learning environments. Finally, in **tertiary entrainment**, music is used as a contingent reinforcer to increase learning behaviors, while at the same time perhaps synchronizing the client to successful cycles of work and play.

While the methods described in this chapter rely largely on music as a means to facilitate learning, there is evidence that the pursuit of music as an end in itself is also beneficial to psychophysiological development. Whether music is viewed as play or rest, it may be tantamount to learning. In his neurophysiological treatise on the subject, Sinclair (1981) has found that rest is not only important in learning, but actually is the part of the cycle of work and rest in which the rate of strengthening of neural connections is greatest. It is the opinion of the authors that the pursuit of music for aesthetic enhancement and emotional enjoyment may serve not only as a tool for synchronizing the senses, but as a means of helping synchronize all the human "oscillators." A major aspect of life may be finding experiences which allow for entrainment and synchronization. Music may provide such ultimate experiences. Perhaps, as Halpern (1978) suggests, we have the power through music to "tune the human instrument."[5]

NOTES

1. Findings through research on the iso-principle show conclusively that music effects changes in mood more dramatically when the mood of the music matches that of the individual (Eagle, 1971; Fisher & Greenberg, 1972; Orton, 1953; Shatin, 1970; Sopchak, 1955).
2. A definitive review of music therapy for children with cerebral palsy can be found in Rudenberg (1982).
3. A definitive review of music therapy for children with autistic behaviors can be found in Paul (1982).
4. For a review of selected studies in this area, see Eagle (1982).
5. The authors are indebted to the following colleagues for their contributions to this chapter: Betsey King Brunk, Charlotte F. Cole, C. Thomas Eagle III, Melissa A. Martin, Babette C. Merwin, and Kathryn S. Mickelson.

REFERENCES

Altshuler, I. A psychiatrist's experience with music as a therapeutic agent. In Schullian, D. & Schoen, M. (Eds.), *Music and medicine.* New York: Books for Libraries Press, (1948).

Anderson, J. C., & Cattell, R. B. *The music preference test of personality,* Champaign, IL: Institute for Personality and Ability Testing, (1953).

Austen, M. J. The effects of music on the learning of random shapes and syllables with institutionalized severely mentally retarded adolescents. *Contributions to Music Education*, (1977), *5*, 54–68.

Bates, F. C., & Horvath, T. Discrimination learning with rhythmic and nonrhythmic background music. *Perceptual and Motor Skills*, (1971), *33*, (Part 2) 1123–1126.

Beisman, G. L. Effect of rhythmic accompaniment upon learning of fundamental motor skills. *Research Quarterly*, (1967), *38*(2), 172–176.

Bellamy, T., & Sontag, E. Use of group contingent music to increase assembly line production rates of retarded students in a simulated sheltered workshop. *Journal of Music Therapy*, (1973), *10*(3), 125–136.

Bentov, I. *Stalking the wild pendulum*, New York: E.P. Dutton, 1977.

Borling, J. E. The effects of sedative music on alpha rhythms and focused attention in high-creative and low-creative subjects. *Journal of Music Therapy*, (1981), *18*(2), 101–108.

Cloudsley-Thompson, J. L. *Rhythmic activity in animal physiology and behavior.* New York: Academic Press, 1961.

Clynes, M. *Sentics: The touch of the emotions.* New York: Anchor Press, 1978.

Clynes, M., & Nettheim, H. The living quality of music: Neurobiologic basis of communicating feeling. In Clynes, M. (Ed.), *Music, mind and brain: The neuropsychology of music.* New York: Plenum Press, 1982.

Collins, C. Personal communication, April 26, 1983.

Dale, E. *Audiovisual methods in teaching* (3rd ed.). New York: Dryden Press/Holt, Rinehart and Winston, 1974.

Dement, W., & Kleitman, N. Cyclic variations in EEG during sleep and their relation to eye movements, body motility, and dreaming. *Electroencephalography and Clinical Neurophysiology*, 1957, *9*, 673–690.

Eagle, C. T., Jr. Effects of existing mood and order of presentation of vocal and instrumental music on rated mood responses to that music. Unpublished doctoral dissertation, University of Kansas, 1971.

Eagle, C. T., Jr. *Music therapy for handicapped children: An annotated and indexed bibliography.* Washington: National Association for Music Therapy, 1982.

Eisenstein, S. R. Effect of contingent guitar lessons on reading behavior. *Journal of Music Therapy*, 1974, *11*(3), 138–146.

Etaugh, C., & Michaels, D. Effects on reading comprehension of preferred music and frequency of studying to music. *Perceptual and Motor Skills*, 1975, *41*(2), 553–554.

Fisher, S., & Greenburg, R. P. Selective effects upon women of exciting and calm music. *Perceptual and Motor Skills*, 1972, *34*, 987–990.

Fogelson, S. Music as a distractor on reading-test performance of eighth grade students. *Perceptual and Motor Skills*, 1973, *36*(3), (Part 2), 1265–1266.

Galloway, H. F., & Bean, M. F. The effects of action songs on the development of body-image and body-part identification in hearing impaired preschool children. *Journal of Music Therapy*, 1974, *11*(3), 125–134.

Gordon, M. V. The effect of contingent instrumental music instruction on the language reading behavior and musical performance ability of middle school students. Unpublished doctoral dissertation, Columbia University Teachers College, 1977.

Halpern, S. *Tuning the human instrument.* Palo Alto: Spectrum Research Institute, 1978.

Hanser, S. B. Group contingent music listening with emotionally disturbed boys. *Journal of Music Therapy, 1975, 11*(4), 220–225.

Haring, N., Lovitt, T. C., Eaton, M., & Hanson, C. *The fourth r: Research in the classroom.* Columbus: Charles E. Merrill, 1978.

Hart, L. A. *How the brain works.* New York: Basic Books, 1975.

Hilliard, O. M., & Tolin, P. Effect of familiarity with background music on performance of simple and difficult reading comprehension tasks. *Perceptual and Motor Skills,* 1979, *49*(3), 713–714.

Hurwitz, I., Wolff, P. M., Bortnick, B. D., & Kokas, K. Nonmusical effects of the Kodaly music curriculum in primary grade children. *Journal of Learning Disabilities,* 1975, *8*(3), 167–174.

Isern, B. Summary, conclusions, and implications: The influence of music upon children. *Proceedings of the National Association for Music Therapy,* 1961, *10,* 149–153.

Jellison, J. A. Accuracy of temporal order recall for verbal and song digit spans presented to right and left ears. *Journal of Music Therapy,* 1976, *13*(3), 114–129.

Johnson, J. M., & Phillips, L. L. Affecting the behavior of retarded children with music. *Music Educator's Journal,* 1971, *57*(7), 45–46.

Johnston, T. F. The function of Tsonga work songs. *Journal of Music Therapy,* 1973, *10*(3), 156–164.

Jones, M. R., Kidd, G., & Wetzel, R. Evidence for rhythmic attention. *Journal of Experimental Psychology: Human Perception and Performance,* 1981, *7*(5), 1059–1073.

Konecni, V. J. Social interaction and musical preference. In Deutsch, D. (Ed.), *The psychology of music.* New York: Academic Press, 1982.

Krauss, T., & Galloway, H. Melodic intonation therapy with language delayed apraxic children. *Journal of Music Therapy,* 1982, *19*(2), 102–113.

Larson, B. A. Use of the motorvator in improving gross-motor coordination, visual perception and IQ scores: A pilot study. *Journal of Music Therapy,* 1978, *15*(3), 145–149.

Lathom, W. The use of music with cerebral palsied children during activities involving physical control. *Bulletin of the National Association for Music Therapy,* 1961, *10*(3), 10–16.

Lathom, W. B. Retarded children's retention of songs, stories and poems. Unpublished doctoral dissertation, University of Kansas, 1970.

Leonard, G. *The silent pulse.* New York: E. P. Dutton, 1978.

Lomax, A. *Folk song style and culture.* New Brunswick, New Jersey: Transaction Books, 1968.

Luce, G. G. *Biological rhythms in animal and human physiology.* New York: Dover, 1971.

Madsen, C. K., & Mears, W. G. The effects of sound upon the tactile threshold of deaf subjects. *Journal of Music Therapy,* 1965, *2*(2), 64–68.

Madsen, C. K., & Forsythe, J. L. Effect of contingent music listening on increases of mathematical responses. *Journal of Research in Music Education,* 1973, *21*(2), 176–181.

Madsen, C. K., Madsen, C. H., Jr., & Michel, D. E. The use of music stimuli in teaching language discrimination. In Madsen, C. K., Greer, R. D., & Madsen, C. H., Jr. (Eds.), *Research in music behavior: Modifying music behavior in the classroom.* New York: Teachers College Press, 1975.

Madsen, C. K., Moore, R. S., Wagner, M. J., & Yarbrough, C. A comparison of music as reinforcement for correct mathematical responses versus music as reinforcement for attentiveness. *Journal of Music Therapy,* 1975, *12*(2), 84–95.

Madsen, C. K., & Geringer, J. M. Choice of televised music lessons versus free play in relationship to academic improvement. *Journal of Music Therapy,* 1976, *13*(4), 154–162.

Marple, H. D. Short-term memory, laterality and chunking. Paper presented at 2nd Annual Loyola Symposium on Hemispheric Laterality and Music, New Orleans, February, 1979.

Maydian, M. J. Melodic rhythms versus non-melodic rhythms in accurate retention and reproduction of rhythmic patterns as presented to college music majors. Paper presented at the 33rd Annual Conference of the National Association for Music Therapy, Baltimore, November, 1982.

Metzler, R. K. The use of music as a reinforcer to increase imitative behavior in severely and profoundly retarded female residents. *Journal of Music Therapy,* 1974, *11*(2), 97–110.

Mickens, A. R. The effect of music on teaching spelling to educable mentally retarded children in an educational setting. Unpublished masters thesis, Florida State University, 1972.

Miller, D. M. Effects of music listening contingencies on arithmetic performance and music preference of EMR children. *American Journal of Mental Deficiency,* 1977, *81*(4), 371–378.

Myers, E. G. The effect of music on retention in a paired-associate task with EMR children. *Journal of Music Therapy,* 1979, *16*(4), 190–198.

Nordoff, P., & Robbins, C. *Music therapy in special education.* New York: John Day, 1971.

Nordoff, P., & Robbins, C. *Therapy in music for handicapped children.* New York: St. Martin's Press, 1972.

Orton, M. R. Application of the iso-moodic principle in the use of music with psychotic and "normal" subjects. Unpublished master's thesis, University of Kansas, 1953.

Ostrander, S., & Schroeder, L. *Superlearning.* New York: Dalacorte Press, 1979.

Oswald, I. Experimental studies of rhythm, anxiety, and cerebral vigilance. *Journal of Mental Science,* 1959, *105,* 269–294.

Palmer, L. L. Auditory discrimination development through vestibulocochlear stimulation. *Academic Therapy,* 1980, *16*(1), 53–68.

Palmer, M. F. Musical stimuli in cerebral palsy, aphasia and similar conditions. *Proceedings of the National Association for Music Therapy,* 1952, *2,* 162–168.

Parry, D. (Producer). *The music child.* New York: Benchmark Films, 1976.

Paul, D. W. *Music therapy for handicapped children: Emotionally disturbed.* Washington: National Association for Music Therapy, 1982.

Piaget, J. *The origins of intelligence in children.* New York: International University Press, 1952.

Premack, D. Toward empirical behavior laws: Positive reinforcement. *Psychological Review,* 1959, *66,* 219–233.

Price, R. D. The effect of selected musical experiences on the actuation of language in young developmentally delayed children. Unpublished doctoral dissertation, University of Toledo, 1979.

Prickett, C. A. A comparison of two rhythmic patterns as aids to digit recall. Unpublished masters thesis, Florida State University, 1974.

Purvis, J. R. The effect of background rock music on the arithmetic performance of sixth grade children. Unpublished master thesis, Florida State University, 1971.

Reardon, D. M., & Bell, G. Effects of sedative and stimulative music on activity levels of severely retarded boys. *American Journal of Mental Deficiency,* 1970, *75*(2), 156–159.

Reid, D. H., Hill, B. K., Rawers, R. J., & Montegar, C. A. The use of contingent music in teaching social skills to a nonverbal, hyperactive boy. *Journal of Music Therapy,* 1975, *12*(1), 2–18.

Rider, M. S. The relationship between auditory and visual perception on tasks employing Piaget's concept of conservation. *Journal of Music Therapy,* 1977, *14*(3), 126–138.

Rider, M. S. The assessment of cognitive functioning level through musical perception. *Journal of Music Therapy,* 1981, *18*(3), 110–119.

Rider, M. S. Transcription of clinical music therapy session in Billings, Montana, 1982(a).

Rider, M. S. A factor analysis of music preferences. Unpublished manuscript, 1982(b).

Rider, M. S. Musical-perception assessment of cognitive development: Test manual. Unpublished manuscript, 1982(c).

Rider, M. S., Floyd, J. W., & Kirkpatrick, J. The effect of music, imagery and relaxation on adrenal corticosteroids and the re-entrainment of circadian rhythms. *Journal of Music Therapy,* In press.

Roederer, J. G. The psychophysics of musical perception. *Music Educators Journal,* 1973, *60*(6), 20–30.

Rosene, P. E. A field study of wind instrument training for educable mentally handicapped children. Paper presented at the 27th National Conference of the National Association for Music Therapy, Milwaukee, 1976.

Rudenberg, M. T. *Music therapy for handicapped children: Orthopedically handicapped.* Washington: National Association for Music Therapy, 1982.

Saperston, B. The use of music in establishing communication with an autistic mentally retarded child. *Journal of Music Therapy,* 1973, *10*(4), 184–188.

Sato, C. A study of rhythm patterns of cerebral palsied children. *Cerebral Palsy Review,* 1962, *23*(5), 7–11.

Schneider, E. H. Relationships between musical experiences and certain aspects of cerebral palsied children's performance on selected tasks. *Proceedings of the National Association for Music Therapy,* 1956, *6,* 250–277.

Schuster, D. H., & Vincent, L. Teaching math and reading with suggestion and music. *Academic Therapy,* 1980, *16*(1), 69–72.

Scott, T. J. Use of music to reduce hyperactivity in children. *American Journal of Orthopsychiatry,* 1970, *40*(4), 677–680.

Sears, W. W. A study of some effects of music upon muscle tension as evidenced by electromyographic recordings. Unpublished doctoral dissertation, University of Kansas, 1960.

Seybold, C. The value and use of music activities in the treatment of speech delayed children. *Journal of Music Therapy,* 1971, *8*(3), 102–110.

Shatin, L. Alteration of mood via music: A study of the vectoring effect. *Journal of Psychology,* 1970, *75*(1), 81–86.

Shehan, P. K. A comparison of mediation strategies in paired-associate learning for children with learning disabilities. *Journal of Music Therapy,* 1981, *18*(3), 120–127.

Sinclair, J. D. *The rest principle: A neuro-physiological theory of behavior.* Hillsdale, NJ: Lawrence Erlbaum Associates, 1981.

Smeets, P. M. The effects of various sounds and noise levels on stereotyped rocking of blind retardates. *Training School Bulletin,* 1972, *68,* 221–226.

Sopchak, A. L. Individual differences in responses to music. *Psychology Monographs,* 1955, *69*(11), 1–20.

Spudic, T. J., & Somervill, J. W. The effects of musical stimulation on distractibility and activity level among retarded subjects. *Education and Training of the Mentally Retarded,* 1978, *13*(4), 362–366.

Stainback, S. B., Stainback, W. C., & Hallahan, D. P. Effect of background music on learning. *Exceptional Children,* 1973, *40*(2), 109–110.

Staples, S. M. A paired-associates learning task utilizing music as the mediator: An exploratory study. *Journal of Music Therapy,* 1968, *5*(2), 53–57.

Steele, A. L. Programmed use of music to alter uncooperative problem behavior. *Journal of Music Therapy,* 1968, *5*(4), 103–107.

Steele, A. L. Contingent socio-music listening periods in a preschool setting. *Journal of Music Therapy,* 1971, *8*(4), 131–145.

Sternlicht, M., Deutsch, M. A., & Siegel, L. Influence of musical stimulation upon the functioning of institutionalized retardates. *Psychiatric Quarterly Supplement,* 1967, *41,* (Part 2), 323–329.

Stevens, E. A. Some effects of tempo changes on stereotyped rocking movements of low-level mentally retarded subjects. *American Journal of Mental Deficiency,* 1971, *76,* 76–81.

Underhill, K. K., & Harris, L. M. The effect of contingent music on establishing imitation in behaviorally disturbed retarded children. *Journal of Music Therapy,* 1974, *11*(3), 156–166.

Wagley, M. W. The effects of music on affective and cognitive development of sound-symbol recognition among preschool children. Unpublished doctoral dissertation, Texas Women's University, 1978.

Wagner, M. J. Effects of music and biofeedback on alpha brainwaves, rhythms and attentiveness. *Journal of Research in Music Education,* 1975(a), *23,* 3–13.

Wagner, M. J. The effect of music stimuli and biofeedback on the production of alpha brainwave rhythms and verbal reports of musicians and nonmusicians. Reviewed by S. Hedden, *Council for Research in Music Education*, 1975(b), *41*, 1–10.

Wagner, M. J., & Manzel, M. B. The effect of music listening and attentiveness training on the EEG's of musicians and nonmusicians. *Journal of Music Therapy*, 1977, *14*, 151–164.

Walker, J. B. The use of music as an aid in developing functional speech in the institutionalized mentally retarded. *Journal of Music Therapy*, 1972, *9*(1), 7–12.

Wingert, M. L. Effects of a music enrichment program in the education of the mentally retarded. *Journal of Music Therapy*, 1972, *9*(1), 13–22.

Wooderson, D. C. The effect of musical and nonmusical media on word reading. Unpublished doctoral dissertation, Florida State University, 1978.

Yarbrough, C., Charboneau, M., & Wapnick, J. Music as reinforcement for correct math and attending in ability assigned math classes. *Journal of Music Therapy*, 1977, *14*(2), 77–88.

Zimmer, J. W., & Brachulis-Raymond, J. Effect of distracting stimuli on complex information processing. *Perceptual and Motor Skills*, 1978, *46*(3), 791–794.

Chapter 10

DYSRHYTHMIA AND DISORDERS OF LEARNING AND BEHAVIOR

JAMES R. EVANS

Introduction

Rhythm may well be the most fundamental and pervasive of all concepts known to man. In this text evidence has been provided for the rhythmic foundations of such already basic processes as attention, memory, language, skilled motor activity, interpersonal interaction, and aesthetic appreciation. Many other texts and scholarly works attest to the pervasiveness of rhythm in our lives from the infradian (greater than 28-hour) periodicities of movements of the planets through the circadian (about 24-hour) periodicities of many bodily functions approximately synchronized with the day-night cycle, to the many ultradian periodicities (less than 20-hour) ranging from rhythms of heartbeats and breathing to rhythmic activity of atoms. [Long considered the basic building blocks of matter, even the atom now is described by some as "a set of relationships operating at a certain rhythm" (Rifkin, 1983)]. (For comprehensive coverage of circadian and infradian rhythm phenomena, see Aschoff, 1981; Ayensu & Whitfield, 1982; Brown & Graeber, 1982; and Moore-Ede, Sulzman & Fuller, 1982.)

Initial sections of this chapter provide an overview of the concept (or attribute) of rhythm. A major goal of those sections is to set the stage for future sections by developing reader appreciation of both the nature and complexity of rhythm and rhythm-realted phenomena. Middle portions primarily consist of the author's speculations concerning relatively well-established and accepted aspects of rhythm in conjunction with human learning and behavior, especially as it may relate to disorders of learning and behavior. In these sections there is an attempt to collate many of the points made by other authors in the present volume and relate these to the topic.

249

The later sections are the author's creative (fanciful?) speculations on rhythm and what it may mean or could mean for many different facets of life. In some cases, research findings or writings of others are cited in support of a view. However, for the most part, it is pure speculation distilled from the author's years of contemplating the phenomena of rhythm. In addition to getting these thoughts into print, the major purpose of this section is to emphasize the fundamental importance of rhythm and related dynamics and to stimulate further thinking which might lead to increased scientific research.

Nature of Rhythm

Definition

Various authors in this volume have provided definitions of rhythm (see especially the chapters by Elliot and Gabriellson); however, none has given a dictionary definition. Such a definition is: "Movement or procedure with uniform or patterned recurrence of a beat, accent, or the like"; and, in regard to speech rhythm, "The pattern of recurrent strong and weak accents, vocalization and silence, and the distribution and combination of these elements in speech" (from the Greek Rhythmos-to-Flow). (**Random House College Dictionary, Revised,** 1975.)

Most definitions emphasize "regularly recurring" and "pattern." By this and other definitions a constant, regularly recurring event with nothing but the simplest pattern would be considered rhythmic. It is common to refer to brain electrical activity as rhythmic, and by this definition even a constant level frequency (for example, 10 Hertz or alpha) would constitute a rhythm. Similarly, regularly recurring oscillations or vibrations could be considered rhythms. From this perspective of the simplest of rhythms it is necessary to proceed to the concept of rhythm hierarchies (rhythms embedded within rhythms) if one is to begin to comprehend the nature of the rhythmic phenomena of the universe. Imagine a spectrum of thousands or more interacting rhythms and one may begin to sense the complexity of our rhythmic universe. Perhaps the best presently available and familiar model of such a confluence of rhythms involves the performances of a symphony orchestra. Following this metaphor, the universe might be considered one all-encompassing symphony!

However, there is more to add to the complexity of rhythmic phenomena. In language and music, for example, the "recurring events" may be accents, pauses, and/or frequency changes (and patterns formed by these). And, as noted by Gabrielsson (this volume) such structural aspects of rhythm are only one aspect of our experience of rhythm. There are motional and emotional aspects as well. Finally, to complicate the matter even further, there are several rhythm-related phenomena which seem crucial to any understanding of rhythm dynamics. These include phase relatedness, harmony, resonance, synchronization, and entrainment.

Aspects of two regularly recurring (periodic) and continuously varying phenomena which co-occur in time are said to be in phase. For example, if all aspects of the EEG wave forms reflecting the rhythmic electrical activity from two or more brain sites are identical at any given instant the wave forms would be in phase. Since rhythmic activity is cyclic (but not all cyclic events are rhythmic) one can conceive of the time between occurrences as constituting the 360 degrees of a circle. Thus, two (or more) periodic events which are not perfectly in phase can be described as out of phase, i.e., one lagging behind the other by a certain degree (up to 360 degrees).

Two or more sounds which, when sounded simultaneously, are pleasing to the ear are said to be in harmony, and those which are not are said to be dissonant. However, the term "harmony" in the more general sense means "accord" and "congruence." Thus whether it be simple sound frequencies or more complex rhythms, one can conceive of certain rhythms being harmonious (congruent, in accord) and others dissonant. It happens that sounds presented simultaneously are harmonious (pleasing to the ear) when each is of a frequency which is an integral multiple of some basic frequency.

When the frequency of an external stimulus is the same or nearly the same as a natural vibration (frequency) of a system there is a tendency toward production of abnormally large vibrations in the system in response to the external stimulus. This is known as resonance. Again, this may be perceived as a rhythm-related phenomenon since vibrations constitute regularly recurring events.

The terms "synchronization" and "entrainment" seem relevant here. Entrainment may be thought of as the modification (or "carrying along") of one rhythmic phenomena by the flow of another—the former conforming more or less to the rhythm of the latter (see also chapters by

Condon and by Rider & Eagle, this volume). Entrainment may be similar to resonance in its operation and may require for its occurrence a certain phase relatedness, harmonious relationship and/or highly similar frequencies between two or more rhythms.

Synchronization (synchronicity or synchronousness) refers to the co-occurrence of events in time. This also is relevant to rhythm dynamics. Whether established by entrainment or otherwise, two or more rhythms (and hierarchies of rhythms) often are synchronized. In fact, one may conceive of many rhythm hierarchies—rhythms embedded within rhythms —as involving synchronization of rhythms. The musical chord (three or more different tones sounded simultaneously) is an example of synchrony of simple rhythms; and both the dynamics of a symphony orchestra and the interactional synchrony discussed by Condon (this volume) provide examples of synchronization of complex rhythm patterns. In many cases, synchrony seems to be actively sought (rather than passively entrained) and this probably is facilitated, if not actually made possible, by the predictability furnished by the regularity aspect of the structure of rhythm.

Disrhythmia Basis of Learning/Behavior Disorders

With the above ideas regarding rhythm and rhythm-related dynamics in mind, this section will discuss a rationale for dysrhythmia as a direct or indirect basis of human learning and behavior disorders. This thesis will be developed with extensive reliance on the writings of other contributors to this text.

General Dynamics

Attention, perception, sensory integration, sensory-motor skills, memory, language, and cognition are basic processes found to be defective or delayed in cases of learning problems and/or abnormal behavior. (Of course, it is rare to find all of these processes defective in any one person.) A case can be made for a dysrhythmia basis to defective functioning of each of these processes. First, however, it should be helpful to discuss rhythm in normal development.

As mentioned earlier, rhythmic activity characterizes all matter, even at the level of the atom. Thus, a normally developing human embryo might be considered from one viewpoint as a mass of oscillators, the vibrations of which create oscillating systems and subsystems, i.e., basically harmonious rhythm hierarchies. At the foundation of the hierarchy may be atomic level rhythms, while of a somewhat higher order may be cellular (including neuronal) rhythms. At still higher levels may be rhythms characteristic of groups of cells constituting specific organs. And at the highest levels there may be overriding rhythms of attention and other behavioral rhythms, perhaps including the "pulse" discussed by Clynes (this volume). Somewhere among these rhythms seems to be a basic reference rhythm, which may function as the "pacemaker"—an internal clock, the timing of which could be fundamental to one's perception of time. Each level may interact with and have the potential to modify other levels, yet be more than the sum of the others. Furthermore, the hierarchy seems to be modified and/or entrained by external rhythms, including not only the well-established effects of the day-night cycle, but also ultradian rhythms such as movement and language patterns of others. It can be speculated that these external rhythms are more influential during earlier parts of life—perhaps when the rhythm hierarchy (which in a sense is the individual) is relatively less complex.

Normal development and normal functioning both pre- and postnatally may require (or may, in fact, be) harmonious cooperation among all levels of the hierarchy. And this cooperation may depend upon appropriate phase relatedness, harmonic relationships, resonance, entrainment, and synchronization. Of course in this model it is obvious that there is much potential for dysfunction; dysrhythmias at higher levels may create (entrain?) lower level dysrhythmias, while excessive lower level dysrhythmias may preclude rhythmic activity at higher levels.

Commonly accepted sources of developmental abnormality include genetic defects (e.g., structural defects of the central nervous system, metabolic disorder), brain damage, nutritional deficiencies and inappropriate parenting (e.g., inadequate mother-child bonding). The first three of these could be conceived of as sources of lower level dysrhythmias in the hierarchy. For example, genetically based structural abnormalities may involve missing, out-of-proper-phase or dissonant oscillators at certain sites. Similarly, damaged brain cells may be dysrhythmic and/or dissonant with others normally constituting systems or subsystems, thus preventing normal operation of those systems. And assuming food (as matter) to involve (or be) unique rhythmic hierarchies, "improper diet" conceivably could translate to "food with rhythmic hierarchies dissonant with (out-of-phase with) the organism's unique rhythms."

On the other hand, sources of dysrhythmia of an entire system may be at higher levels of the hierarchy. Jones (this volume) notes that "the child's attentional rhythms may adapt to the particular rhythmic gestures and patterns of gestures (auditory and visual) of the performer;" and Condon (this volume) states, "It seems that an infant's motor behavior reacts to and is synchronized with the organized speech behavior of the others in his environment." Thus it should follow that these rhythmic gesture patterns (or speech patterns) by adult models may hinder development of rhythmic attentional, motor and linguistic patterns in the child. If these are seen as patterns higher in a rhythm hierarchy affecting (as well as being affected by) lower level patterns, the lack of interactional synchrony may have wide ranging effects on development.

Specific Disorders

Although dysrhythmias may relate to many different learning and behavioral disorders (or perhaps to all disorders), only two will be considered here. Certain other will be referred to briefly in a later section.

Autism. Infantile autism is considered to be a pervasive developmental disorder with onset before the age of 30 months, and characterized by lack of responsivity to others, gross deficits in language development, resistance to change, peculiar attachments to objects, and bizarre behaviors such as appearing to explore objects through the five major senses sequentially rather than simultaneously. If an infant inherited—or acquired through damage to the central nervous system—dysrhythmias at certain lower or middle levels of a rhythm hierarchy, he/she may not develop those higher order rhythmic patterns which normally can be entrained by (be synchronized with or resonate to) attentional, gestural and speech/language patterns of others. Even if some potential for entrainment remained, it seems likely that other persons would—consciously or unconsciously—note the lack of synchrony (perhaps perceived as lack of empathy or responsiveness) and find little or no reward in further interactions with the child. This would help guarantee that no synchrony would develop. In this regard it probably is true that certain parents and siblings of autistic children cease interaction with them more readily than others.

Lacking appropriate synchrony with others, autistic children could be expected to find it difficult to focus attentional energies in the flexible, adaptive manner of most persons, to experience little, if any, empathy with others (in fact, perhaps to experience only dissonance in regard to interpersonal relations), to experience disorganization of motor movements, and to fail to develop an appreciation of language [especially its rhythmic (prosodic) aspects]. (See also Condon, in this volume, for further speculation on the link between autism and dysrhythmias.)

Normal language and gestural rhythmicities undoubtedly are complex and may be expected to require for entrainment more complex synchronizations and/or resonances than simpler rhythms. Similarly, however, inanimate objects can present as complex stimuli especially if all facets are considered simultaneously, i.e., if they are experienced in a holistic and multisensory fashion. The autistic child would be expected to have trouble due to lack of appropriate (or stable) internal rhythmicities. However, he/she might be expected to comprehend objects more readily if they were treated more simply, e.g., if only one sensory aspect (rhythmic aspect) were monitored at a time. Thus it would not be surprising to find such children examining objects in a sequential "sense-by-sense" fashion and developing attachments to the objects [movement sequences or language sequences (as in echolalia)] once they finally interpret them. Furthermore, they could be expected to seek the comfort of sameness rather than face the dissonance of the unfamiliar. As mentioned above, such symtoms and behaviors define autism.

Specific learning disabilities. A recent definition of learning disabilities (LD) is:

> Learning disabilities refers to a heterogeneous group of disorders manifested by significant difficulties in the acquisition and use of listening, speaking, reading, writing, reasoning or mathematical abilities. These disorders are intrinsic to the individual and presumed to be due to central nervous system dysfunction. Even though a learning disability may occur concomitantly with other handicapping conditions (i.e., sensory impairment, mental retardation, social and emotional disturbance) or environmental influences (e.g., cultural differences, insufficient/inappropriate instruction, psychogenic factors), it is not the direct result of those conditions or influences (p. 336). (Hammill, Leigh, McNutt, & Larson, 1981.)

In addition to a discrepancy between ability and academic achievement characterizing LD, the most commonly reported problems for these children are attentional deficits, perceptual disorders, problems with intersensory and sensory-motor integration, memory impairments, and language deficits (especially in regard to written language). As noted in the definition given, the causes are believed to be intrinsic to the child and presumably a result of central nervous system dysfunction.

This disability seems especially appropriate in arguing for a dysrhythmia model of learning/behavior disorder. In some respects LD symptoms appear similar to those of autism, but on a much smaller scale. In fact, Condon (this volume) has observed a continuum of interactional synchrony-dyssynchrony ranging from that of normally learning children through moderate problems in dyslexics, to severe dysynchrony in autistic children. (Dyslexia refers here to the LD child with a severe reading disability.) In this regard it is of interest that in the earlier days of study of LD children, one of the several terms applied was "the dysynchronous child." Since it seems that synchrony among behavioral, neural and other patterns implies some regularity (rhythmicity) among patterns, the term "dysrhythmic child" appears to be equally appropriate and perhaps more basic. In the following paragraphs, a rationale will be presented for the manner in which dysrhythmias (especially internal dysrhythmias) may detrimentally affect basic processes which, in turn, precludes normal academic achievement in LD children.

Difficulty selectively attending to stimuli (attentional deficit disorder) is a common symptom of LD. The arguments of Jones (this volume) for "attentional rhythmicities" seem highly relevant to this. She notes that, "attending may reflect an interplay of a rhythmical organism with rhythmicities in the environment." This suggests that, when attending, we as complex rhythm hierarchies have aspects of that hierarchy synchronized with (resonating to; in harmony with) those other patterns of energy over time (and/or space) which are the stimuli to which we are attending.

Jones suggests that as infants we may be entrained by patterns of language, movements, etc. of others in our environments, i.e., rhythms may be induced in us which become our early attentional rhythmicities. This implies that when an infant is exposed several times to, for example, his mother's face and voice, rhythms are induced within him/her matching the time/space pattern of those stimuli. In the future that face and voice may be more easily recognized and hence, be more readily attended to. Sufficient exposure to any stimuli may lead to similar results; however some constraints may be imposed on attention in general by the unique characteristics of those rhythms of others to which we became entrained as infants, e.g., their unique background tempos, pulses (see the "inner pulse" discussed by Clynes in this volume). In any event, once a synchrony is established between an internal and an external rhythm pattern, it may be manifest consciously as familiarity with the stimulus; and, as suggested above, this may orient and facilitate attention to those stimuli in the future.

Jones suggests still other ways in which rhythmic patterning facilitates attention. In addition to dynamics of entrainment and familiarity, organismic needs such as hunger and thirst also affect attention. Environmental stimuli are seen as having various dynamic structural patterns (rhythm hierarchies?) certain of which may match a person's present organismic needs. The needs may elicit specific internal energy shapes (patterns) which match one or more of the patterns inherent in the external stimuli. Those pattern aspects of the stimulus then will be attended to. One may speculate here that the internal energy patterns elicited by needs relate closely to the time-form prints found by Clynes (this volume) to be internal representations of specific emotions.

Finally, Jones proposes that the rhythmic character of internal and external patterns enables anticipation/prediction of when a future event (in a rhythmic sequence) will occur. This may be most readily understood in terms of music and poetry where, for example, hearing an early part of a melody or verse enables prediction of later sections. It is suggested that this not only helps focus attention to certain points in the rhythmic sequence which may carry a higher information load, but also focuses attention to unexpected breaks (dysrhythmias) in the sequence. The latter could become sites of placement of new information to be learned—perhaps learned in the context of familiar (i.e., previously patterned) information.

In all these views of attention as the matching (or interplay) of excited rhythmicities within an individual with environmental patterns, it is readily seen that internal dysrhythmias could cause the impairments in selective attention so commonly observed in children labeled "LD."

The term "perception" generally refers to the process of organizing and interpreting sensory stimuli. "Perceptually handicapped child" is another term which once was commonly applied to persons with specific learning disabilities (Hallahan & Cruickshank, 1973). This was because LD persons very frequently show symptoms such as inability to select one part of a stimulus as figure (foreground) and the remainder as background, fail to note differences among easily confused (mirrored) words such as "was" and "saw," and fail to organize adequately the verbal utterances of others into meaningful groupings, e.g., syllables, words, phrases.

Although the separation of attentional processes from perceptual processes may be at times arbitrary and vague, some argument may be made for a dysrhythmia basis to perception as a distinct process. For example, proceeding on the assumption that organization and "recognition" of a stimulus occurs when a sufficient matching (resonance, harmonious relationship) of internal and external rhythm patterns occurs, certain internal dysrhythmias might be expected to interfere. In such cases partial, or unstable, organizations might lead to misperceptions such as hearing "enemy" as "emeny" or reading "was" as "saw."

Furthermore, there is evidence (see chapter by Martin, this volume) that the rhythmic nature of stimuli facilitates "chunking," i.e., the perception of groups or gestalts as opposed to element by element perception. As mentioned earlier, the rhythmic nature of stimuli also is believed to enable prediction of future aspects of a stimulus sequence from perception of earlier aspects. Both chunking and prediction are said to enable vastly more efficient information processing than otherwise would be possible. That is, by chunking many different discrete elements into a few units, limited human processing capabilities are expanded. That is the few units (but much information) then can be processed. And the ability to predict accurately certain elements in a sequence provides some redundancy which, in turn, permits more time and/or energy to be allocated to processing the more difficult perceptual or semantic aspects of a sequence.

Finally, in regard to perception and rhythm it may be speculated that one's perception of (meaning assigned to) a stimulus is greatly enriched if the stimulus is perceived in a multisensory fashion, i.e., with all its sensory attributes. For example, the congenitally deaf-blind person's perception of a dog probably would be limited to its tactile and olfactory attributes and hence, likely would not be as rich as the perception of a person with all senses functioning normally. Assuming that each sensory aspect of a stimulus has its own characteristic energy pattern which is rhythmic in nature, it can be speculated that an integrated (multisensory) perception of the object might require simultaneous matching of each pattern to appropriate internal rhythm patterns. (Alternatively it can be speculated that the stimulus patterns corresponding to each sense may combine to form also a higher order pattern which then may be matched by a corresponding internal pattern, thus permitting a true multisensory perception.)

As with attentional disorders, rhythm dysfunctions in persons with LD may cause perceptual disorders by precluding adequate matching of internal to external rhythm patterns. And, apart from any internal-external matching requirements, a failure to appreciate the rhythmic qualities of sequential stimuli may interfere with chunking and prediction, and hence with perception. The latter reasoning will be mentioned again in a later section on language and LD.

Memory deficits, especially in immediate memory for sequences, are another very commonly reported symptom in persons diagnosed as LD. Payne and Holzman (this volume) discuss the significance of rhythm in memory functioning. For example, it has been suggested that grouping (encoding) of discrete stimuli into chunks is facilitated by rhythmic presentation (and by rhythm appreciation). Such chunks, when stored in a limited storage "memory bank," may permit a greater absolute amount of information storage and may enable retrieval (recall) of more information than would be possible without such grouping. That is, by recalling chunks, one has in effect also recalled the elements. Payne and Holzman cite research in support of these ideas.

Commensurate with the above-mentioned matching (synchronizing, harmonizing) of internal and external rhythm patterns is a notion once advanced by Pribram (see Goleman & Pribram, 1979) that memory functions by mathematical principles similar to those involved in the hologram. In this view, the environment apparently is seen as a domain of many different frequencies or vibrations, and specific cell groups in the human brain are seen as specialized to resonate to specific ones of those frequencies. [Although environmental stimuli may present as highly complex wave forms, the brain supposedly functions to perform mathematical transforms (Fourier Transforms) on such wave forms, breaking them down into component simple frequencies.] The wave fronts resulting from the resonances presumably meet to form interference patterns which then are stored in the central nervous system as holograms. Wave forms in the environment thus are isomorphic to wave forms in the brain. The hologram-like stored interference patterns will be reactivated any time the person encounters identical (or very similar) frequency patterns, that is, encounters similar stimuli. In this model the reactivation processes apparently are the basis of one's conscious experience of recall. Thus, dysrhythmias within an individual could be expected to hinder memory, preventing both initial coherent formation of the "hologram" and its later activation.

One of the more popular theories of LD (at least in regard to specific reading disability) is that it is due to a basic deficit in language (Vellutino, Smith, Steger, & Kaman, 1975). Basing much of their reasoning on the writings of Miller (1956), Vellutino et al. claim that for human speech perception to be efficient there must be ways to overcome our limited spans of absolute judgment for discriminating one stimulus from another and our limited spans of immediate memory. A major way this is believed to be accomplished is by "chunking" the distinctive features of speech articulation into well-organized structures (units) which we come to perceive as familiar whole events in and of themselves. It is believed that such reorganization occurs at semantic levels as well with groups of words processed simultaneously as meaningful chunks. Furthermore, it is hypothesized that when normally hearing persons learn to read they rely upon such chunking to expedite visual information processing; that is, they translate the visual information from the printed page into an auditory-verbal code and then process it (apparently as if they are "hearing" the printed page).

Both Martin and Hanes (this volume) discuss such aspects of language perception, and relate them to rhythm. For example, the rhythmic character of speech (prosody) is said to facilitate "chunking"; and the ability to analyze written text into meaningful units such as sentences and phrases (parsing) is believed to involve, through mediation, the "reconstructing" of the prosodic (rhythmic) character of spoken language. In other words, parsing during reading is seen as a natural consequence of appreciation of prosody. Both Martin and Hanes, however, consider the rhythmic nature of language to have information processing significance that goes beyond more traditional views of the value of chunking.

Martin (this volume) notes that aspects of the rhythm of speech may carry information about stress (perhaps "pointing to" words, phrases, and other units with a heavy information load, and may generate moment-to-moment expectancies (predictability component) regarding later aspects of the speech stream. Speech rhythm thus presumably facilitates perception by the listener. Furthermore, his writings suggest that "chunks" may be hierarchically organized, with dynamic interactions occurring among them.

Hanes (this volume) also stresses the importance of rhythmic factors in language—both oral and written. She notes that prosodic features of language have been shown to carry the heaviest information load of all features. She suggests that efficient reading strategies include parsing into the largest meaningful units possible, and using a given unit for such purposes as: (1) a site for searching and researching for meaning; (2) a means of attacking unfamiliar words; (3) a source of prediction of future information in the passage, and (4) a sort of "echo" to maintain in short-term memory the meaning of the material read up to that point. As mentioned above, this type parsing refers to the reorganization of written material into an auditory-verbal code (inner language) which retains the prosodic features of auditory language.

Up to this point, emphasis primarily has been upon relationships of rhythm and rhythm-related phenomena to receptive aspects of information processing and language. However, as Martin (this volume) suggests, rhythm may be the natural link between reception and production of speech. As one learns the speech rhythms of others, these patterns (relative timings of elements) may be incorporated and later accessed during speaking. Hanes (this volume) notes that speaking involves "on-going movement aimed at achieving in real time a reproduction of the anticipated pattern." She suggests that truly fluid (rhythmic) speech production involves temporary adjustments in tempo, etc. which may require reference to both some constant internal sense of timing (internal clock) and to internalized speech rhythm patterns. In this regard, it seems likely that other skilled motor acts such as handwriting and eye movements during reading also involve internalized motor patterns and an internal clock reference.

Of special relevance here is the theory of a motor basis to speech perception (see Liberman, Cooper, Shankweiler, & Studdent-Kennedy, 1967). In this view, speech is perceived via motor processes which are also involved in speech production, i.e., there is an interdependence of perceptual and productive processes. It is assumed that "at some level or levels there exist neural signals standing in one-to-one correspondence with the various segments of the language—phoneme, word, phrase, etc." Liberman et al. proposed further that there is overlapping of signals between neural networks that "supply control signals to the articulators and those that process incoming neural patterns from the ear." It is suggested that this auditory-motor linkage facilitates oral language perception because the fact of limited numbers of acoustic signals which can be readily and rapidly identified is circumvented by linking perception to a "system of physiological coordinates more richly

multi-dimensional—hence, more distinctive—than the acoustic signal."
Evidence for such speech-movement linkage also is provided by the
work of Condon (this volume) in regard to self-synchrony and interactional
synchrony, i.e., synchronization of a speaker's own movements and the
movements of listeners with the speech of the speaker.

The motor theory of speech perception has several implications for
the field of LD. For instance, it suggests that motor skills may be at least
as basic to language as auditory-perceptual skills, and that efficient
reorganization of written material may involve recoding it into auditory-
motor verbal form (or initially to motor and then to auditory-verbal
form). Furthermore, one can readily hypothesize that rhythm factors are
even more basic, that is, that the "neural networks" mentioned by Liberman
et al. consist of patterns (rhythms of neural activity) initially generated
via entraining by the movement/speech patterns of persons in the infant's
environment.

As with the processes of attention, perception and memory discussed
earlier, it is apparent that internal dysrhythmias and/or lack of rhythm
appreciation may disrupt language functioning, including reading, in
any of several ways. Drake (1964) reports that only 2 of 300 dyslexic
students in one research study showed even minimal musical talent, but
showed many deficits in patterning of fine motor skills. And Langille
(1977) found a correlation of .34 between children's scores on her tests of
rhythm perception and reading vocabulary (the correlation between IQ
test scores and reading vocabulary was .44).

There are, of course many possible sources of dysrhythmia, many of
which were mentioned earlier, e.g., brain damage, structural abnormalities at cellular levels, inappropriate (dysrhythmic) speech/movement
models in one's early environment. In regard to models, it is likely that,
as Langille (1977) states, "The word and sentence structure of the English
language present their own unique rhythm pattern to which the young
child must become aurally sensitized." Superimposed upon this unique
structure may be dialectical variations (such as "non-standard English")
—not to mention the unique "pulse" characterizing an individual speaker's
rhythm. It is speculated here that such variations from some English
language "norm" in one's entrained inner language patterns would make
perception of standard English more difficult in both its oral and written
forms. That is, there would be less precise matching of rhythms and less
potential for using prosody and parsing to facilitate processing. Dialect-
related difficulties in matching rhythm patterns might be further exacer-

bated by other sources of dysrhythmia. It may be, for example, that the rather high coincidence of poverty, dialect variation, bilingualism, high risk for brain damage, and school reading failure is due to the common denominator of dysrhythmia. In this regard, Condon (1982) suggests that a black child raised in a ghetto may find it very difficult to relate to "a white kind of rhythm."

Any dysrhythmia explanation of LD (or other disorder) must confront the fact of apparently excellent rhythmic skills in many children with learning and behavior problems, and of severe (but often isolated) dysrhythmias in persons with normal, or even superior learning ability, e.g., cerebral palsied persons, those with cardiac or certain EEG (brain wave) dysrhythmias. In attempting to resolve these apparent contradictions, the complexity of the human body as a "collection of oscillating systems and subsystems" must be considered. It seems reasonable to assume that certain systems remain sufficiently independent of others to preclude significant interference of all other normally functioning systems by a dysrhythmic one. Thus, for example, rhythm in gross motor activities may not be affected by dysrhythmia of systems involved primarily in auditory processing. It might be speculated that only those systems which are physically close to each other and/or whose rhythms or rhythm hierarchies are similar or have some harmonic relationship to each other will show mutual interference when one is dysrhythmic. Furthermore, as mentioned above, it is not necessarily a dysrhythmia, as such, which causes language difficulties; a mismatch between internal and external rhythms can also be a source of such problems.

Treatment Possibilities

Dysrhythmia models of disorders such as autism and LD have implications for preventative and remedial measures. If a person is dysrhythmic, it should follow that treatment could take one or both of two general forms: (a) attempts to develop appropriate rhythmicity within the individual; or (b) presentation of learning materials (stimuli) in such a fashion that rhythmic processing is facilitated.

In terms of prevention, it may be useful to insure adequate exposure of infants and young children to persons accurately modeling the movement/language patterns of the larger culture in which he/she will be educated. One may even speculate that exposure to good models of several languages at very early ages might not cause confusion, but, in fact, help build into the child a potential for efficient learning of these languages. This might be thought of as entraining "time-form prints" for future matching (see Clynes, this volume).

If an intrinsic dysrhythmia already exists, certain remedial procedures might be designed to modify it, i.e., make it rhythmic. Fraisse (1974) stresses the dependence of rhythm on our body movements. Relevant to this, the so-called "movement therapies" prevalent in the LD field in the 1960's (variations of which still are practiced by professionals in fields such as adaptive physical education) stress training of rhythmic movement sequences, synchronization of movements of various muscle groups, and coordination of input from various sense modalities. There were reports that such activities often led to improved academic functioning, e.g., Kephart (1960) and Kallan (1970). If so, one possible mechanism by which this occurred could be regularization of motor patterns thus enabling accurate matching to oral language patterns (with subsequent appreciation of prosody and parsing in oral and written language). Another mechanism might be the facilitation of intersensory integration (synchronizing of the rhythmic patterns characterizing each sense). In regard to the latter, the author (Evans, 1972) used an approach labeled "multiple simultaneous sensory stimulation" in which severely retarded subjects were exposed to children's songs accompanied by lights which changed in intensity and color in synchrony with amplitude and frequency characteristics of the music. Limited gains in fluency of movement and language were observed in some subjects. Variations of this might help establish learning-related rhythms in dysrhythmic persons. For example, computer technology should enable precise synchronization or harmonic relationships among rhythmic auditory, visual and tactile stimuli, and dysrhythmic persons could try to move in synchrony with such correlated rhythms. Such training might help develop an inherent rhythmicity as well as coordination among the senses involved.

Other approaches to developing internal rhythm include music therapy and biofeedback training of specific brain rhythms. Rider and Eagle (this volume) discuss the unique values of music for entraining and/or synchronizing physiological rhythms. As they note, music is rhythmic in both its horizontal (e.g., melodic continuance) and vertical (e.g., pitch, overtones) structure. Perhaps such rhythmic complexity makes it especially effective in this regard. There has been speculation that the alpha (8–13 Hertz) frequency of brain electrical activity is a "fundamental reference which temporally organizes experience" i.e., that it may be or may reflect, an internal clock. However, Treisman (1984) cites evidence that there is no simple relationship between alpha frequency or prevalence and time judgments. To the degree that alpha frequency is important in time perception, EEG biofeedback procedures might help in developing and reinforcing it at appropriate brain sites—with possible beneficial effects for time and rhythm appreciation. EEG biofeedback also might be used to develop rhythm relationships among brain sites to conform to patterns which may exist in normal (or superior) learners, and/or to reinforce already existing patterns of this sort so that they might endure despite dysrhythmic influences from surrounding sites [see Evans (1977) for relevant research on cortical coupling among children with specific reading disability].

Finally, treatment might take the form of emphasizing the rhythmic character of stimuli to be learned. Hanes (this volume) mentions the "neurological impress" method in which a fluent reader reads a passage orally while the remedial student tries simultaneously to read the same passage. This may focus the student's attention on the model's language rhythm, perhaps enabling him/her to perceive the relationship between oral prosody and the printed page. It also may facilitate eventual entrainment to the rhythm of standard English.

Other means of emphasizing rhythm include embedding materials to be learned in a song or verse. In a study involving two groups of children labeled "LD", Bottari and Evans (1981) found such procedures associated with more efficient learning and recall (as compared to regular oral presentation). Successful use of "melodic intonation therapy" (Berlin, 1976) may involve similar dynamics. In this procedure sometimes used with aphasic patients, short phrases or sentences to be learned are embedded in simple melody patterns. Some formerly non-speaking patients are able to sing the phrases or sentences, and often later regain many speech/language skills. It seems possible that this could occur because music is usually more rhythmically patterned than speech (thus facilitating perception, and perhaps re-entraining internal patterns). A related technique is reported by Martin, Meltzer, and Mills (1978). They found reading to be facilitated by preparing sentences in such a manner that they appeared on a TV screen with each syllable timed, syllable by syllable, as if it were spoken, i.e, words were presented in a visual rhythm corresponding to the auditory rhythm of a speaker.

Finally, it is suggested that rhythmic background stimuli (such as certain music) may facilitate learning in some situations by serving to enhance the stability of one's internal clock. Clynes' (this volume) finding that music can be "time's measure" seems relevant here. Perhaps this is one of the means through which the Suggestology technique of Lozanov (1978) functions to enable more efficient learning. In that technique materials to be learned (such as definitions of words) are spoken in a monotone by the teacher while classical music is played in the background.

Miscellaneous Speculations and Summary

As mentioned earlier, the disorders of autism and LD seem well suited to a dysrhythmia hypothesis. Application of that hypothesis in above sections involved some conceptual leaps, but it did seem to fit a great many of the observed and known facts about such disorders. The dysrhythmia explanations of other human behaviors and phenomena which will be suggested in this section may involve even greater leaps, but hopefully will make interesting reading and stimulate further thinking and research on the topics.

Dysrhythmia in Disease

Many diseases have an obvious rhythmic or dysrhythmic component, e.g., regular increases in fevers at night, the periodic cycles of insomnia and manic-depressive disease, cardiac and respiratory dysrhythmias, the chaotic (dysrhythmic) firing of neurons in epilepsy. Manic-depressive illness has been described as involving circadian rhythms free running (unlocked from day-night cues) and out-of-phase with each other (Kripke et al., 1978). And some psychosomatic disorders have been viewed as due to stress-caused disorganization of 90-minute cyclic behavior of certain physiological processes leading to erratic hormone output and unstable autonomic nervous system activity (Friedman, 1978).

While scientific research is finding increasing evidence for dysrthythmic components in many diseases (sometimes referred to as "periodic diseases"), there are writers who believe rhythm to be intimately related to a great many aspects of health and sickness. Some perceive the human body as a collection of oscillating subsystems more or less in harmony with each other; and the greater the harmony among the systems the less the "dis-ease," while the greater the dissonance the more severe the "dis-ease." According to some such views, internal order can be increased and hence the quality of the human "body symphony" enhanced by exposure to ordered stimuli such as certain music (Halpern, 1978), poetry and rhythms of nature and/or by participation in rhythmic movement activities as diverse as dancing, jogging, and certain martial arts (e.g., see Leonard, 1978). One might guess that dancing to music under the stars on a beach would be highly conducive to reestablishment of internal order!

There are still other notions which can be advanced regarding stimuli and activities with the capability of resetting (or enabling the resetting) of one's internal clocks and physiological rhythms. Clynes' (this volume) concept and findings of "music as time's measure" suggests that musical thought may provide a reference for programming or reprogramming certain biological clocks. Furthermore, it is known that the day-night cycle has a strong effect on phase timing of circadian rhythms; some believe this to be mediated by the effects of light (itself a wave/particle phenomenon) upon neuromelanin molecules (Barr, 1983). Thus, exposure to light also may be seen as potentially facilitating internal order. And in regard to depressive illness and the disruption of biological clocks, one may even hazard the guess that electroshock's effectiveness as a treatment may be due to the entraining power of the alternating (rhythmic) electrical current involved.

There have been reports of meditation, progressive relaxation, hypnosis and biofeedback procedures being related to increasing amounts of rhythmic brain wave activity, especially of alpha (8–13 Hertz) frequency. If, as mentioned earlier, alpha is an index of functioning of an internal clock, this suggests the possibility that some aspects of these procedures affect settings of this clock. Intuitively it seems to the author that such procedures may, in effect, "level" the previously variable strengths of individual rhythms in the total rhythm spectrum (or hierarchy), thus perhaps making them more vulnerable to entrainment by external rhythms. This "leveling" may be facilitated by such procedures as the simple, monotonous rhythm of a hypnotist's voice, and by the prolonged concentration on the rhythm of one's breathing, rhythmic organization of a visual stimulus (mandala) or rhythmic repetition of a sound or word (mantra) during meditation exercises.

Internal **dissonance,** on the other hand, may be seen as facilitated by dissonant (i.e., nonrhythmic) stimuli in one's environment (although there are instances of **rhythmic** stimuli causing dysrhythmic phenomena as in epileptic attacks triggered by music or by light flashes of a specific frequency). The physiological "dis-ease" associated with air travel involving crossing of time zones and becoming out of synchrony with one's usual day-night cycle is a generally accepted example of body-environment dyssynchrony. However, if it is true that all aspects of the universe are rhythmic in nature (e.g., light and sound as wave phenomena, objects as coalescences of vibrations), then anything in one's environment may have the potential to cause disruption in one or more oscillating subsystems of the body if its rhythm is dissonant with or out of synchrony with the subsystem. One might even speculate that such processes could occur at cellular levels and be part of the dynamics of diseases such as cancer. A certain piece of music or art discordant with one's "body symphony" might be disruptive of certain internal rhythms. Similarly, street noise and non-rhythmic light (such as florescent bulbs) may have detrimental effects. Finally, if dissonant stimuli within the ranges detectible by the human senses can cause internal disruption, it is likely that other frequencies in the electromagnetic spectrum have the same potential for disruption as well as hormonization.

These ideas of environmental dysrhythmias as causes of disease (and "dis-ease") have been suggested occasionally by others for several years and now seem to be increasing in popularity. In the author's opinion, it is an area where there is a major need for further consideration and research.

Rhythm in Other Life Experiences

In this section there will be brief discussion of the possible effects of rhythm and dysrhythmia in three other general areas: interpersonal relationships, aesthetic experiences, and paranormal phenomena.

Interpersonal relations. The research of Condon (this volume) and that reported in Davis (1982) suggest that human interactions normally are synchronized and hence, rhythmic. Relevant to this, it may be surmised that persons with (composed of?) similar rhythms or rhythm hierarchies find it easier to resonate with or entrain to each other. If so, it seems reasonable to speculate further that ease of entrainment may be positively correlated with such phenomena as empathy, "intuitive" like or dislike for another person and "love at first sight." Of course it is such rhythm dynamics that are implied in statements like "We are on the same wavelength" and "I get good vibrations from him/her."

Following some of the reasoning of earlier portions of this chapter, it seems likely that entrainment by rhythmic environmental stimuli such as music and parental speech and movement patterns is a basic source of one's rhythm hierarchies. If so, it may be that persons sharing exposure to similar music and speech are more likely to feel mutual empathy and attraction. For example, this may help explain generally greater empathy within than between families, generations, geographical regions, countries, and religions. From this viewpoint, the words of a recent popular song, "I'd like to teach the world to sing in perfect harmony" should have strong implications for world peace!

Aesthetic experiences. Tastes in music, art, poetry, and other fine arts and performing arts vary widely across individuals as well as across generations, nations, and cultures, yet a few have almost universal appeal and remain popular over the ages, i.e., are considered "classics." It seems possible that rhythm and rhythm-related phenomena are involved in such aesthetic likes and dislikes.

Perhaps, "ideal" forms exist and we are inherently attracted to them. These may involve mathematically precise tonal (vibration) ratios in the auditory realm, and specific spatial proportions in the visual realm. Thatcher (1985), considers proportion to be the characteristic of rhythm in visual space, and notes the frequent occurrence of specific, mathematically precise proportions in nature. It can be speculated that aesthetic appreciation is one's participating (via resonance?) in the rhythmic order pervading nature. A mathematically precise relationship inherent in some music and art, for example, may reinforce or "re-program" the same "ideal" organization within the listener or viewer.

Another (perhaps related) view of aesthetic experience may be deduced from the research of Clynes regarding essentic forms. Clynes presents evidence (this volume) that such forms are a property of the central nervous system for the production **and perception** of expressions of pure emotional qualities. They may be manifest externally through touch quality (as shown in sentographic records) or through the melodic pitch contours and amplitude contours of music. Thus it seems reasonable that music, art, movement or other stimuli with properties more closely resembling the qualities of pure essentic forms might evoke those forms (specific central nervous system activity) in the perceiver, giving rise to more intense aesthetic experience.

Finally, one may speculate as to possible rhythm-related sources of popular appreciation of music and art forms which professional musicians, artists and others who appreciate classical works find "vulgar," "gross," or lacking in artistic value, e.g., much "popular" music. Assuming again the view of humans as coalescences of rhythm hierarchies in various stages of complexity and with varying degrees of internal harmony and synchrony, it could be predicted that we would resonate more readily to certain rhythmic hierarchies than to others, i.e., prefer certain songs and performers to others. Entrainment could be a related mechanism; hearing certain pieces of music several times may entrain some aspects of our own rhythm hierarchy, thus making it easier to attend to those pieces in the future, and perhaps providing a comfortable (but often temporary) sense of "familiarity" with them.

Paranormal phenomena. There has been some discussion of the possible relationship of rhythm to paranormal phenomena such as mental telepathy and precognition (prediction of future events). If, as Condon (this volume) notes, we unconsciously interact in a rhythmic fashion with others (interactional synchrony of movements/speech) and if movement patterns carry meaning regarding emotion, then our "mirroring" of others' movements may evoke, via resonance, matching emotions in ourselves. Since we are not consciously aware of the interactional synchrony, this might be perceived as "extrasensory" perception of the others' feelings and feeling-related thoughts, i.e., as mental telepathy. (Incidentally, this seems to be one of the dynamics involved also in the phenomena of "emotional contagion" in groups.) Somewhat similarly, if the notion can be accepted that thoughts are patterns of rhythmic firings of neurons in the central nervous system which modify and are reflected in other aspects of one's total rhythm hierarchy or "body symphony," then it could be surmised that one might perceive these patterns as variations in a sense of resonance with another. In some cases these variations may be accurately decoded and "telepathy" therefore occur.

Some writers (e.g., Goleman & Pribam, 1979) have suggested that underlying our perceived world may be a world of frequencies and vibrations where time and space are meaningless—where an instant is not discriminable from a century. It may be speculated that for some unknown reasons we can gain occasional glimpses into that realm where future, past, and present are identical. At such times, "future" events may be sensed and remembered.

Concluding Remarks

The notion of vibrations and rhythm as basic to physical forms, consciousness and all life experience has been speculated upon in a great many ancient scriptures and myths about creation of the universe. And in the early days of experimental psychology rhythm research was prominent [e.g., see McDougall (1903) and Wallin (1911)]. Between those early twentieth century years and approximately 1975, however, the scientific study of rhythm was relatively neglected (with the exception of a few active researchers studying circadian rhythms and others studying rhythm in music). Since about the middle 1970's there have been many more references to rhythm and related phenomena in fields ranging from music, linguistics, medicine, aesthetics and developmental psychology to parapsychology and paraphysics. Several of the contributors to this volume have been pioneers in this renewal of interest.

It is now generally accepted that many infradian and circadian rhythms affect biological functioning, and that rhythm appreciation and expression are critical to development in infancy. Regarding the latter, for example, Condon (this volume) notes that infants can entrain to adult speech only twenty minutes after birth (and perhaps even before birth); and several others have noted that newborn infants are "sensitive" to the rhythmic, intonational, frequency, and phonetic composition aspect of human speech. Perhaps such scientific support of the basic importance of rhythm will lend greater credibility to related research in the diverse topical areas covered in this chapter.

A great many questions can be asked in relationship to rhythm and life, and many seem amenable to scientific investigation. Some general questions which seems especially in need of research, and/or are of special interest to the author include:

(1) To what extent does "information processing" consist of the brain performing mathematical transforms (or spectral analyses) on frequencies and rhythm hierarchies? Are processes of harmony, entrainment, resonance, synchrony and phase relationships involved, and if so, how and at what brain sites?

(2) Can music, light, rhythmic movement and/or rhythmic vocal and visual patterns re-program internal clocks and thus have prophylactic or curative properties in disease, "dis-ease," and learning disability?

(3) Can exposure of infants to various different (but rhythmic) patterns of language and/or movement facilitate later learning of those languages and greater empathy with persons in which those patterns are standard?

(4) Are there commonalities among brain processes, mathematics, music, art and dance?

(5) What are the primary sources of rhythm appreciation—limb

movements, brain electrical activity, heartbeat, breathing, activity of an internal pacemaker somewhere in the brain?

(6) Can different medications, foods, and allergens have therapeutic (or undesirable) effects by processes of entrainment or resonance with the rhythms of bodily systems and subsystems?

(7) Can thoughts (considered as rhythmic patterns of neuronal firing) affect functioning of bodily systems (considered as oscillating sub-systems) through procedures such as entrainment or resonance? If so, are "positive" thoughts more apt to normalize functioning and "negative" thoughts disrupt functioning, perhaps commensurate with Christian Science doctrine or with other views of the "power of positive thinking"?

Among the special needs in this area are a comprehensive theory of rhythm and precise measurements of rhythm, resonance, harmony and synchronization at various hierarchical levels. The microanalyses of interactional synchrony via motion picture frames as used by Condon, computerized spectral analyses of EEG wave forms using mathematical Fourier transforms, the sentographic techniques of Clynes, the use of a "macroscope" (Ferguson, 1984) to enable visual representation of sound, and methods of "checking" bodily organ integrity with auditory resonance represent attempts to study many of the phenomena discussed in this chapter. With recent technological advances in electronics and computer processing, greatly improved methods should be on the horizon. Any "body symphony" would be incredibly complex, but even if only a few of the speculations in this chapter are correct its scientific study should be very fruitful.

Perhaps today's aspiring researchers on rhythm-related topics would find it most useful to study "naturally" occurring examples of apparent extremes of rhythmic performance and of dysrhythmia. The former might include highly skilled musicians, artists, dancers, athletes, psychotherapists who are unusually empathic and effective with a wide range of clients, fluent readers and persons who experience synesthesia (unusual coordination and/or equivalence of sensory input in which, for example, colors may be experienced as tones). Naturally occurring examples of dysrhythmia may include persons with autism, epilepsy, cerebral palsy, specific learning disabilities, or major lack of empathy with others. A method of study which the author often contemplated, and which may be feasible with present technology, involves transforming aspects of the brain electrical activity of persons from these categories into auditory and/or visual form for analysis of rhythm and proportion. If this were possible, it may be speculated that output from the rhythmic performers might provide evidence for some "true" or ideal pattern—a pattern to which dysrhythmic persons could then be exposed in order that resonance and/or entrainment might occur as a form of treatment.

It seems fitting to conclude this chapter by referring to Charles Elliott's statement in Chapter 1 that some scholars believe clues to an understanding of the basic nature of the universe may be found in the study of rhythmic phenomena. Certainly the wide variety of topics shown in this volume to be rhythm-related attests to its universality. It has been suggested that all matter is coalesced vibrations or "frozen light" (light being a spectrum of frequencies) (Bohm, reported by Ferguson, 1983). From this perspective, there was great significance in a statement my son made as a six-year-old: "Maybe God is a rainbow." Could rhythm (vibration, frequency) be an essence of a force, reciprocally interwoven in the patterns of all of nature? Paraphrasing words of a once-popular song: "the answer my friends remains blowing in the wind."

REFERENCES

Aschoff, J. *Handbook of behavioral neurobiology, No. 4: Biological rhythms.* New York: Plenum Press, 1981.

Ayensu, E., & Whitfield, P. *The rhythms of life.* New York: Crown Publishers, 1982.

Barr, F. Melanin: The organizing molecule. *Medical Hypotheses*, 1983, 11, 1–140.

Berlin, C. On "melodic intonation therapy for aphasia" by R. W. Sparks & A. L. Holland. *Journal of Speech and Hearing Disorders*, 1976, 41, 287–297.

Bottari, S., & Evans, J. R. Effects of musical context, type of vocal presentation and time on the verbal retention abilities of visual-spatially oriented and verbally oriented learning disabled children. *Journal of School Psychology*, 1982, 20, 329–338.

Brown, F., & Graeber, R. *Rhythmic aspects of behavior.* Hillsdale, NJ: Lawrence Earlbaum, 1982.

Condon, W. Cultural microrhythms. In M. Davis (Ed.), *Interaction rhythms.* New York: Human Sciences Press, 1982.

Davis, M. *Interaction rhythms.* New York: Human Sciences Press, 1982.

Drake, C. Reading, riting and rhythm. *The Reading Teacher*, 1964, 202–205.

Evans, J. R. A cortical coupling pattern differentiating good from poor readers. *International Journal of Neuroscience*, 1977, 7, 211–216.

Evans, J. R. *Multiple simultaneous sensory stimulation with severely retarded children.* Paper presented at meeting of Southeastern Psychological Association, Atlanta, 1972.

Ferguson, M. Of math, music and vibrations. *Brain/Mind Bulletin*, 1984, 9, 4–5.

Ferguson, M. Bohm views matter as condensed light. *Brain/Mind Bulletin*, 1983, 8, 7.

Fraisse, P. *Psychologie du rhthme.* Paris: Presses Universitaires de France, 1974.

Friedman, S. A psychophysiological model for the chemotherapy of psychosomatic illness. *Journal of Nervous and Mental Disease,* 1978, 166, 110–116.

Goleman, D., & Pribram, K. Holographic memory. *Psychology Today,* 1979, February, 71–84.

Hallahan, D. P., & Cruickshank, W. M. *Psychoeducational foundations of learning disabilities.* Englewood Cliffs, NJ: Prentice-Hall, 1973.

Halpern, S. *Tuning the human instrument.* Palo Alto, CA: Spectrum Research Institute, 1978.

Hammill, D., Leigh, J., McNutt, G., & Larson, S. A new definition of learning disabilities. *Learning Disabilities Quarterly,* 1981, 4, 336–342.

Kallan, C. Rhythm and sequencing in an intersensory approach to learning disability. *Journal of Learning Disabilities,* 1972, 5(2), 68–74.

Kephart, N. *The slow learner in the classroom* (2nd ed.). Columbus, OH: Charles E. Merrill, 1960.

Kripke, D., Mullaney, D., Atkinson, M., & Wolf, S. Circadian rhythm disorders in manic-depressives. *Biological Psychiatry,* 1978, 13, 335–351.

Langille, C. M. An investigation of the relationship of aural rhythm pattern perception to reading skills of second grade students. *Dissertation Abstracts International,* 1977, 38 (6-A), 3355.

Leonard, G. *The silent pulse.* New York: Dutton, 1978.

Liberman, A., Cooper, F., Shankweiler, D., & Studdent-Kennedy, M. Perception of the speech code. *Psychological Review,* 1967, 74(6), 431–460.

Lozanov, G. *Suggestology and outlines of suggestopedy.* New York: Gordon and Breach, 1978.

Martin, J., Meltzer, R., & Mills, L. Visual rhythms: Dynamic text display for learning to read a second language. *Visible Language,* 1978, 12, 71–80.

McDougall, R. The structure of simple rhythm forms. *Psychological Review, Monograph Supplement 4,* 1903, 309–411.

Miller, G. A. The magical number of seven, plus or minus two: Some limits on our capacity for information processing. *Psychological Review,* 1956, 63, 81–97.

Moore-Ede, M., Sulzman, F., & Fuller, C. *The clocks that time us.* Cambridge, MA: Harvard University Press, 1982.

Random House College Dictionary. New York: Random House, Inc., 1975.

Rifkin, J. *Algeny.* New York: Penguin Books, 1983.

Thatcher, R. W. Personal communication, 1985.

Treisman, M. Temporal rhythms and cerebral rhythms. In J. Gibbon and L. Allan (Eds.), *Timing and time perception,* New York: New York Academy of Sciences, 1984, 542–565.

Vellutino, F., Smith, H., Steger, J., & Kaman, M. Reading disability: Age differences and the perceptual deficit hypothesis. *Child Development,* 1975, 46(No. 2), 493–497.

Wallin, J. E. Experimental studies of rhythm and time. *Psychological Review,* 1911, 18, 100–131.

AUTHOR INDEX

SUBJECT INDEX